PSYCHOLOGY LIBRARY EDITIONS: SPEECH AND LANGUAGE DISORDERS

Volume 7

THE INFANCY OF SPEECH AND THE SPEECH OF INFANCY

THE INFANCY OF SPEECH AND THE SPEECH OF INFANCY

LEOPOLD STEIN

Routledge
Taylor & Francis Group
LONDON AND NEW YORK

First published in 1949

CATALOGUE NO. 5025/U
PRINTED IN GREAT BRITAIN BY
THE CHAPEL RIVER PRESS, ANDOVER, HANTS
9.49

FOREWORD

BY

E. J. BOOME, M.B., M.R.C.P., F.R.A.I., F.C.S.T.
Consultant in Speech Therapy, London County Council

MUCH has happened since the International Conference of Speech Training in 1927 at which there was a section devoted to Remedial Speech. In those days there were only a few pioneers who took any interest in this subject; but happily since then there has been widespread research by students of speech therapy and a widening interest taken by the medical and educational professions and also by the general public.

Great Britain was for many years a long way behind the Viennese school of speech therapy of which Dr. Stein was an active and eminent member for over twenty years, but latterly I feel that this country of ours is no longer in the rearguard but in the vanguard of the advance of speech therapy. This has further been enhanced by the remarkable success of the International Speech Conference which was held in London in September, 1948.

One cannot but think back to the evolution of our own language and the effect the Norman Conquest had on it. The Normans and the English were subsequently welded into a Nation. The English language, which was then that of a socially inferior class, disappeared for about two centuries and French was then the ordinary language of the courts. A statute of 1362, however, ordered the use of English instead of French in the pleadings of the Law Courts. It is, moreover, interesting to note that the French language was modified considerably and as A. Gordon Smith tells us in his 'Short History of Medieval England' so much so that it was a French that sounded strange in the ears of a Frenchman. More important than this, he tells us, was the revival of English itself as a literary language which dates from the early part of the 13th century. It was about 1205 when Layamon, the parish priest of Ernley, composed his 'Brut,' a legendary chronicle of the ancient heroes of Britain, and from then onwards other works in English appeared. The English language was spread throughout the world and is now considered by students of other languages, including the author, to be rich and flexible.

I have known Dr. Stein since he came to England. In those days his knowledge of the spoken word in English was limited but anyone reading his books to-day will realise the mastery he has achieved in our language. This book is an example of patient and erudite study and shows how deep he has delved into anthropology and linguistics. His method of approach to the subject is at times definitely provocative and will stimulate students of linguistics and anthropology to further researches. He has collected a set of illustrations and diagrams which are apt, explanatory and amusing; and enhance the value of the book.

Dr. Stein's thesis sets out to prove that the speech of primitive communities throws a light on modern speech disorders and that modern speech disorders suggest how primitive man spoke. He has attempted to conjure up the past in speech and language and I think he has succeeded.

April, 1949   E. J. B.

APOLOGIES, JUSTIFICATION AND THANKS

To the minds of some readers this book may hardly deserve to be regarded as a serious work. Rather would the twaddle I seem to be talking in it invite the reader to include it in the class of what the Romans called *ineptiae* written down by a scribbler.

The reason is not difficult to find. The attempt at describing types of speech spoken in bygone ages, some of them as much as half a million years back, may well be derided as a piece of folly. This attitude may be strengthened as the patient reader finds that the book is based on a scatter of facts, some of them confirmed some of them not, some of them accurate some of them apparently distorted, misunderstood or misrepresented, some of them obvious, some of them obscure and obtuse. I may be accused of having plunged myself into an unforgivable adventure by using a smattering of knowledge in such fields as anthropology, archæology, prehistory, philology, etc., with which I confessedly have only a bowing acquaintance. What makes matters worse is that in an attempt at moulding those facts into a coherent whole I have arranged them in a seemingly fanciful and capricious manner. To those who take exception to this mixture of fact and fantasy I offer my apologies.

To the benevolent opponents who will nevertheless read on, I should like to exonerate myself by telling them how this misadventure has come to pass. The idea of elucidating the beginnings of human speech was conceived during a span of my life when in the midst of bombing, destruction and grief an escapist attitude would explain and perhaps justify the headlong flight into a golden past. Yet, whatever man does is not only dictated by unconscious drives, but is also determined by conscious needs and purposes. For many years I have been engaged in the treatment of speech disorders. Close examination of these has revealed many symptoms strongly reminiscent of archaic linguistic features. At first sight they seem to be no more than scattered pieces of a jig-saw puzzle. To help the patient to re-arrange them, the data have to be determined in space and time. In other words, since treatment is nothing but the testing of one's knowledge, it has become imperative to arrive at albeit fictitious assumptions regarding the growth and structure of human speech. That is why I have not confined myself to the task of the chronicler or to that of a compiler of linguistic facts. In an attempt at 'recapturing the atmosphere and reconstructing the life' (John Buchan) of bygone ages I have tried to conjure up the modes of utterance which our forbears may have employed, and which, I believe, are still lying dormant in all of us. Thus the narrative has forcibly assumed the form of the historical novel. Bulwer Lytton has inspired me with the courage to do so. He suggests that one way of utilizing historical data consists in 'lending to ideal personages, and to imaginary fable, the additional interest to be derived from historical groupings.' The narrator should, it is true, strictly adhere to the data furnished by the historian. Yet, faithful to Lytton's precept I have claimed 'the privileges of fiction,' and have 'employed the agency of the passions to illustrate the genuine nature of the beings who had actually lived, and to restore the warmth of the human heart to the images recalled from the grave' insofar as I have endeavoured to re-enliven their 'inward life' and its manifestation in their speech. True, the modes of speaking described in these pages are of a somewhat fictitious character. To present them to the public as 'true' is, however, justified by the fact that under their guidance it has been possible to re-integrate the speech of human beings inflicted with speech disorders.

The manuscript was ready for the printer a considerable time ago. It has, therefore, not been possible to revise it in the light of a number of publications not accessible at the time.

I have selected Reichert's drawings of the brain (Plate 8) made a century ago, for their beauty.

While writing this preface I was asked whether the book would be dedicated to someone. Indeed, I said, it would be.

In the first place it is my heartfelt desire to thank the members of the staff of the Tavistock Clinic, my fellow speech therapists, my patients, and many friends, who all have supplied some tangible evidence, have enlightened me with their interpretations, and have encouraged the flow of ideas.

Once again I wish to put on record my gratitude to Miss Ruth Bennett, L.C.S.T. who helped me with her criticism and corrections, while the work was in the making.

Mrs. Mary J. B. Williams, Psychiatric Social Worker to the Tavistock Clinic, who for some time has been assisting me in the treatment of speech disorders, has with painstaking care helped in the correction of the proofs. Her scrupulous labour, and deep understanding of the emotional aspect of human behaviour has enabled me to eliminate certain ambiguities and inaccuracies, and to put the finishing touches to the work.

Many thanks are due to Miss Harborough, Mr. Massey, Mr. Hubner, and Mrs. Stenger for supplying the photographs of babies, and to Miss Shiels for compiling the index.

Tavistock Clinic, London L. STEIN
1948

CONTENTS

Chapter		Page
	Foreword	v
	Apologies, Justification and Thanks	vii
I.	SHORT HISTORY OF THE PROBLEM	1
	Proem	1
	The Problem Restated	5
	History and Evolution	15
	The Annal	22
	Narrator's Parenthetical Remark	23
II.	THE FORERUNNERS	25
	The Scene of Action	25
	The Cast	26
	Animals	28
	Animal Language	30
III.	THE HUMAN STOCK	38
	The Protagonist Introduced	38
	Pithecanthropus	39
	Pithecanthropus' Behaviour Analysed	45
	The Respiratory and Alimentary Tracts	49
	The Larynx	50
	Voice	52
	Vocal Attacks	56
	Aspirated Attack or Sighing	56
	Soft Attack	56
	Hard Attack or Glottal Stop	57
	Nasality	59
	Linguistic Use of the Attacks	61
	Mouth and Throat	65
	Sucking	67
	In the Beginning was the Need	68
	Clicks	70
	Rhythm	72

Chapter		Page
IV.	UNFLEDGED LANGUAGE	76
	The Three Rungs of Meaning	76
	The Lowermost Rung of Meaning	79
	Sinanthropus	83
	Piltdown Man	86
	Heidelberg Man	88
	Chellean Culture	89
	Chellean Language	91
V.	NEW-FLEDGED LANGUAGE	97
	Amalgamation of Sucking and Voicing	97
	The Stages of Babbling	97
	The Meaning of Babbling	102
	Rhodesian Man	104
	Negroes	106
	Mousterian Man (*Homo Primigenius*)	106
	Acheulian and Mousterian Cultures	111
	Mousterian Language	112
	Half-clicked Sounds	114
	Consonants	117
	Reiteration	124
	Lalling	134
	Aurignacian Man	142
	Aurignacian Culture	146
	Aurignacian Language	154
	The Second Rung of Meaning	158
	Magic Speech	159
	Onomatopœia	161
	Symbolic Language	165
	The Magdalenian Age	166
	Magdalenian Language	171
VI.	FULL-FLEDGED LANGUAGE	177
	The Azilians	177
	Azilian Language	180
	The Uppermost Rung of Meaning	181
	Non-reiterative Speech	186
	Grammatical Categories	189
	Word Coinage	192
	Here Endeth the Narrative	196
	Index	199

TEXT ILLUSTRATIONS

Fig.		Page
1.	Geological Time Table	25
2.	Lateral Surface of the Brain	33
3.	Heads of Prehistoric Man	40
4.	Genealogy of Pithecanthropus	41
5.	Upper Respiratory and Alimentary Tracts	49
6.	Larynx	51
7.	Approximation of the Vocal Cords	51
8.	Infantile Cry	55
9.	Head of a Horse	58
10.	Position of Passavant's Cushion	66
11.	Field of Reference	76
12.	Field of Reference	77
13.	Chronological Survey	87
14.	Anthropometric Measurements	88
15.	Chellean Scraper	90
16.	Cultural Ages	91
17.	Early Palaeolithic Implements	95
18.	Early Babble	97
19.	Babble	98
20.	Clicks	116
21.	Sorcerer from Les Trois Frères	148
22.	Magical Symbolism	148
23.	Capsian Art	149
24.	Bushman Art	150
25.	'Canalisation'	156
26.	Solutrean Flints	168
27.	Magdalenian Flint Implements	169
28.	Magdalenian Art	170
29.	Azilian Art	178
30.	'Under Cover'	196
31.	'From whatever angle you look at it'	196

PLATES AT END

1. MOUTH GESTURES IN APES
2. MOUTH GESTURES IN CHILDREN
3. MOUTH GESTURES IN CHILDREN
4. EARLY AURIGNACIAN OUTLINE-PICTURES
5. A. AURIGNACIAN SCULPTURE
   B. SUPERPOSED PAINTINGS
6. MAGDALENIAN ART
7. ' VENUS ' STATUETTES
8. A. BRAIN-STEM FROM BELOW
   B. BRAIN-STEM FROM ABOVE
   C. INNER SURFACE OF THE BRAIN

ACKNOWLEDGEMENTS

The following illustrations, tables and plates have been drawn from various publications, listed below, for which grateful acknowledgements are made to the authors and publishers.

Text Illustrations :—*Man Rises to Parnassus*, Osborn (Oxford), Figs. 1, 3. *Ophthalmo-und Oto-Neurologie*, Spiegel and Sommer (Julius Springer, Berlin), Fig. 2. *Prehistory*, De Pradenne (Harrap), Fig. 4. *Kehlkopfkrankheiten*, Grünwald (Lehmann, Munich), Figs. 6 and 7. *The Child*, Chamberlain (Walter Scott), Fig. 8. *Le Pharynx*, Chauveau (Baillière et Fils, Paris), Fig. 9. *Sprach-und Stimmstörungen*, Stein (Weidmann, Vienna), Fig. 10. *Dating the Past*, Zeuner (Methuen), Fig. 13. *The Antiquity of Man*, Keith (Williams and Norgate), Fig. 14. *The Old Stone Age*, Burkitt (Cambridge), Fig. 16. *Der Geist der Vorzeit*, Schmidt (Scherl and Keil Verlag), Fig. 17. *Practical Phonetics for Students of African Languages*, Westerman and Ward (O.U.P. and International African Institute), Fig. 20. *Ancient Hunters*, Sollas (Macmillan), Figs. 15, 22, 24, 28. *Our Prehistoric Ancestors*, Davison (Methuen), Figs. 21, 23, 26, 27, 29. *Speech and Voice*, Stein (Methuen), Figs. 18, 19.

Plates:—W. Suschitsky: *Personality of Animals*, Munro Fox (Penguin), Plates 1A & B. Dr. Kurt Priemel, *Sprechen Sie Schimpansisch?* Schwidetsky (Verlag Deutsche Gesellschaft für Tier u. Ursprachenforschung, Leipzig), Plate 1C. A. Houghton Broderick, *Illustrated London News* (London Electrotype Agency, Ltd.), Plate 4. *Ancient Hunters*, Sollas (Macmillan), Plates 5A & B, 6A. *Adam's Ancestors*, Leakey (Methuen), Plate 6B. *Prehistoric Foundations of Europe*, Hawkes (Methuen), Plate 7. *Der Bau des Menschlichen Gehirns*, Reichert (Engelmann, Leipzig), Plate 8C.

CHAPTER I

SHORT HISTORY OF THE PROBLEM

PROEM

THE EXISTENCE of 'language' has always puzzled its possessors. Uncountable are the attempts which for thousands of years have been made towards solving the problem of its origin. It is customary as a mark of the appreciation due to them, to introduce a fresh inquiry by an account of the findings of one's predecessors. If I do not now do so, it should not be taken as a sin of omission. My chief reason for not dealing with previous research in detail is the difference in my approach to the problem. Many of the older theories can be neglected because they are derived from speculation, i.e., a procedure which aims at acquiring coherent knowledge under the guidance of logic, but which, although proceeding logically, bases the inquiry on ideas, especially theological, which transcend experience, and not on facts.[1]

Thus, for example, the religious (traditionalistic) theories claim that language was created as one of the inherent faculties of man, that man derived the use of language from supernatural interposition, or that it was made known to him through divine revelation.

The Brahmans in the Veda raised language to the rank of deity, speech being called the Supreme Brahman.[2] The Old Testament [3] holds a similar view. Democritos regarded names as sounding pictures fashioned by the gods themselves.[4] As late as 1767 Süssmilch [5] attempted to furnish proof of the assertion that language was created by God.

Such doctrines, founded as they are upon the evidence only of emotions, dreams and superstitions, we must regard to-day as unscientific. Thorndike [6] defines Science as 'systematical and ordered knowledge, a consistent body of truth, attained through

---

[1] Eisler, R. (1922). *Handwörterbuch der Philosophie*. Mittler, Berlin. S.v. *Speculation, Tatsache*.
[2] Müller, M. (1882). *Lectures on the Science of Language*. Longmans, Green & Co. Ltd., London. I. p. 92 f.
[3] Genesis, 2. 19 f.
[4] See Plato's *Philebos*.
[5] 'Versuch eines Beweises, dass die erste Sprache ihren Ursprung nicht vom Menschen, sondern vom Schöpfer allein erhalten habe.' Berlin, 1767.
[6] L. Thorndike (1941). *A History of Magic and Experimental Science*. Columbia University Press, New York. Quot. from Brit. Med. Journ. (1941), p. 479.

sense-perception, introspection and reflection, aided by mechanical and mathematical instruments, independently of faith, emotion, prejudice, appetite, pleasure, and the like.' Magic is ' a systematized and ordered marvel-believing and marvel-working, a consistent body of error, attained through sense-perception, introspection, reflection and dreaming, influenced by faith, emotion, appetite and pleasure, marked by unwarranted associations of ideas, without adequate means of correcting error and without proper standards of measurement.'

Strangely enough, similar solutions of the problem of language have persisted right up to our present age. How are we otherwise to account for a book, published by the Eirean Publishing Company of New York in 1943, " which, it is claimed, proves that the Bible was written by Irishmen and that Hebrew is only a dialect of Gaelic."[1]

Other explanations such as—to mention only a few—the invention theories and the nativistic theories, are growing more and more unsatisfactory, because they sin mainly against one now ' common sense ' principle by ignoring the proper arrangement of the relevant facts in space and time, and treating universals as representations of fact.

Nativism attributes all achievements to the unfolding of the individual's innate constitution, the direct antithesis of Empiricism which regards man as an initial blank filled gradually from outside experience.

The Empiricists assert that language was invented by individuals and owed its origin to human choice and convention laid down arbitrarily.[2] The Nativists hold that language is innate, and that from the onset there has been existent a definite correlation between sounds on the one hand and objects and images on the other.[3]

Augustinus, Thomas Aquinas, Locke,[4] Gerber,[5] Hagemann[6] believe that only the general faculty of language is primordial.

Lucretius[7] had already asserted that language was an impulsive

---

[1] *Evening Standard*, 5.3.43, p. 2.
[2] See Whitney (1874). *Die Sprachwissenschaft*, p. 71 ff. Plato, *Cratylus* ; Aristotle and the sophists.
[3] Wundt, W. (1900). *Die Sprache*. Engelmann, Leipzig. Steinthal, H. (1881). *Abriss der Sprachwissenschaft*. Dümmler, Berlin. See also Marty, A. (1916). *Gesammelte Schriften*. I. 2. Niemeyer, Halle, and Paget, R. (1930). *Human Speech*, Kegan Paul, London.
[4] *Essay* III, Ch. 1. 1 ff.
[5] *Die Sprache und das Erkennen*, 1889.
[6] Hagemann (1911). Psychologie 8, S. 295.
[7] Lucretius. *De rerum natura*, V, 1027-1031 (Translated by J. Munro). Deighton Bell & Co., Cambridge, 1873.

SHORT HISTORY OF THE PROBLEM 3

activity, the impulses entailed becoming eventually conventionalized and systematized : ' But nature impelled them to utter the various sounds much in the same way as the inability to speak is seen in its turn to drive children to the use of gestures, when it forces them to point with the finger at the things which are before them.'[1] This view was later expounded by Herder, W. von Humboldt, Renan, Steinthal, Lazarus and others.

The empiristic-genetic theories of Schleicher, Tylor, Marty [2] and others [3] denied the primordial association of images and sounds, but held that the correlation evolved through the ages.

Marty took great pains to prove that "the sounds of language (*die artikulierten Laute*) came to their function neither through innate association with images, nor through chance, but through human choice and intention."[4] The German version referring to the speech sounds shows that much confusion is bound to spring from the German participle '*artikuliert*' which may mean both '*articulated*' and '*articulate*.' We shall revert to the question of 'articulateness' on a later occasion (see p. 99). A similar confusion between 'articulate' and 'articulated' is found in Rae's paper on Polynesian : ' Language is definite articula*te* sound. Its general progress therefore would be from the slightly articulat*ed* to the strongly articulated. That is to say from being but little broken by what we term consonants, to being greatly broken by them ; speaking in the general therefore, the fewer the consonants the older the language.' [5]

These brief examples also show that the approach of earlier workers was mainly anthropomorphic in so far as ' forces,' ' powers,' ' faculties ' were searched for and hypostatized. It was not sufficiently realised that language as such, which was supposed to be engendered by such forces, was itself an abstract notion as opposed to the particular features observed in languages.

Even those who, in a somewhat materialistic manner, attempt to reduce psychological events to physiological (physical) processes cannot be acquitted.

To comment briefly on one of the often propounded ' modern '

---

[1] At varios linguae sonitus natura subegit mittere, et utilitas expressit nomina rerum : Non alia longe ratione, atque ipsa videtur protrahere ad gestum pueros infantia linguae, quom facit, ut digito, quae sint praesentia monstrant.
[2] Marty, A. (1916). *Gesammelte Schriften*. Niemeyer, Halle, I. 2.
[3] Cf. Kreibig (1909). *Die inteliektuellen Funktionen*, pp. 52 ff.
[4] Marty, l.c., p. 1.
[5] Dr. J. Rae in Paget, R. (1930). *Human Speech*. Kegan Paul, London, p. 326.

B

views ; that man from his very beginnings has owed his speaking faculty to the extensive development of the cerebral cortex, and that language is thus a kind of by-product of the brain. No doubt the cortex is a *conditio sine qua non* of speech. But to regard it as the only essential is a serious fallacy, since, as we shall try to make clear, other parts of the nervous system are equally indispensable. Moreover, the concept of causation involved in describing the nervous system as the sum total of the *causes* with language as its *effect*, cannot stand philosophical scrutiny.

A serious deficiency of many works, old and new, lies in their assumption that everyone, including the inquirer, knows precisely to what subject matter the word ' language ' refers. So it happens that the general concept of language as a ' faculty ' is confused with particular modes of speaking. We need only recall such phrases as : articulated speech, articulate speech, human speech, parrots' speech ; human language, animal language, and so forth, to realize the confusion of terms.

No wonder that under such conditions the controversy about the origin of language had led to such a confusion that the *Société de Linguistique* of Paris in 1866 saw fit to forbid any further discussion on the subject. It apparently assumed the problem to be insoluble.

Recent years, however, have seen a vigorous revival of the desire to unravel the origin of language. Most of the attempts have been fruitless, strangely enough, because workers like Niessl-Mayendorf,[1] Naunyn,[2] R. A. Wilson,[3] and others have again stepped into the same traps as led to previous failures.

The memory of the state of affairs in the 19th century seems to have induced such eminent scholars as Sir Richard Paget[4] to apologize for a renewed attempt at solution. How far such restraint is justified the following pages will show.

There is, it must be admitted, a grain of truth in the notions underlying the above-mentioned theories, provided they are properly defined and fitted into the body of knowledge about the world in general. Thus, their brief enumeration helps here in so far as their at least partial denial serves as an encouragement in the search, and as a warning to free ourselves from the tyranny of words

---

[1] Niessl-Mayendorf, E. (1914). *Das Geheimnis der menschlichen Sprache*. Bergman, Wiesbaden.
[2] Naunyn, B. (1925). *Die organischen Wurzeln der Lautsprache des Menschen*. Bergmann, München.
[3] Wilson, R. A. (1941). *The Miraculous Birth of Language*. British Publishers Guild, London.
[4] Paget, R. (1930). *Human Speech*. Kegan Paul, London, p. xiii.

SHORT HISTORY OF THE PROBLEM

which was imposed on former writers. It will then also become clear that some of the above-mentioned theories only seemingly contradict one another.

By confining the abstract notions strictly to their respective fields, and by taking care to arrange those fields in the right temporal order, we shall avoid confusion, and may turn contradiction into agreement, putting to good use the material furnished and the results obtained by many eminent scientists of language.

The outcome may seem to be a reconciliation of the nativistic and empiristic theories, which as regards the development of speech in the child was successfully attempted by W. Stern.[1] Révész[2] has made a similar attempt in respect of the pre-history of language. By carefully stating our premises we, too, shall endeavour to unify the existing theories. It will then be seen that such a scheme bears the solution of the riddle in the bud.

THE PROBLEM RE-STATED

The first essential, then, is to be unmistakably certain of just what it is that we are going to talk about. Can we be sure of knowing the objects to which the term ' language ' refers ? Such a question may at first cause a frown. A short etymological consideration, however, shows that a not uncommon misconception still lingering in some minds, is caused by the tyranny of the word itself. Like many others this term for the communication of our thoughts and feelings expresses a metaphor, while still retaining its literal meaning. Thus the German *Zunge*, the Greek *glossa*, the Latin *lingua*, and its Romance derivatives (such as French *langue*), Czech *jazyk*, English *mother-tongue*—to mention only a few—all denote the fleshy organ in the mouth which is used for taking in, pushing, chewing, grinding and tasting food.

There is no need to explain the metaphor as everyone knows the important part which the tongue plays in articulation. Yet the co-operation of the tongue is by no means essential. First, a language without lingual sounds such as *t, d, n, l, r, s, sh* can easily be imagined. Secondly, speech pathology has furnished cases demonstrating that individuals who, owing to disease, have been

---

[1] Stern, William (1914). *Psychologie der frühen Kindheit*. Quelle & Meyer, Leipzig, p. 19.

[2] Révész, G. (1946). *Ursprung und Vorgeschichte der Sprache* Franke, Berne. Chapters I-VI.

deprived of the greater part of the root of the tongue can still speak intelligibly.[1]

In spite of such facts some historians, anthropologists and linguists are inclined to deduce the more or less highly developed faculty of speech from the conformation of the lower jaw, and the insertion, shape and mobility of the tongue in (fossil) man. (See p. 35.) It is obvious that these workers are influenced by the concrete meaning of the term for articulate utterance.

Having examined the term itself we are confronted with the task of dealing with the object to which the word refers, is believed to refer, or should refer. These alternatives derive from the widespread belief that where there is a word there is also an object. Now, 'things' are recognized by their properties, spatial and temporal, which in their turn are dependent on the observer's probing. These processes must be properly observed and described before they can be logically arranged and classified.[2] The classification of objects or events entails the synthesis of properties common to their class. The results of this procedure are the 'concepts,' i.e., mere logical ideals as opposed to concrete data. A concept embraces a number of objects and the relationships of their properties.

It is doubtful whether things can be perceived properly without being brought into some frame-work of classification however crude and primitive this may be, and here it is that we commit the commonest error, namely, the mistaking of a class of things for one of its individual items. The word which labels the thing in question is then used for the class or the concept. The latter in its turn is hypostatized, i.e., regarded as concrete and independent in its existence from the classifying mind.

The entanglement increases when two concepts are brought into relation with one another in a logical proposition, which is usually expressed by a sentence consisting of two words, denoting these concepts and a word which indicates that relationship. The latter belongs to a class of words, termed (first, it seems, by Abaelard) 'copula,' i.e., 'that which couples,' usually represented by the word 'is.' It thus appears that the words 'is' or 'is not' do not indicate *real existence*.[3] Nor do the subjects and predicates

---
[1] Louis (1774). Mém. de l'acad. de chir. Paris. T.v., p. 486.
Twisleton, E. (1873). 'The Tongue not essential to Speech.' London.
[2] As to the scientific approach, see Lenzen, V. F. (1938). *Procedures of Empirical Science*. The University of Chicago Press.
[3] See Eisler, R. (1922). *Handwörterbuch der Philosophie*. Mittler, Berlin. S.v. Kopula.

connected by the copula exist in their own right or by their own might; they are only distinctions within the judgment which alone is the primary act of thought.[1] Such judgments are of rather high standing and therefore have to be handled with the utmost care lest the inquirer get into entanglement and commit a blunder.

The word ' is ' (or its equivalents) has a long development behind itself which has made it a powerful and indispensable instrument of thought. If the full extent of its grown-up capacity be disregarded or misunderstood, it can, despite its diminutive size, lead us into serious mischief.

In primitive languages copulas are not yet developed. There we can see them in their infancy, as different from their adult shapes as are tadpoles from frogs. The normal type of the substantive sentence even in Indo-European languages has no copula, and is known as the substantive sentence in its pure form. The attribute is simply placed next to the subject, the respective order of the two elements being fixed in each language by special rules.[2] In Indo-European languages the verb which is to act as copula starts its function as an intransitive verb, later being stripped of concrete meaning and colour to an extent which enables it to act as a pure mental counter. Thus, the root *es-* which yielded the copula at a very early period really signifies existence or life ; the participle *sat*, in Sanskrit, means a living being, and its derivative *satyas* means true ; in Greek *ta onta* signifies " reality." . . . Quite a number of substitutes for the verb " to be " are used as copulas. One of the most extensively used is a verb whose proper meaning is ' to grow, to increase.' It has retained this meaning in the Greek *phyein*; but *bhavati* in Sanskrit has acquired the meaning of " it becomes " and finally " it is." In Old English *béo* signified " I am " like *biu* in Irish ; Latin derived its preterite *fuit* " he was " from the same base; Slavonic derived from it a series of substantive verbal forms (*byti* " to be," *bychu* " I was," etc.). Still other roots have been placed under contribution: the meaning of Greek *gignomai* " I become " is akin to that of " to be," like the Latin *uersor*. Latin *stare* was the source of the French imperfect *j'étais*; and from a root signifying *to inhabit* (Sanskrit *vasati* " he dwells ") Germanic has taken some of the forms of its substantive verb (German *ich war, gewesen*). Russian, perhaps, contains the greatest variety of substitutes for the verb " to be." According to the

---

[1] Schiller, F. C. (1929). *Logic for Use*, p. 218.
[2] Vendryes, J. (1925). *Language*. Kegan Paul, London, pp. 122-3.

exact shade of meaning required, it employs *sidjêt* (to be seated) *ležat'* (to be lying down), *stojat'* (to be standing), *sostojat'* (to be composed), *predstavljat' soboiu* (to appear as), etc.[1] However, the sentences in which these verbs are used are only partially substantives, for the significance of the copula, which is fundamental to their use, is overlaid with shades of meaning derived from the real meaning of these verbs. They are akin to sentences frequently used in old languages, where the adjective-attribute was attached to some verb : Gr. *kolakes akouousin* (they heard themselves called flatterers), Gr. *chthizos ebe kata daita* (he went to the feast yesterday); Latin *ibant obscuri* (they walked in the dark); Old Slavic *pade nici* (he fell down).[2] Here one cannot help recalling such English phrases as ' *he goes, went*, or *has gone mad*,' expressing the process of ' becoming.'

Here, then, is another instance showing how necessary it often is to explain the hierarchy of meaning of a given word, if we want to avoid entanglement.

To avoid that danger in this special case it is essential that a word's more abstract meaning, and a word's concrete meaning should be treated separately.[3]

It now becomes obvious that our inquiry into the nature of language should start with the observation and description of an immense multitude of individual languages and the internal and external events related to them, a task which surmounts human power. A certain amount of abstraction will therefore be needed, but will do no harm provided we remain aware of what we are doing.

Having collected as many properties as possible, we may carry the procedure of abstraction further and further and arrive at such definitions as the one given by Dittrich, which says : " Language is the entirety of all human or animal instances of successful expression which ever have or can become actual, in so far as they are (can be) attempted to be understood by at least *one* other individual." [4]

---

[1] Boyer, P. and Spéranski, N. (1905). *Manuel de langue russe*. Paris, p. 249 ff. Substitutes equally varied are frequent in Polish.
[2] Vendryes, pp. 124–5.   [3] See p. 9, imposition.
[4] " Sprache ist die Gesamtheit aller jemals aktuell gewordenen bzw. aktuell werden koennenden Ausdrucksleistungen der menschlichen bzw. tierischen Individuen, insofern sie von mindestens *einem* anderer Individuum zu verstehen gesucht werden (koennen)." Dittrich, O. (1913). *Die Probleme der Sprachpsychologie*. Quelle & Meyer, Leipzig, p. 12. Cf. also Gardiner, A. H. (1932). *The Theory of Speech and Language*. Clarendon Press, Oxford.

SHORT HISTORY OF THE PROBLEM

This broad definition has been given preference because it entails that all language has been imposed on individuals by their evolutionary make-up ; that it is " the offspring of need and the foster child of social feelings ; "[1] that it presupposes a community ;[2] that it exists to promote communication, as was first emphasized, so far as I know, by Hugo Schuchardt.[3]

We are of course permitted, indeed compelled, to use terms in a general sense. But this endeavour must not make us overlook the fact that they are verbal abbreviations and do not indicate definite realities.

And here we are back again at our starting point, more puzzled than ever. Do we really mean those generalities ? And if we do, do we not behave like children who attribute every happening to gremlins, spirits, and the like, in brief, to some mysterious agents ?

It can now clearly be seen who the tyrants are that have induced us to believe in such agents. It is the very words we are using.

The scholastic grammarians have warned us to bear constantly in mind the ' impositions ' and ' intentions ' of the words we are using at a given moment. " Impositions " are ' uses that have been put upon them ' (Latin *impono* '. I put upon '). ' A word has first imposition when it is used to signify or point out something else, as when I say "table" and mean the thing I am writing on. A word has second imposition when it is used to refer to itself, as when I say " table is a noun " ; I am then making " table " refer to itself as a word.'[4]

' When terms in the first imposition refer to concrete objects or groups of them the terms have first intention. When they refer to universals they have second intention. . . . Terms may have both first and second intention, and when they do, we feel the ambiguity due to the presence of the ghostly universals in the concrete objects.'[5]

It is relevant here to point out how long it has taken mankind to analyse those elements which common sense nowadays has accepted as constituent parts of language, and where this procedure has led us.

The first grammarians were probably those who had to teach

---
[1] Wieland (1871). As quoted by Weise, O, (1909). *Language and Character of the Roman People*. Kegan Paul, London, p. 75.
[2] Cf. Van Wijk, N. (1938). ' La delimitation des domaines de la phonologie et de la phonétique.' Third Congress of Phonetic Sciences. Ghent. p. 8.
[3] Abhandlungen über den Sprachursprung.
[4] Buchanan, S. (1938). *The Doctrine of Signatures*. Kegan Paul, London, p. 8.
[5] Buchanan, l.c., p. 17.

foreign languages. The idea of learning a foreign language probably did not dawn on people until at a comparatively late stage of history, with the advent of general travel and commerce.[1] Kipling's poem, "The Stranger," brings home to us the uneasy feeling which was bound to spring up when an alien was entering a dwelling place.

'The stranger within my gate,
he may be true or kind,
but he does not talk my talk—
I cannot feel his mind.
I see the face and the eyes and the mouth,
But not the soul behind.'[2]

The Greeks analysed their language in a way which, surprisingly, still forms the basis of present day grammar.

Everyone who has had some schooling has been taught that a coherent utterance consists of sentences. These can be divided into smaller units, called words. They in their turn are divisible into syllables and further into sounds.[3]

The schoolboy also knows that the different parts of an utterance may be given more or less prominence by enouncing them with more or less force or loudness (stress), and in a higher or lower pitch, thus basing articulateness on vocal melody (intonation).

He has been taught that the constituent parts can be represented visually. The units of written or printed language are the letters of the alphabet. They are arranged in smaller or larger units said to refer to spoken units. This representation and the grouping of letters is as arbitrary as that of sound sequences and is often dictated by convenience of classification, historical considerations and false etymologies. Cf. black bird—blackbird, Ital. *finiró*<*finir*+*ho* (I have to finish, i.e., I shall finish), *fight* pronounced [fait], French *bonheur*, ' good fortune,' Latin *bonum augurium*, ' good augury.'

The school boy, to his disappointment, soon recognises that the written representation by no means always corresponds to the spoken units. Hence the difficulties he finds in acquiring the necessary ability in spelling. But not only does he find it difficult to establish the reference between, e.g., the verbal noises [endaitmənt], [rʌf], [plau] and the verbal pictures ' endictment, rough, plough '; simple syllables also cannot easily be seen to consist of the ' sounds ' he has learned. Many of us may have noted that to a child taught

---
[1] See Müller, M., l.c. I. pp. 92 ff.
[2] Kipling, R. Verse. Hodder & Stoughton Ltd., London, p. 616.
[3] See Aristotle, *Metaph.* IV. 3.

SHORT HISTORY OF THE PROBLEM 11

in the alphabetical method it is not at all obvious that M and O when placed next to one another is MO [mo^u]. A link seems to be missing which is essential in the concept of the syllable as an ' unbroken unity ' of sound. We shall soon see what this ' link ' is and how essential it is to realise its nature and the role it plays in the evolution of language. (See pp. 97 ff.)

The sound elements can be analysed down into smaller constituent parts by means of the scientific methods of modern physics such as kymography, phonography and the like. Thus it is now known that the speech sounds are peculiar resonances, built up in the same way as other resonances such as musical tones, noises and chords.

There need be practically no limit to this analysis except that it tends to distract us from other qualities. It goes without saying, for example, that one of the features which distinguish language from other noises is the fact that it must at least be performed by living beings [1]; but living beings—we are told—have in common the essential components of ' Body ' and ' Mind.' Now what precisely do these terms mean ? Theories of language are usually built on psychological theories, and much must evidently depend on the underlying concepts. It is not the place here to enumerate and evaluate the theories on the interrelation between entities usually classified as and termed Body and Mind ; the traditional distinction between bodily (or material) and mental processes had—according to Carnap—its origin in the old magical and later metaphysical mind-body dualism.[2] I submit as a working hypothesis the theory of identity adumbrated by Spinoza,[3] Goethe, and later workers, which seems to be the best way of escape from magical belief. According to this doctrine, the Corporeal and the Mental, the Physical and the Psychical, the Objective and the Subjective ' though distinguishable under abstractive analysis ' and ' diverse in kind ' are not interconnected in some mysterious way, but are merely two *aspects* of one unique, and as such, indivisible identical substance. There is ' one course of events within the organism ; just one, though these events are always two-fold in relatedness, physical and mental, diverse in kind, yet inseparable, but none the less

---

[1] See the enumeration of animals gifted with language in Huxley, J. and Koch, L. (1938). ' Animal Language.' Country Life, London.
[2] Carnap, R. (1938). ' Logical Foundations of the Unity of Science.' *Int. Encyclopedia of Unified Science.* University of Chicago Press. Vol. I, Number 1 p. 47.
[3] Spinoza, *Ethics* II,.' Concerning the Nature and Origin of the Mind,' prop. VII. London, Dent & Sons, pp. 41 f.

distinguishable under abstractive analysis.' There is, in the words of C. Lloyd Morgan a certain hierarchy of modes of relatedness in every living being. Just as there is physical relatedness so there is ' mental ' relatedness co-related with it from bottom to top. " In the evolutionary advance of events there is not a new kind of relatedness, called mental, that slips in at some stage of hierarchical progress ; nor is the physical kind absent at any stage even the highest ; nor is either kind derivative from the other kind." [1]

The foregoing basic principle, although only briefly outlined, hints at the fact that we have by no means enumerated all the data referring to beings described as gifted with speech. It would be necessary to give a more or less complete account of the structures and mechanisms co-operating in speech, such as the so-called speech organs (lips, tongue and so on), the nervous mechanisms operating them and the social groups within which languages can be observed. But this would constitute a textbook of anatomy, physiology, psychology, phonetics and so on, which it is not our purpose to write. Reference shall, however, be made to the relevant structures in the appropriate places.

There is also another reason for postponing the account of the mechanism concerned. If the analytic way of approach induced us to split the properties enumerated above into smaller and smaller units, we might perhaps arrive at considerable knowledge of infinitesimal parts. Yet this mode of analysis would not furnish us with that thorough understanding which it yields when applied to purely physical phenomena.

According to Kerr,[2] ' our knowledge is, and always must be, comparatively superficial as compared, say, with the physicist's knowledge of physical phenomena, for the reason that we cannot apply to living substance the method of analysis—the method of splitting the complex into its simple components, and the investigation of these in the isolated condition—the method which has yielded to physics and chemistry their triumphs.' For even if we take into account all the information afforded by natural and mental sciences we get no further than the catalogue stage—with an inventory of the parts of a complex machinery. Looking at those parts we still wonder how and why they have come to work in the peculiar way observed, why they have their particular shapes and

---

[1] Morgan, C. Lloyd (1929). *Mind at the Crossways*. Williams & Norgate, London, pp. 28/9.
[2] Cf. Kerr, J. G. (1926). *Evolution*. Macmillan, London, p. 10.

positions, and why together they form their particular patterns. The necessary degree of comprehension can be attained only through re-instating the peculiar relationships between the atomic facts which the analytic mind has disregarded ; such relationships usually referred to by terms like context, pattern, mode, and so forth.

Language has so far been analysed into elements, which can be subjected separately to further study. Although there can be no doubt that without this procedure we should not have reached such knowledge as is set out in the works on phonetics, and grammars, it seems that we must now reverse the whole process of analysis and so re-establish the primary units step by step without losing sight of the elements. In recombining the isolated components into more complex sets, we must beware of two possible errors. Firstly, the overlooking of some determining factor which during our analytical efforts may have seemed irrelevant. The main factor which is generally overlooked is the position on the time scale of a given element or event, a mode of relatedness to which we shall presently return (see *Evolution and History*, p. 16).

Secondly, the analysing mind tends—according to Smuts—to conserve the elements it has isolated ' as the natural factors of the situation ' and indeed to regard ' the situation itself as a sort of result brought about by them.' ' The analytical elements thus become the real operative entities, while the situation or phenomenon to be explained becomes their product or resultant. As a matter of fact,' continues Smuts, ' just the opposite is the case. We started in nature with the complex situation or sensible phenomenon as the reality to be explained. The analytical elements or factors were merely the result of analysis, and might even be mere abstractions. But because they are simpler and admit of closer scrutiny and experiment, we have come to look upon them as real or constitutive, and upon the situation from which they were abstracted or analysed as artificial or constituted. Thus it has come about that in physical science, for instance, the elements of matter or force into which bodies have been analysed have tended to become the reals. Thus scientific entities like electrons and protons, and the physical energies or forces which they represent, are taken to be the real entities in nature, and sensible matter or bodies as something derivative and merely resulting from their activities. The abstract thus becomes the real, the concrete is relegated to a secondary position. This inversion of reality is very much the same procedure as was condemned in the case of the scholastic and other philosophers who attributed reality to universals instead of to concrete particulars. This may be called the error of abstraction or generalisation. Against both these forms of error we have to guard, if we wish faithfully to interpret Nature as we experience her.' [1]

If we disregard the above rules we may—and very often do—fall into a trap which has been pointed out by Blanshard in his warning that ' we must not confuse what is analytically simplest with what is historically first,' since ' what is first in order of nature tends, as Aristotle said, to be last in order of thought.' [2]

Being ignorant of such principles some of the older philologists fell into the error of regarding the so-called ' roots ' as the primordial elements of language.

The early Indians before 500 B.C. had arrived at the conception of roots as the simplest and central elements of meaningful speech.[3] The Jewish grammarian, Abu Zachariyà Hayudj, introduced the idea into Hebrew grammar.

In Europe the same idea was taken up in the 16th century by Henry Estienne.[4]

According to Jespersen,[5] a root should be properly defined as ' what is common to a certain number of words felt by the popular instinct of the speakers as etymologically belonging together.' Everyone has a certain framework for the language he employs. It is constructed by a classification—not always correct—of words according to their meaning and sound-structure. Thus, for instance, $dr.nk$, $s.t$, are formulas abstracted from the English words drink, drank, drunk ; sit, sat, seat, set, which are naturally felt to belong together.

Thus ' roots ' are mere mental concepts arrived at through a more or less ' scientific ' process of classification which takes place in all speakers and at all times. The classification is carried out according to a certain, but as it were, arbitrary principle or purpose, say time, thing, mode of action, spatial relation and so on. (See below, pp. 17 ff.)

From this it appears impermissible to assign to these merely conceptual and timeless " units of partial resemblance between

---

[1] Smuts, J. C. (1926). *Holism and Evolution*. Macmillan, London, pp. 19 f.
[2] Blanshard, B. (1939). *The Nature of Thought*. Allen & Unwin, London, pp. I. 55–56 ; 217.
[3] Müller, M. l.c., I. p. 93.
[4] Müller. *Ibid.*, footnote 2.
[5] Jespersen, O. (1922). *Language*. Allen & Unwin, London, p. 374.

words,"[1] the role of the *real*, i.e., primary linguistic elements out of which prehistoric speech was formed.

Yet up till not so long ago[2] it was strongly believed that primeval language consisted " of nothing but formless roots " which passed through an agglutinating stage, wherein formal elements had been developed, independently of them, to the third and highest stage found in flexional languages, in which formal elements penetrated the roots and made inseparable unities with them.[3] Only in recent times has this fallacious doctrine been abandoned.

HISTORY AND EVOLUTION

The foregoing considerations bring to mind the method in which Herbert Spencer used to approach a problem. He most aptly showed that objects or events cannot be adequately comprehended unless we persistently ask ourselves : ' How came it thus conditioned ? ' and ' How will it cease to be thus conditioned ? '[4]

The inquirer's attitude is thus historical in that it refrains from dealing with facts without referring to their temporal framework.

Thucydides' assertion ' that only through a knowledge of how things came about can we understand what they are '[5] finds an echo in Tylor, who urged that ' they who wish to understand their own lives ought to know the stages through which their opinions and habits have become what they are.'[6]

Before going any further it may be advisable to take a look at ' history ' as a term applied to this method of approach. The English word is a loan-word from French where, as in cognate Romance languages, it is the direct descendant of the Latin *historia*. The Romans borrowed it from the Ionian Greeks who applied the term ' to the "inquiries" or investigations which characterized the whole intellectual movement rather than to that one branch to which it was ultimately limited. The " historian " was the " inquirer " or truth seeker. The word was already used in this sense in the Iliad, where quarrelling parties in disputes at law came shouting " Let us make Agmemnon, Atreus' son, our arbitrator, our ' histor ' (ἵστωρ). " Obviously, by the word " histor " Homer had in mind

---

[1] Bloomfield, L. (1933). *Language*. New York, p. 240.
[2] Cf. Müller. *The Science of Language*.
[3] Jespersen, l.c., p. 367.
[4] Spencer, H. (1867). *First Principles*. Caldwell, Boston—New York, p. 235.
[5] As quoted by Shotwell, J. T. (1939). *History of History*, pp. 15, 234.
[6] Tylor, Edward (1871). *Primitive Culture*.—See also Sherrington, C. (1940). *Man on his Nature*. Cambridge University Press, p. 30.

the wise man who knows the tribal customs and can get at the rights of the case by " inquiring " into the facts. . . . The Roman *quæstor*—' he who inquires '—carried the office over into the formal magistracy.'[1]

The word *histor* ' one who knows ' and its derivatives sprang from a base *wid, woid*, which is otherwise preserved in Germanic, and Old English *witan* ' to know,' modern English *wit*.

The adoption of the Greek word into English is felicitous, since only through setting it against its temporal background can we gain true knowledge of a present occurrence.

The introduction of the term betrays a fine sagacity since the Germanic word ' *geschehen*,' old High German *gisechan* from which German " *Geschichte* " is derived refers solely to the narration of what has happened. Similarly for instance Czech *dějiny* (*děje se* ' it happens ').

Yet the mere taking into account of the time factor does not turn a classification gained from another, say analytical, angle into a historical, let alone a genetic one. It necessarily involves a re-shuffling and rearranging of the facts so far known, so that whole blocks different from those gained by static analysis come to be established. And even then we shall not have set up more than a succession of " mere panoramas."

Polybius would have us to know that *history* must answer the question ' *why* ' in terms of *cause, principle* and *motive*, if it is to be of abiding value (see above) and if it is to transgress the purview of a mere *chronicle*. Briefly, then, chronicle, i.e., the enumeration of events becomes history by introducing interpretation, i.e., the revelation of the meaning of the events.

The nature of interpretation has been well described by Shotwell. ' Anyone knows that you answer the child's " Why ? " by telling another story. Each story, is, in short, an explanation, and each explanation a story. The schoolboy's excuse for being late is that he couldn't find his cap. He couldn't find his cap *because* he was playing in the barn. Each incident was a cause and each cause an incident in his biography. In like manner most of the reasons we assign for our acts merely state an event or a condition of affairs which is in itself a further page of history. At last, however, there comes a point where the philosopher and the child part company. History is more than events. It is the manifestation of life, and behind each event is some effort of mind and will, while within

---

[1] Shotwell, l.c., p. 168.

each circumstance exists some power to stimulate or obstruct.'[1] 'History and its interpretation are essentially one, if we mean by history all that has happened, including mind and matter in so far as they relate to action.'[2]

The historical approach holds good not only in respect of such events as are known from written records, but also to happenings previous to strictly historical ones. Zilsel has shown that 'the realm of history comprehends human occurrences and their causes which are slower by one degree than the reactions of the individuals and faster by one degree than biological evolution.'[3] 'Thus history with its prelude pre-history becomes a continuation of natural history.'[4]

It is, therefore, on natural history that our inquiry should be based since 'a history of language that sees in the customs which it records merely the conventional and not the natural as well, will remain a senseless learned chronicle of words.'[5]

Pursuing in this way the succession of events we arrive at sets of patterns which are said to have 'evolved' out of each other, in a manner comparable to such processes in every-day life as the transition from seed to plant, to flower and to fruit. To give these stages the epithet "transitional" is only possible if we assume substances which are by definition permanent. But it must be borne in mind that only the different configurations are given; that these should be only growth-stages of one and the same thing, i.e., of an identical substance, is a mere postulate of the mind,[6] arrived at probably because the conscious mind usually conceives itself as a permanent entity.[7]

Viewed in isolation, taken out of their temporal and causal context, many configurations and phenomena, such as purple as distinct from red and blue, copper sulphate as distinct from copper and sulphuric acid, the flower as distinct from its seed appear to us as 'new.' Aggregates of a certain kind displaying qualities which cannot be observed in their components are said to be the result of 'emergent evolution.'[8]

---

[1] Shotwell, l.c., pp. 15, 234.
[2] Shotwell, ibid. p. 17.
[3] Zilsel, E. (1940). 'History and Biological Evolution.' *Philosophy of Science*, vii, I, pp. 121-8, Baltimore.
[4] Childe, Gordon (1942). *What happened in History*. Penguin Books. l.c., p. 7.
[5] Vossler, l.c., p. 98.
[6] Schiller, F. C. (1912). *Formal Logic*.
[7] For the meaning and nature of analogy, see below, pp. 20 ff.
[8] See Haldane, J. B. S. (1937) *The Inequality of Man*. Penguin Books, p. 114.

Occurrences agreeing in all their qualities are said to be " *the same.*" It is obvious that this assertion entirely depends on the more or less acute discriminating power of the observer. The 'man in the street'—himself a fiction of the mind—holds that the English language of to-day is 'the same' as that of 1940 or even 1930, but the trained philologist refutes this opinion both in respect of utterance and of the underlying mental states.

The differences grow bigger and bigger the more we plunge into the past which becomes increasingly 'patchy' and deprived of 'perspective.' Events pertaining to those dim and distant epochs are then said to be totally different, i.e., not kindred. Such propositions express our disability to perceive the data necessary for the construction of a clear cut 'line' of development.

Thus the course which the line may have taken between two or more points found can only be guessed. This synthetic procedure which traces the march of time, establishes causal relations and continuity of existence by filling in the gaps in the material furnished by observation is known as *interpolation*.[1]

In employing it we must always remember that, permissible though it may be to insert a detail in its probable place, there may be other less readily apparent details and their relationships correlated to it, which with patience would lead to a considerably more accurate conjecture.

This precaution has often been disregarded when linguistic changes and their causes have been assumed by analogy with known changes, whilst it has been tacitly presumed that the factors related to them have remained identical—an error particularly common when dealing with early historical or prehistoric occurrences, which the present writer himself cannot feel quite certain of being able to avoid.

The more we peer back into the past, the more we have to guard against taking for granted such mere possibilities as have been arrived at by interpolation. On retracing the stages of the unfolding process the number of 'facts' becomes increasingly scanty, continuity increasingly intermittent, the historian thus increasingly the chronicler.

What is then more natural for the imaginative mind than to insert hypothetical data? And what is more dangerous than an

---

[1] Liebmann, O. (1904). *Gedanken und Tatsachen.* II, p. 51 ff. *Die Klimax der Theorien* (1884). Ch. 7.

SHORT HISTORY OF THE PROBLEM

approach which is bound to be guided by preconceived plans or patterns, and by predilections and expectations of all kinds ?

The disadvantage involved in the scarcity of ' points ' necessary for the construction of the evolutionary ' line ' is compensated for by the knowledge of the stage so far reached. Aristotle, and after him Fernel, insisted that to know a thing we must know where it is going to.[1]

The narrative must, nevertheless, in order to avoid rash conclusions, start deliberately as an annal in the sense given to it by Ennius, Vergil and the old grammarians. In their view the word *annal* was much more the synonym for " history " than *historia*. Not only was it used in the general sense which it has in such English phrases as " the annals of the poor " or the " annals of the Empire " but in the eyes of the grammarians it was the only correct term for history of the past. Historia was properly used only of contemporaneous narrative.[2] So Ennius called his epic *Annales* ; and when Vergil refers to the content of early history he uses the same general term.[3]

' The annal is potentially historical. The past not the present, gives it its value and interest. Moreover, the step from the annal to the chronicle is a short one. Prefix a few genealogies or the legendary deeds of the sovereign's divine ancestors and the narrative becomes historical. Where such a narrative follows a rigid scheme of years, as in the annals, we term it a chronicle.' [4]

Our inability to perceive relevant changes may often tempt us to regard certain correlative facts as static and to shift them into the background as more or less irrelevant, although we cannot deny that they may at some time be found to be fundamental and essential.

This is where our intentionally scientific procedure necessarily gets a touch of art, in so far as art satisfies our desire to comprehend the significance of a whole by stressing the relationships between its component parts.[5] A quotation from D. S. MacColl's article on " Action, Direction, Movement " may best express what we mean : " If I wish to express in words the fact that a man passed rapidly through a room, I shall commit an elementary error in description if I linger to make a careful inventory of its furniture. To do this would be to indulge in a realism untrue to fact, for

---
[1] Sherrington, C. (1940). *Man on his Nature*, pp. 105-6, 112.
[2] Shotwell, l.c., p. 273 f.
[3] Vergil, *Aeneid*, Book I, line 373 : *et vacet annales nostrorum audire laborum*.
[4] Shotwell, l.c., p. 61.
[5] See Eisler. *Handwörterbuch*. s.v. ' Aesthetik.'

C

these objects would be present in such insistent detail neither to the actor nor the onlooker ; and destructive of effect, because to describe at such length would be to slacken the expression of speed in the event by the lounging style of its narration. . . . A hint that the china rattled on the chimney-piece may be to the purpose as indicating a vigour of tread, but to be full of information at that moment about the maker's mark on the under-side, is to convince the ' reader that a leisurely saunter was on hand. . . .' " [1]

As we cannot help demonstrating more or less complex occurrences in the above manner before we place them on a given rung of the time-ladder, we have to be particularly careful not to misuse the freedom of inquiry and exposition. For ' in a piece of historical writing, arrangement is argument ; statements of fact, every one of which is true, can be arranged in many ways ; and as some arrangement is always necessary, no historian can be truly " impartial." [2]

Having thus worked out a scheme for making and arranging our observations, we have now only to pass in review the bodies of knowledge which are likely to furnish the mass of data necessary for the construction of the line of development.

These are (1) anthropology ; (2) the descriptive, historical and comparative grammars of existing and extinct languages ; (3) the psychology of primitive races ; (4) the observation of the growing human being especially in respect of gesture and speech ; (5) the comparative anatomy of the nervous system ; (6) the observation of animal behaviour ; (7) the pathology of speech.

As regards primitive [3] peoples, it would be rash to infer that their languages reflect the primordial state of speech for which we are searching, since it is known that these people are themselves backed by a long cultural history ; their present state is therefore to be regarded as only *relatively* primitive. It should, none the less, be possible to detect in them certain relatively stable qualities which may be inferred to be links between a past level and the present.

---

[1] MacColl, D. S. (1940). *What is Art ?* Penguin Books, Ltd., Harmsworth, p. 205 ff.
[2] Shotwell, l.c., p. 198, footnote.
[3] ' The word " primitive " . . . does not carry with it the connotation of " inferior " or even " backward," but rather indicates a condition in which some of the basic factors governing human life are more clearly seen, because less overlaid, than in the so-called " higher " civilisations which have been built up on these earlier foundations.' Layard, John (1942). Stone Man of Malekula. Chatto & Windus, London, p. 25.

To reach this still lower level of speech, other evidence is required (see below, pp. 22ff.). Where can we find it ? Are there any living beings who display features no longer observable in primitive peoples ?

The evidence seems immediately available in the young baby in whom we all anxiously watch the eternal rebirth of the faculty of speech. No one will doubt that babies, besides animals which can for the moment be left out of consideration, are the only beings that do indeed exhibit primitive patterns of utterance. Yet, what assurance have we that the ejaculations of babies resemble the sound patterns which early man may have uttered ?

Observations in other fields have led to the formulation of a general rule which comes to our aid and warrants the inclusion of infantile speech in our inquiry. It is now common knowledge that 'the human embryo passes through phases entirely in agreement with the past history of man' as is shown by the successive appearance of the single cell or zygote representing the Protozoan phase ; the gill-clefts used by the fish for breathing ; the great arteries in the form of aortic arches ; the noto-chord ; the unossified cartilages of the skeleton, characteristic of the lowest fishes ; the tail; the coat of fur . . . ' this agreement is continued in post-natal development.' We need only think of the infant's creeping movements, ' his power of supporting himself by hanging on with his hands, his feeble mentality.' [1]

Von Baer felt justified in deducing from the comparison of embryonic stages of development and the genealogy of animals that " the young stages in the development of an animal are not like the adult stages of other animals down the scale but are like the young stages of those animals." Haeckel, on the other hand, asserted that " the adult stages of the ancestors are repeated during the development of the descendants, but are crowded back into the earlier stages of ontogeny, therefore making the latter an abbreviated repetition of phylogeny." To put the matter in a nutshell, " ontogeny epitomises phylogeny, in the sense of recapitulation, i.e., sums up " [2] and phylogeny is " the procession of ontogenies along a given phyletic line of modification." (The Biogenetic Law.)[3]

---

[1] Kerr, l.c. 212.
[2] Garstang, W. (1921). Journ. Linn. Soc. (Zool.) 35, pp. 84, 98-9.
[3] As to the controversy briefly set out here, see Swinnerton, (1938). ' Development and Evolution.' Report of the British Association for the Advancement of Science, p. 57 ff.

Assuming, then, that the phases through which the child's speech passes reflect those of primitive man, we can avail ourselves of many facts which, though known to previous writers such as Romanes,[1] Kussmaul,[2] Egger,[3] Ament,[4] and others, have not been given adequate consideration by recent workers.

We intend to make full use of the conjectured correlation between infancy and primitivity in an effort to reconstruct the general features of the remote past history of speech. The Biogenetic Law also warrants the telling of another story, namely, that of animal language, in order to ' explain ' infant speech.

Our inquiry is thus making use of the comparative method of approach by means of the analogy :

Structural development of the individual (ontogeny) (A)	:	Structural development of present man's precursors (phylogeny) (B)
Development from infant speech to adult speech (C)	:	Progress from primordial language to present day language (D)

Trusting that the analogy is well built we can attempt to reconstruct the language of our ancestors.

This procedure holds good, of course, mainly in so far as genetically fixed structures and functions are concerned. Our story will therefore end at the point where, rooted and stemmed speech begins to blossom forth in a multitude of environmental circumstances bringing about as many conventional patterns.

THE ANNAL

Having thus outlined our method of approach we will now peruse the annals on which to base our inquiry.

Where are they to be found ? They are comprised, if the well worn metaphor be permitted, in the Grand Book of the Earth. It is a curious book. Its pages are the layers of the Earth's crust. To turn the pages in this volume is not easy. The pages are of different thickness and not always bound in the right order. The events seem to have been entered in a careless and slovenly way,

---

[1] Romanes (1888). Mental Evolution in Man.
[2] Kussmaul, A. (1877). Die Störungen der Sprache. Vogel, Leipzig.
[3] Egger, E. (1903). Beobachtungen und Betrachtungen über die Entwicklung der Intelligenz und der Sprache bei Kindern. Wunderlich, Leipzig.
[4] Ament, W. (1899). Die Entwicklung von Sprechen und Denken beim Kinde. Wunderlich, Leipzig.

for instance, when records relating to different epochs appear on the same page, i.e., on the same level. Many pages have been left empty, some have stuck together or have crumbled away (erosion through the influence of wind and water on the strata); some show a few remarks, others more, but often the record is blurred, illegible or incomprehensible owing to holes (e.g., burrows dug by animals).[1] Even where the ' facts ' are recorded with accuracy they are often incoherent owing to the lack of genealogy or other relationships.

To read the Book of the Earth is thus uphill work, particularly for one like the present writer who by no means gives himself out to be an expert in deciphering the epigraphs engraved in the Earth with a clumsy stencil.

NARRATOR'S PARENTHETICAL REMARK

Scholarly commentators have certainly furnished us with data relating to man's accomplishments throughout the ages. Yet they themselves do not pretend to have presented us with a complete series of well staged scenes of action. Thus, if we are to compose the drama, we cannot help transgressing the field of the mere chronicler by such rational activities as we have above referred to as interpolation, analogy, and so forth.

As Goethe was aware of the more or less unconscious influence of imagination and fantasy in the construction of a narrative out of certain given facts when he entitled his life story : ' Dichtung und Wahrheit ' (Fiction and Truth), so we, in combining the chronicler's task of collecting facts with that of the historian, are anxious to keep in mind the potential distortions involved in the attempt to arrange and interpret them. The writer is aware that the foregoing lengthy remarks on the scientific approach and his efforts to pin himself down to hard and fast rules are merely clumsy attempts which conceal his desire to let his fantasy wander. Imagination is, however, an essential activity in the formation of a hypothesis and is justifiable if it seems likely that the hypothesis can be verified.

In terms of space-time wholes what, then, are the primary wholes which gave rise to human language and how, where and when are we to find them ? It seems at first futile to try to picture the debut of vernal language on the world stage, since, as is well known,

---

[1] See De Pradenne, A. V. (1940). Prehistory. Harrap, London, p. 48.

the records of language cannot be traced back farther than a few thousand years. Careful examinations estimate the age of *Homo Sapiens* at some scores of millenia.[1] Even if such early records as picture writing, cuneiform writing, hieroglyphics and the like dated from that time, they could by no means satisfy our curiosity regarding the archegenesis (Huxley) of language.[2]

Thus we must shift the inquiry from the safe ground of the verifiable as furnished by philology (i.e., that branch of history which examines the linguistic achievements of sundry peoples past and present) to that of prehistory which deals with human beings whose languages have irrevocably perished. This inevitable step has at least the advantage of enabling us to avoid the principal mistake of most writers on the origin of language, who ' treated the problem as though it were a philological one, as if the origin of *language* were one with the origin of *languages*.' [3]

The term ' prehistoric,' incidentally, as Shotwell points out,[4] should be used ' not so much for the pre-known past—since much inside the field of history remains unknown and on the other hand much beyond is known—as for the preinscriptional or preliterary past. . . . The field of prehistory is joined with that of history by archaeology, which works with impartial zeal in both, though with different methods. In the prehistoric field, since the documents are lacking, it can only verify its conclusions by the comparison of the remains of the culture of unknown peoples with the output of similar cultures to-day. This is the *comparative method* of anthropology which has thus been called into service to enable us to recover the unrecorded past before history began.'

Let us, then, see to what extent archaeology enables us to watch the stage and the shifting scenes, and the actors taking part in the grand drama of the *Logos prophorikos*—the thought given tongue.[5]

---

[1] Cf. Leakey (1935). *Adam's Ancestors*.
[2] See Marty, l.c., p. 237.
[3] Vendryes, l.c., p. 5. My italics.
[4] Shotwell, l.c., pp. 37-38.
[5] Sext. Empir. Pyrrhon. hypotyp. I. 65. (As quoted by Eisler, s.v. Logos.)

CHAPTER II

THE FORERUNNERS

THE SCENE OF ACTION

ALTHOUGH THE origin of our earth is of no special interest here, it may be of value to pass in review the periods of its earliest evolution as established by the natural sciences.

According to some geologists our earth is approximately 3,000 millions of years old.[1] Its solid crust suitable for living beings was

Era	Period	Minimum Age Based on Uranium-Lead-Helium Content	Round Numbers for Reference
QUATERNARY Age of Man	Recent Pleistocene	Years 1,000,000	Years 1,000,000
TERTIARY Age of Mammals	Pliocene Miocene Oligocene Eocene	6,000,000 12,000,000 16,000,000 20,000,000	50,000,000
MESOZOIC Age of Reptiles	Cretaceous Comanchian Jurassic Triassic	40,000,000 25,000,000 35,000,000 35,000,000	150,000,000
PALAEOZOIC Amphibians and Fishes	Permian Pennsylvanian Mississippian Devonian Silurian Ordovician Cambrian	25,000,000 35,000,000 50,000,000 50,000,000 40,000,000 90,000,000 70,000,000	300,000,000
PRECAMBRIAN Beginning of Life on Earth		1,000,000,000	1,000,000,000

Recent geologic time table, in which the whole geologic life-period of the earth is estimated at a thousand million years and subdivided as above. After W. A. Parks, F.R.S.C., published in 1926 by the Royal Society of Canada.

Fossil remains of man are now known in the entire Quaternary Age of Man era and in the upper part of the Tertiary Pliocene period.

FIG. 1. (From Osborn)

---

[1] Zeuner, F. E. (1946). *Dating the Past.* Methuen & Co., Ltd., London.

formed—so chemists tell us from their radioactive methods of estimation—a moderate multiple of a thousand million years ago.[1] Astronomers assess the age of the sun and the hot stars as of a hundred thousand million years.[2] (See Fig. 1.)

It was a world in which ' matter ' seems to have obeyed purely physico-chemical rules. That earliest age is termed Azoic (*a*, privative prefix, *zoon*, ' life '). The Azoic Rocks in North America which cover the first half of a period of about one thousand million years [3] reveal no vestiges of life. This does not necessarily mean that there was no life then, since creatures without bones or other hard parts would naturally have left no traces. Anyhow, at some remote age—perhaps some five hundred million years ago [4]— matter became so integrated as to be capable of maintaining itself by reacting to stimuli—that is to say, it began to ' live.'

The genesis of the first living creatures, probably of microscopic size, is one of the eternal puzzles. It was a process of " constant inflow and outflow of matter and energy at their surface, between the living substance within and the non-living world without." [5] " Perhaps in some warm runnel of tidal mud or frothy ooze " specks arose endowed with the capacity to build themselves up and break themselves down, chemico-physical systems, integratively organized, autonomous moving systems so constituted as to establish and maintain themselves in a dynamic equilibrium, self-centred and self-balanced units.[6] The faculty of maintaining the intrinsic fundamental *rhythm* of life, i.e., the alternating disintegration and re-integration of matter, has been perpetuated ever since. (Cf. pp. 72ff.)

THE CAST

We are fortunate in that Nature has preserved many specimens of the hierarchy of living creatures, which have remained on lower rungs of the evolutionary ladder, while their descendants began ' to venture ocean and in time to populate it. To populate it with countless millions of feeding mouths, and to feed them, while their fins oared them about, fins prophetic of the bird's wing, and of the

---

[1] Lord Raleigh (1921). Report, British Association, pp. 413-15. As quoted by Poulton (footnote [5]), p. 13.
[2] Nernst, W. (1921). *Das Weltgebäude*. Springer, Berlin, pp. 22, 29.
[3] Wells, H. G. (1927). *A Short History of the World*. Heinemann, London, pp. 6-8.
[4] Zeuner, l.c.
[5] Kerr, p. 241-2.
[6] Sherrington, C. (1940). *Man on his Nature*, pp. 73-84.

human hand. Millions of feeding mouths voiceless but yet potential of bird's song and human speech.'[1] It will be our endeavour to demonstrate *how* the potentialities referred to by Sherrington in his prophetic statement may have become realities.

We can thus follow up the differentiation both in structure and in function of living (i.e., reacting) beings, from the appearance of unicellular beings (Palæozoic or Primary Period, *palaios*, ' ancient ') through multicellular beings such as the Invertebrates (Molluscs, Arthropods) and the backboned Fishes, Amphibia, Reptiles and Birds (Mesozoic or Secondary Period, *mesos*, ' middle '). The two latter were dominating the living world up to about 200 million years ago.[2]

The next period, the Cainozoic (*kainos*, ' recent ') divides into two main halves, the Tertiary and the Quaternary periods. The former is subdivided into the geological systems of the Palæocene (*palaios*, ' ancient '[3]), Eocene[4] (*eos*, ' dawn '), the Oligocene[5] (*oligos*, ' scarce '), the Miocene[6] (*meion*, ' smaller ') and the Pliocene[7] (*pleion*, ' more,' ' fuller,' [8]), the latter into the Pleistoæne (*pleistos*, ' most ') and the Recent systems.

Since by language we imply, for our present purpose, communicative sound produced by the respiratory and alimentary systems (or by such analogous systems as the air bladder of fishes), we need not consider here the buzzing insects (Lower Palæozoic Period), which produce noises with their wings. The amphibians, however, must be remembered for their voice-producing faculty, as also birds (Upper Palæozoic). (See below, p. 37.)

The Mammals, i.e., animals which suckle their young (Latin *mamma*, ' breast ') originated probably in the Kainozoic (Older Tertiary), or at the earliest at the end of the Mesozoic System Group characterized mainly by reptiles and Ammonites.

The profound differences between the Mesozoic Period (200,000,000–70,000,000 years ago)[9] and the Kainozoic Period have

---

[1] Sherrington, C. (1940). *Man on his Nature*, p. 91.
[2] Zeuner, l.c.
[3] i.e., more ancient than Eocene.
[4] Dawn of living molluscs.
[5] Few living molluscs.
[6] Minor proportion of living molluscs.
[7] Major proportion of living molluscs.
[8] See Baily, E. B., and Weir, J. (1939). *Introduction to Geology*. Macmillan, London, p. 468.
[9] Zeuner, l.c. It should be noted that throughout this book the more or less conjectural lengths of periods are given merely for the sake of comparison with recorded historical periods.

been well described by H. G. Wells. We do not profess to know much about the 'mental' aspect of reptile life, but assume that a fundamental difference between the mental life of the two periods " arises essentially out of the continuing contact of parent and offspring which distinguishes mammalian, and in a lesser degree bird life, from the life of the reptile. With very few exceptions the reptile abandons its egg to hatch alone. The young reptile has no knowledge whatever of its parent, its mental life such as it is begins and ends with its own experiences. It may tolerate the existence of its fellows, but it has no communication with them; it never imitates, never learns from them, is incapable of concerted action with them. Its life is that of an isolated individual. But with the suckling and cherishing of young which was distinctive of the new mammalian and avian strains arose the possibility of learning by imitation, of communication, by warning cries and other concerted action, of mutual control and instruction. A *teachable* type of life had come into the world." [1]

Before the end of the Eocene the primitive lemurs had come into existence. They are notable for their ' chattering that quickens into shrill barking and at length into prolonged yellings. . . . One will begin. Then another answers and another, till the air clangs with the loud, harsh chorus. It doesn't mean anything much, but how exhilarating to utter such a ringing volume of sound all in unison.' [2] Exhilarating just because the symphony knits them into a group.

Fossils of the earliest man-like ape were found in 1911 in the Egyptian Fayum in beds of Early Oligocene Age [3] (*Propliopithecus*). The apes differentiated into several species in various parts of the world during Miocene times.

ANIMALS

Before introducing man on to the stage let us look more closely at the creatures of the preceding scene.

The four surviving types of the order Primates (Chimpanzee, Gorilla, Gibbon and Orang) have several features in common with Man. Apart from minor disparities, they are all plantigrade, have nails on fingers and toes, and have an opposable thumb (an adaptation to arboreal life); their brain case is relatively large, the face is

---
[1] H. G. Wells, l.c., pp. 25 ff.
[2] Henderson, Keith (1927). *Prehistoric Man*. Harrap, London, p. 6.
[3] Elliott Smith (1934). *Human History*. Jonathan Cape, London.

comparatively small, and the eyes are directed forwards.[1] Like other animals (cats, dogs, beasts of prey, birds), they have developed the senses to a high degree, especially the faculties of vision, and of hearing. The latter reached a high capacity [2] in the monkeys which sprang from the Tarsioids as far back as the end of the Cretaceous System.

While it is doubtful whether animals lower than monkeys and apes can perceive peculiar aggregates of tones as integers to the same extent as the latter, it seems to be safe to say that dogs [3] and Cebus monkeys [4] can perceive visual configurations such as letter and words, and react appropriately to them. This must not, of course, lead to the belief that they grasp the dictionary meaning of the words utilized. (Cf. pp. 31, 36.)

Apes share with Man several behavioural peculiarities, chief among which are their tendency to live in groups and their response to musical patterns.

Lemurs and apes tend ' to pick up bits of wood, even to brandish them about in a vague, rather feeble manner, or throw things down upon enemies passing below.' [5] Chimpanzees readily break off a stick for the purpose of knocking down a fruit.[6] Such tendencies foreshadow the achievements of later descendants in the art of making and using ' tools ', which marks the boundary between nature-enslaved and nature-dominating creatures.

Yet there are mental activities in which modern man differs outstandingly from the animal.

Cats for instance are known to be clean animals. A young kitten readily defæcates in a box filled with earth, in which it will instinctively bury the fæces. When, at the age, say, of three months, it is let into the garden, the defæcation reflex will not be elicited by the garden earth. Nor will it respond if the box be placed in the garden. The kitten does not recognize ' earth ' in isolation, it has not ' analysed it out ', it cannot ' abstract ' from accompanying features, it has not got the ' concept ' of ' earth '.

It seems safe to say that animals are stimulated by and respond to the environment only in so far as a given situation constitutes one whole or one unique, hardly divided, impressionistic configuration.

[1] Bailey and Weir, l.c., p. 348.
[2] Shepherd, W. Y. Some mental processes of the *Rhesus* monkey. *Psychol Rev. Monogr.* Suppl. 12.
[3] Lubbock, J. (1887). *Die Sinne und das geistige Leben der Tiere.* Leipzig.
[4] Thorndike, E. L. (1911). *Animal Intelligence.* N.Y., 2nd Edn.
[5] Henderson, Keith, l.c., p. 9.
[6] Henderson, Keith, p. 15.

They cannot separate ' qualities ', classify them as ' relevant ' and ' irrelevant ' and do not respond solely to essential ones.[1] This mode of reaction still lurks in human beings.

It will be seen below how great a role this way of looking at things played in the evolution of language.

Older animals seem able to acquire some rudimentary capacity of analysis, though we must beware of becoming anthropomorphistic in the interpretation of animal behaviour. If, for instance, ' cats or monkeys do not require to be shown the use of a fresh rug or cushion . . . '[2] or if cats like to creep into baskets, boxes, drawers, cupboards of all kinds, this need not be attributed to their conceptual thinking, but can be explained by instinctive urges to find a suitable hiding or resting place.

ANIMAL LANGUAGE

Animals can, it is true, utter a notable variety of sounds and noises more or less resembling human sounds : Dogs bark, growl, snarl; wolves and hyenas howl, yelp, ' laugh '; lions roar; sheep bleat; horses neigh; donkeys bray; cats mew and purr; cows moo; geese, swans, snakes and cats hiss.

Monkeys produce an explosive noise in the larynx, and several vowel sounds, such as [i], [I], [œ], [e], [o], [ɔ], [ou], [u], [ʊ].[3] (Letters in square brackets are phonetic symbols. See Index.)

The vowel sounds just referred to are to be regarded as resonatory modifications of laryngeal sound, brought about by the shaping of the mouth. Apart from laryngeal sound very few noises activated by other means can be observed in animals.

Side by side with vocal utterances and independent from them, oral gestures can be observed in the higher animals. In most cases, however, mouth gestures [4] represent a mere segment of the animal's general behaviour. (See the mouth gestures of apes and infants on Plates 1, 2 and 3.)

When performed simultaneously with voice they naturally contribute to its modification, but are not themselves noise-producing, although they are in themselves significant. We need only think of the dog, which by drawing back the corners of the

---

[1] Cf. Blanshard, l.c., p. 254.
[2] Tylor, E. B. (1937). *Anthropology.* Watts, London, p. 41.
[3] Paget, R. (1930). *Human Speech.* Kegan Paul, London, p. 128.
[4] Yerkes, R. M., and Learned (1925). *Chimpanzee Intelligence.* Baltimore, p. 55, report on the scarcity of imitative, mostly mute lip movements in their apes.

mouth and displaying the teeth, reveals his aggressive impulse, while uttering a snarl.

Paget observed mouth gestures made without sound by the Pig-Tailed Monkey and by the Mandrill (London Zoological Gardens).[1] If he regards them as expressive of pleasure it is merely the observer's interpretation which " makes " them " expressive."

The same author describes some very expressive gestures which the Chimpanzees make " when ' asking ' for food—in particular a projection of the lips, which is often coupled with the projection of the hands, and an open-mouthed gesture with the lips drawn back so as to show the teeth." [2]

The fact that the word " asking " stands in inverted commas seems to indicate that the observer meant to say that the gestures were performed " as if " the animals were asking for food. The last but one observation is, however, of value as it shows the natural wholeness of behaviour in the integral unit consisting of hand and mouth gesture as the natural reaction to food. Who can tell whether it is not on the threshold of symbolism ?

Köhler [3] definitely denies the ability of apes to designate objects even by gesture, and Blanshard, [4] admitting that animals can utter diverse noises, states the almost trivial truth that they do not use nouns.

This opinion is not contradicted by the fact that Dr. William H. Furness [5] claims to have taught a young female orang-outang to imitate " papa," which she finally recognized as her teacher's name, and " cup," which she used of her own accord when she was thirsty.

Similar successes have been claimed by many animal lovers. Such remarkable results of training do not prove that the animals concerned were able to " talk," i.e., express ' ideas '.

Once I saw a dog (described by Fröschels) which could count from one to three, say sugar when this was shown to him, and so on. All that can be said about this dog's achievements is that he somehow imitated the vowels, but hardly the consonants. Nothing suggested that he associated these sounds with ideas.

To the latest report from America that " a sheep has been taught to talk," Punch found the appropriate answer : " Says ewe ! " [6]

---

[1] Paget, l.c., p. 128.
[2] Ibid.
[3] Köhler, W. C. (1929). The Mentality of Apes, p. 305.
[4] Blanshard, l.c., p. 252.
[5] ' Observations on the Mentality of the Chimpanzees and Orang-Outangs. Proc. Amer. Philos. Soc., 1916, 55, pp. 281-90. As quoted by Paget, l.c., p. 129.
[6] ' Punch ' (1943), Vol. CCIV, No. 5319, Jan., p. 65.

It can, nevertheless, be said that in their mouth gestures apes shape their mouth in such a way as to pave the way for the production of articulated noises. The few that occur in apes owe their origin to the rarefaction of air in the mouth, of which more will be said below (p. 67). Phonetics has reserved the term ' clicks ' for such noises. (Represented here by inverted symbols.)

Baboon, chiromys (a prosimian) and macaco produce a labial click.[1] The latter and long-tailed monkeys utter [ʇ-ʇ-ʇ], the young mandrill says [ʮ].[2] Other apes such as the Orang-outan possess [ɗ] and [ʯx].[3] We shall turn to this kind of speech-sound and its significance below (p. 70).

In apes, the cortical area from which movements essential for sucking, chewing, swallowing and so on can be elicited lies in the *genu inferius* of the *sulcus centralis*. Lowermost in this area the lips (pouting of the lips, retraction of the angle of the mouth) are represented. The lip area neighbours that of the nose. There follow those of the ear, eyelids, neck, hands, arms, shoulders, chest, abdomen, hips, legs.

Adjacent to the lip area lies a very large area from which tongue movements can be evoked. Sherrington [4] stresses that in his experiments " they were extremely varied in their form and sequence, almost baffling verbal description. For the most part they could be grouped under the headings retraction, protrusion, rolling on long axis, upcurving of base or tip, and hollowing of upper surface from side to side." . . . " Protrusion very rarely carried the tongue beyond the lips. The appearance of the movements frequently suggested that they were part actions in mastication, licking, lapping, and swallowing. Thus one not infrequent was a thrusting of the tongue against the inside of the cheekpouch as though to remove food thence ; again a rhythmic movement of licking or lapping ; again a heaping of the back of the dorsum against the back of the palate, followed by contraction of the faucial opening as though in swallowing. Occasionally the tongue was drawn back or thrust forward straight ; much more commonly the retraction or protrusion was deviated, the deviation being sometimes to the ipsilateral, sometimes to the contralateral side. Retraction and protrusion were evidently much commingled in their representation in the

---

[1] Schwidetzky, Georg (1931). *Sprechen Sie Schimpansisch?* Deutsche Gesellschaft für Tier und Ursprachenforschung. Leipzig, p. 44.
[2] Schwidetzky, p. 71.
[3] Schwidetzky, pp. 48, 56.
[4] Sherrington, C. (1939). *Selected Writings*, p. 411 ff.

cortex, but on the whole protrusion seemed situated lower down the convolution than was retraction. Sometimes the protrusion of tongue was accompanied by closing of jaw, and then occasionally

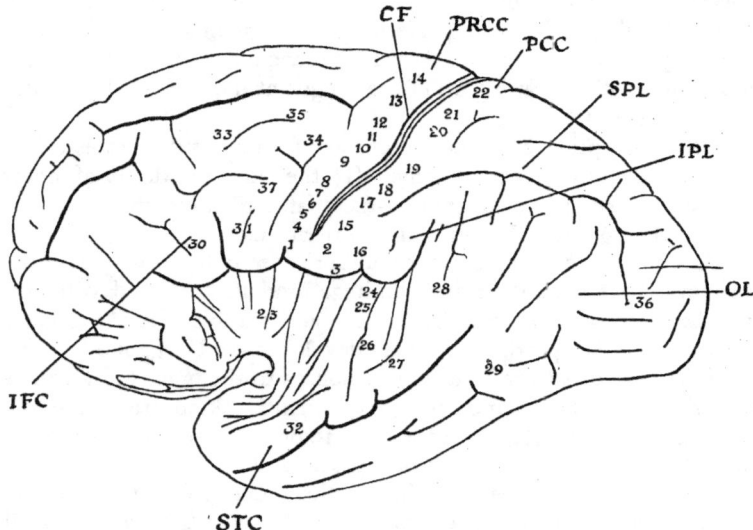

FIG. 2
Lateral Surface of the Brain. (After Economo-Koskinas. From Spiegel-Sommer)
1. Rhythmic chewing and swallowing.
2. Movements of the pharynx.
3. Movements of the larynx.
4. Movements of the jaw.
5. Movements of the tongue.
6. Movements of the mouth.
7. Movements of the face.
8. Movements of the neck.
9. Movements of the fingers.
10. Movements of the arm and hand.
11. Movements of the shoulder.
12. Movements of the trunk.
13. Movements of the diaphragm.
14. Movements of the leg.
15. Sensibility of the face.
16. Taste. (?)
17. Sensibility of the mouth.
18. Sensibility of the hand.
19. Sensibility of the arm.
20. Sensibility of the shoulder.
21. Sensibility of the leg.
22. Sensibility of the foot.
23. Smell. (?)
24. Appreciation of noises.
25. Appreciation of high tones.
26. Appreciation of low tones.
27. Appreciation of words heard.
28. Comprehension of word-meaning. (?)
29. Recollection of words.
30. Singing.
31. Word utterance.
32. Appreciation of melody.
33. Prying.
34. Writing.
35. Instrument playing.
36. Visual images.
37. Gestures.

CF. Central fissure.
PRCC. Pre-central convolution.
PCC. Post-central convolution.
SPL. Superior parietal lobe.
IPL. Inferior parietal lobe.
OL. Occipital lobe.
STC. Superior temporal convolution.
IFC. Inferior frontal convolution.
F. Frontal lobe.

the tongue was nipped by the teeth, recalling the biting of the tongue in epilepsy. On many occasions the points of excitable cortex farthest down of all in the convolution evoked movement confined to the tongue tip."

Stimulation of the jaw area, lying forward from the tongue area, brought about closing and more often opening of the mouth. Rhythmic chewing movements could be evoked from points far forward at the foot of the convolution. Movements of the jaws, generally elicited from the posterior part of the lingual region about half-way down and from a quite restricted region, were often associated with a heaping up of the tongue at the back of the mouth. (See Fig. 2.)

This description bears out important features which foreshadow new sets of movements to come: (1) the close proximity of motor centres governing movements characteristic of eating and prophetic of articulating ; (2) their rhythmical performance.

To sum up we can say that animals seem to form a natural, primeval unit with their surroundings, and to be linked with one another through their gestures visible and audible. It is the vocal power which is particularly well developed and organized. The peculiar sound patterns and the responses to them are more or less genetically fixed. Sounds of a ' consonantal ' kind are scarce and rudimentary. To state that they talk to or converse with each other would be a rash, anthropomorphic assertion.[1]

The bulk of movements including the sound producing activities of the larynx [2] indicating a certain attitude towards events inside or outside the animal, can be called *gestures* in the earliest sense of the word which is derived from Latin *gerere*, " to carry " (cf. English *carriage*, " behaviour ").

Throughout the animal kingdom many and diverse exclamations are found ; they ' mean ' something only in so far as they are an *integral* part of the whole of the natural and more or less vegetative behaviour of animals. They are produced even by congenitally deaf animals just as is the case with deaf mutes.

It is difficult to decide whether animals can use such sounds as *intentional* signs for objects, actions, desires and the like.

The foregoing remarks bring to mind the often heard question : Since animals are obviously endowed with the organs necessary for speech, and produce the elements underlying civilized language, why do those sounds and noises not evolve into what we call articulate speech ?

To this a very simple, if seemingly facile, answer can and must be

---

[1] See Fox, Munro (1940). *The Personality of Animals*. Penguin Books. Chapter II.
[2] See below, p. 50.

given : Because they are animals of a certain species and not of the genus *homo*. The calls, songs, and ululations of animals form part and parcel of their very nature. In animals evolutionary ' growth comes, in this respect, to a standstill, in so far as it does not bring about changes of configuration and organization.' [1]

In man emergent evolution has progressed further, and new cortical layers have developed which are now overriding more ancient ones. The above-mentioned noises are, therefore, still found in the lower strata of human speech.

We must at this point repudiate an explanation which is so often reappearing in print ; namely, that apes cannot speak partly on account of the interlocking of the front teeth, partly because their lower jaws are too narrow and their chins non-existent.[2] Others maintain that the ' hanging position of the head in quadrupeds makes the *free* passage of sounds impossible, and prevents the evolution of such vocal organs as are compatible with articulate speech.' [3]

It is evident that the argument hinges on the definitions of speech and language. The upholders of the above opinion contradict the assertion that speech is the communication of mental states, when they refer to the ' jabbering ' which accompanies the gatherings of lemurs and apes, and which may be regarded as adequate expression.

Should the assertion refer to the articulation of speech sounds, it must be stated that such articulation hardly ever involves any lateral movements of the organs of the admittedly narrow mouth of apes and other animals.

The activities of the sides of the tongue are essential only in a few human speech sounds, such as [*l*], [*s*], [*ʃ*], and these are by no means of fundamental importance for achieving diversity of utterance.

It has been pointed out earlier (see p. 5) that fairly articulate speech may be achieved without the use of the tongue, and so it stands to reason that anthropoids and their descendants, in spite of the conformation of a jaw and tongue different from ours " might have jabbered well enough to convey a good many discriminated, objective meanings if they had needed to do so." [4]

Stress should be laid here upon the word ' needed.' ' The

---

[1] See Gesell's definition of growth : Gesell, A. (1933). ' Maturation and the Patterning of Behaviour.' *Handbook of Child Psychology*. Clark Press, p. 210. Cf. Valentine, C. W. (1942). *The Psychology of Early Childhood*. Methuen & Co. Ltd., London, p. 44.
[2] Henderson, K., l.c., p. 13.
[3] Murphy, J. (1927). *Primitive Man*. Oxford University Press, p. 14.
[4] Read, C. (1925). *The Origins of Man*. Cambridge University Press, p. 33.

gibbon, most social, is also the most vocal of anthropoids ; but having no common task in which united action is necessary, he uses his remarkable power of voice (apparently) merely to express his feelings and to keep the troop together. The chimpanzee and the gorilla enjoy probably a close and affectionate family life, but one that makes little or no demand for concerted effort. Hence their vocalization is very rudimentary.'[1] For similar reasons the 'language' of most birds has remained in a comparatively crude state.

So far we have referred mainly to utterances of animals in their natural state. Domestication, i.e., the process of taming and associating animals with man, brings up a further perfection of linguistic gesture. Munro Fox[2] mentions the well-known fact that 'some domestic animals learn from us to ask for what they want. A dog learns to ask for food ; a cat learns to mew until a door is opened.' He then poses the question, ' Do any wild animals learn to express their desires to others of their kind in this way ? Young animals may cry for food by inborn instinct, but as far as we know adult wild animals do not learn to beg. It looks as if domestic animals learn a sort of language that wild animals have not got.'

The peculiar vocal sound of wild animals also undergoes modification under the influence of domestication, and vice versa ; ' in certain conditions dogs cease barking, in others captive wolves begin barking like dogs.'[3]

In contrast to the motor part of language, the sensory part, i.e., the comprehension of a sound complex offered, undergoes a marked development in domesticated animals. It is well known that they can be made to respond promptly and invariably to certain command words. Most of them are of an interjectional, i.e., pre-articulate character ; their meaning is entirely arbitrary. /brrr/, for instance, means ' stop ' in Germany, and ' go ' in Italy, the click /ʯ/ starts or urges the horse in America and several European countries, but stops it in India. *Psp* urges horses in America, stops them in South Africa, and quietens them in Austria and other countries.[4]

Here we may profitably digress to the way in which birds learn their songs.

---

[1] Read, C. (1925). *The Origins of Man*, Cambridge University Press, pp. 32-3.
[2] Fox, Munro (1940), l.c., p. 21.
[3] Huxley, J. (1942). *Evolution.* Allen & Unwin, London, p. 307.
[4] See Bolton, H.C. (1897). ' The Language used in Talking to Domestic Animals.' *Amer. Anthr.* X, pp. 65-90, 97-113. Quot. by Chamberlain. *The Child*, p. 122.

Some song-birds, e.g., the blackbird, the chiffchaff, the grasshopper bird, the warbler and the short-toed treecreeper produce the song peculiar to their species, even if reared in isolation. Others depend on models for their singing capacity. In the absence of a model, ' Baltimore orioles (*Icterus galbula*) . . . developed a song totally unlike the normal, and retained it throughout their lives.' [1]

The whitethroat, the tree and meadow pipits, the greenfinch, the chaffinch, the yellow-hammer, the skylark, and others ' learn ' their songs by copying others.

Huxley remarks that there is no strict correlation between simplicity or complexity of a song and genetic fixation. ' While this is true for simple songs like the chiffchaff's and far more elaborate songs like the whitethroat's, the elaborate song of the blackbird is innate, and the relatively simple song of the chaffinch has less innate basis than the blackcap's very elaborate song. . . . One might further expect that learnt songs would be more variable in nature than innate ones ; but this does not seem to be the case (except possibly for the chaffinch).' [2]

Considering the almost negligible development of the cortex in birds, one cannot help thinking that their proverbial echoing impulse, like mimesis in general, seems to be controlled by the older and well developed striatal system, which in man plays a predominant role in the expression of emotions. This fact in its turn accounts for certain other features in the evolution of language. (See below, pp. 47ff.)

---

[1] Huxley, J. *Evolution*, pp. 305–6.
[2] Huxley. *Ibid.*, p. 307.

CHAPTER III

THE HUMAN STOCK

THE PROTAGONIST INTRODUCED

LET US now follow up the series of events which ushered into the world those creatures which because of their distinctive qualities may be regarded as the archetypes of man. These creatures originated probably in various parts of the then surface of the earth and lived for scores of thousands of years. All of them, such as the *Australopithecus africanus* (Taungs, Bechuanaland), *Australopithecus transvaalensis* or *Plesianthropus* (Sterkfontein) and the *Paranthropus robustus* (Kromdraal, South Africa) [1] finally died out with the exception of one which had diverged furthest [2] from the anthropoids in pre-Miocene times,[3] the genus *homo*.

It would be of little use or consequence to attempt to determine the age of mankind in absolute figures of any magnitude. But in order to give a clearer idea of the velocity with which the evolution of man has been going on, it may be expedient to give figures which should be taken as comparative measures.

The geological layers in which the first bones thought to be human were found, are generally believed to be those of the early Pleistocene period, but flints indicating human craftsmanship have been dug out of Pliocene strata.[4] It is assumed that the Pleistocene and Recent epochs have lasted from 300,000 or 400,000 to one and a half million years.[5]

The fact that human fossils have been discovered in those geological layers indicates the relative abundance, rather than the first appearance of human creatures.[6]

The emergence of beings displaying features hitherto unknown was probably due to one of the greatest revolutionary changes in the world. Hundred thousands of years ago the great ice caps which covered the polar regions of both hemispheres began to creep towards the equator. This climatic change altered the habitable

---

[1] De Pradenne, l.c., p. 181.
[2] See Kerr, l.c., pp. 210-211.
[3] Keith, Sir A. *The Antiquity of Man*, p. 732.
[4] Bailey and Weir, l.c., p. 472.
[5] See tabulated survey in Keith, l.c., frontispiece. Sollas, l.c., p. 40 ff.
[6] Kerr, l.c., p. 213.

THE HUMAN STOCK 39

surface of the earth so much as to cause many animals, among them the apes, to immigrate into regions more congenial to their make-up.

In front of the ice sheet there was the tundra, many hundreds of miles deep, covered with moss and interspersed with lakes and swamps, the land where the reindeer reigned.

Next to it lay the steppe, where grazed bison, wild horse and zebra.

Farthest from the ice was a temperate zone with rich pastures and woodland. It was populated by the gigantic *Elephas trogantherii*, the ancestor of the mammoth, and the Etruscan rhinoceros. In the forests could be found elks, trogantheriums, stags and roes.

Some groups of apes retained the ancient habit of living in trees;[1] others which remained in their ancestral region adapted themselves to the new woodlands with their light growth of trees. The new environment compelled the half-erect anthropoid creature to progress more and more habitually upon the foot-bearing earth; and this new mode of life developed the arched foot, and the human prehensile hand. 'For the completion of both these tasks, the posture became increasingly upright, in the course of many generations.'[2]

PITHECANTHROPUS

It was from this stock of creatures that Pithecanthropus Erectus Dubois (*pithekos*, 'ape', *anthropos*, 'man'), found at Trinil in Java, and his almost contemporary relative the Sinanthropus Zdansky, found in China, took their rise about 500,000 years ago.[3] Owing to some still considerable differences between them and the now living human races they are included in a class labelled 'hominids.'

These ancestors of man had a low and flat skull with a low, narrow receding forehead with very prominent ridges over the eyes (*torus supraorbitalis*), and a well-developed musculature of mastication. The jowl was very large, but without a chin. (See Fig. 3.) All these features vividly bring to mind the now existing anthropoids. The same can be said of the height of the cranial vault.[4] But in total length and width of brain Pithecanthropus was more man-like.[5] (See Fig. 3.) It must not, however, be forgotten that

---

[1] Bailey and Weir, l.c., p. 348.
[2] Schmidt, R. R. (1936). *The Dawn of the Human Mind.* Sidgwick & Jackson, London, p. 38.
[3] Zeuner, l.c.
[4] De Pradenne, l.c., p. 192.
[5] Keith, l.c., p. 130.

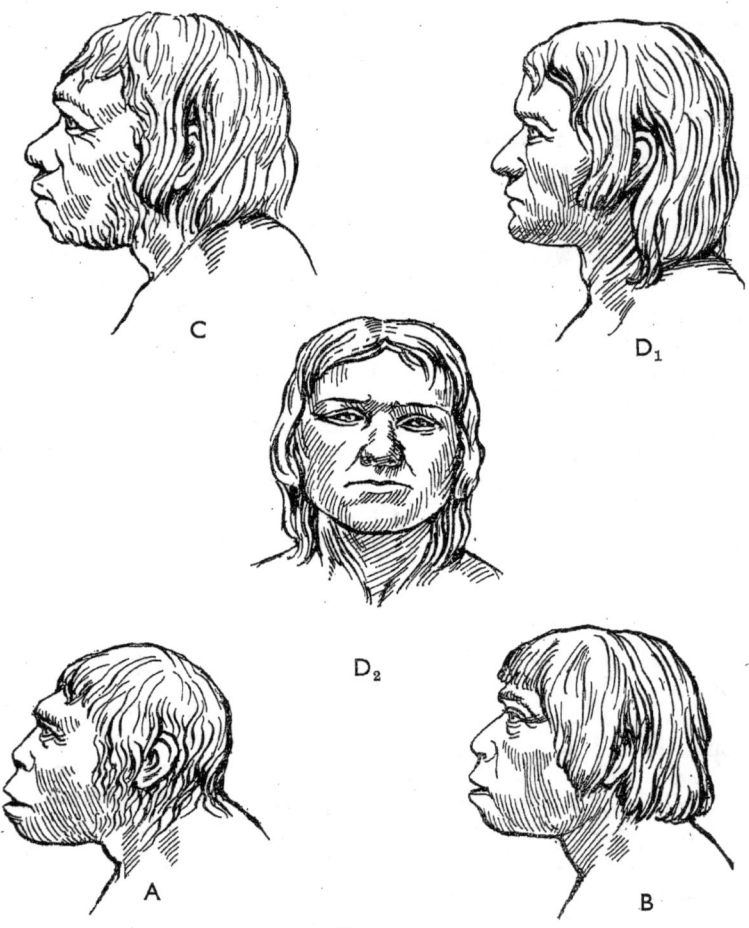

FIG. 3
Heads of pre-historic man modelled by J. H. McGregor on restored skulls. Re-drawn. (From Osborn)
A, Pithecanthropus.
B, Piltdown Man.
C, Neanderthal Man.
D_1 and D_2, Cro-Magnon Man.

as a whole his brain was small in comparison with that of present-day man (cranial capacity 55–73 cub. ins. in Sinanthropus) if larger than that of the anthropomorphous apes. (Cranial capacity 24–37 cub. ins.; 79–98 cub. ins. in modern man.) [1]

---

[1] De Pradenne, l.c., p. 192.

THE HUMAN STOCK 41

Although it is now generally accepted that Pithecanthropus sprang from an ancestor common to him and the anthropoids, there remain some doubts as to the lineage, demonstrated in Fig. 4. (After De Pradenne, l.c., p. 25).

Confronted with these alternatives of genealogy we are obliged to assume that the conjectural ancestors of the human types possessed essential qualities in the bud, which they transmitted in a straight line to " higher," i.e., more fully developed and younger types. The peculiar features which may have characterized the speech of prehistoric people have irrevocably perished, but our ignorance in this respect need not invalidate our argumentation as to the main

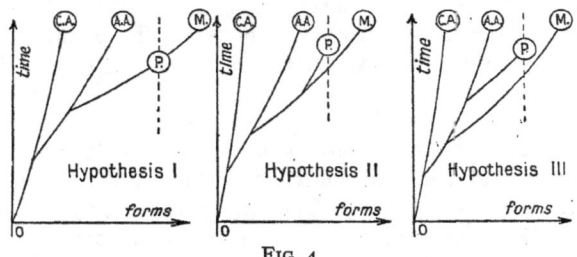

FIG. 4
Illustrating three possible hypotheses as to the position of Pithecanthropus (P.) in relation to Anthropoid Apes (A.A.) and to Man (M.). C.A., cynomorphic apes.

trend of speech evolution. Our surmises will in the main be based on certain vestiges from the past, which, we believe, can still be detected in existing languages. In the following chapters we hope to free that keenly perceptive, delicate part of the reader's mind, which can appreciate those speech patterns.

Many writers, such as Childe, Elliott Smith,[1] Kerr,[2] Davison and others assume that Pithecanthropus possessed some, albeit crude, speech.

Childe[3] infers from ' a rudimentary swelling over the area devoted to speech in our brains ' (usually referred to as the temporal and frontal lobes) that ' Java man was already talking and investing sounds with socially approved meanings.'

Dubois, in describing the frontal convolutions of Pithecanthropus, also emphasizes that ' the important inferior frontal convolution has attained a fair development.' He found that the average area

---
[1] Elliott Smith, G. *Human History;* p. 50.
[2] Kerr, l.c., p. 214.
[3] Childe, V. G. *What Happened in History.* Penguin Books, p. 26.

of the exposed superficies equalled half the average area in twelve European hemispheres, but at least double that in the brain of a large chimpanzee or an orang-outang. This seems to indicate that our fossil being (Pithecanthropus) possessed already a certain amount of power of speech.[1]

Dorothy Davison recognizes that the area concerned with thinking and skill which develops latest in children, was very small. Nevertheless, she assumes that, ' though Pithecanthropus must have been a very slow and clumsy fellow, he possessed one of the greatest assets of the human race—he could, in some primitive way, speak.' She infers this ' from the impression made by his brain on the skull, where just over the ear the speech area bulges slightly.'[2]

Fallaize cautiously surmises that the Ape Man of the Pliocene or Pleistocene periods ' may even have been able to talk in rudimentary fashion.'[3]

We should regard with some care inferences commonly drawn from anatomical facts. There is no reason to doubt that Pithecanthropus was able to emit sounds, but what is still to be determined is the qualities of those sounds and what meanings they conveyed.

Recalling that we are to examine speakers and not speech, let us first picture the surround to which those creatures are assumed to have been reacting by some manner of speaking.

The rather warm subtropical climate of the Eocene period which engendered the common stem of monkeys, and of the Oligocene period which generated the anthropoid and human stem had begun to give place to a cooler one (although in Britain it was still warmer than in our days).[4]

The strata in which the remains of Pithecanthropus were discovered also contained those of the rhinoceros, horse, bison, camel, deer and elephant.[5] It was swampy ground, covered in places by huge forests of mangroves and cypresses, partly decaying into peat.[6]

Our minds can conjure up a vision of a small gang wandering

---

[1] Dubois (1921). ' On the Cranial Form of Homo Neanderthalensis and of Pithecanthropus erectus.' Konin. Akad. van Wetensch. te Amsterdam. Vol. xxiv, Pts. 6, 7. As quoted by Keith, l.c., p. 434. For further references, see Sollas, l.c., Chapter II.
[2] Davison, Dorothy (1934). *Men of the Dawn*. Watts & Co., London, pp. 40-41.
[3] Fallaize, E. N. (1928). *The Origins of Civilization*. Benn, London, p. 23.
[4] Bailey and Weir, l.c., p. 472. Fallaize, l.c., p. 42.
[5] Keith, l.c., p. 420.
[6] See Bailey and Weir, l.c., p. 47.

about the jungles and forests, isolated from other such groups, picking up a berry here, digging out a root there, climbing up a tree to get hold of some eggs or young shoots, fruits or nuts. As its members went on gathering food they always took care not to lose sight of each other, recognizing that only the pack could stave off attacks from wild beasts. All the objects in their environment were embedded in a great spectrum of shining colours, at times cast into the shade of trees, clouds or overhanging rocks. No doubt they had to prick up their ears to distinguish the noises and sounds made in their neighbourhood by an orchestra of ever-changing size. It was a strange and bewildering symphony which filled the air, composed of the burring of insects, the humming of bees, the fizzing of flies, the swishing, wheezing, whizzing, shrill shrieking and whistling of birds of all kind, the hissing of snakes, the coarse howling of the hyena and of the wolf, the horrisonous roaring of the lion, the trumpeting of the mammoth, the chirping and twittering of little birds and insects, the manifold rustlings of the vegetable world, the rippling, whispering and creaking of the trees, the occasional fulminate cracking of thunder, the gurgling and murmuring of little streams, and the thundering and rushing of torrents.

It may have been a considerable strain for those early people to grasp and adapt themselves to the acoustic world which we have described above in onomatopœic terms used by the modern Englishman. The noises and sounds that usually surrounded primitive man blended into a homogeneous pattern and formed, as it were, a protecting screen in his waking hours and to some extent in his sleep. It had ' tentacles, cast near and far, for the approach of an enemy. . . . The sudden cessation of one of its constituents would break the pattern and put him on the alert and in a mild state of fear. The hearing of the pattern then meant safety. . . . Absolute silence, which is a rarity in the natural world and meant to man that he is without his acoustic protection, still brings a feeling of awe.'[1] Conversely, the sudden change of loudness caused alarm as it still does both in babies and adults.

Taking it all in all, Pithecanthropus' physical make-up was certainly inferior to that of his next of kin and of some more remote relations.

Yet he could make headway against his competitors, for he was handed on an enormous heritage which he could put to good use and which gave him some—perhaps only slight—superiority over

---

[1] See Lancet (1941), p. 465.

the creatures surrounding him. It would lead too far into the field of fancy were we to discuss all the specific functions, attitudes, behaviours with which he was endowed. We shall therefore have to content ourselves with some generalities.

His capacities to preserve and perpetuate life by responding to outside stimuli had been developed throughout evolution from the amœba onwards, a process which had taken many millions of years. Many of them had become highly automatic, that is to say, they were directed by inner stimuli, without being influenced by the conscious self. They had become inherent qualities of the life process. Thus, for instance, in the early stages of consciousness of the primitive, brutish, untamed children of nature, as of the young child, stimuli coming from without were not always distinguished from those coming from within; they still formed a unity.

It is difficult for our analytic mind to grasp the idea of that wholeness. Yet reference to some unmistakable examples from the animal world and our own enables us to arrive at it through interpolation.

Early man had probably inherited from his ancestors the faculty of making the most of such objects as were necessary and useful for the maintenance of life. It remains doubtful, however, whether they could perceive them in isolation, as " animals do not easily recognise objects out of their usual setting." [1] Even monkeys are rather clumsy in recognizing and appreciating objects in isolation. " A monkey was trained to find its food behind a door marked by a card with a red circle on it, and to take no notice of another door marked with a blue triangle. When the monkey had learnt this and made no mistakes, the blue triangle was changed for a blue circle. This completely confused the monkey; it no longer knew that its food was behind the red circle. Evidently it had learnt the situation as a whole." .' Many animals which have good eyes, perhaps most, see situations as a whole and do not easily recognize objects out of their usual setting. We ourselves are just the same until we get to know a thing or a person well; often we do not recognize a casual acquaintance in unusual surroundings.' [2]

Primeval man was still dominated by the surround, he had not even begun to master it, as we may infer from the negative fact that the Pithecanthropus site itself was archæologically sterile. He did not possess the technical dexterity to manipulate and to fashion his

---
[1] Fox, H. Munro, l.c., pp. 10–11.
[2] Fox, H. Munro. Ibid., p. 11.

materials into tools planned to fulfil a specific purpose. " He lived under cover of the woods, in a sub-tropical region which was highly fruitful : consequently he was not dependent upon animal food, and therefore was not forced to take this decisive step." [1]

It is open to doubt whether the rude implements of quartzite discovered in the same layers [2] and in the Sinanthropus site [3] were really man-made.

It is, however, conceivable that Pithecanthropus employed sticks, clubs, stones, and bones, which he found ready to hand for digging roots, reaching fruits, catching little fish, and so forth.[4] ' Arms of old,' says Lucretius,[5] ' were hands, nails and teeth and stones and boughs broken off from the forests.' [6] Such ready-made implements have, of course, withered away through the ages, but recalling that apes can utilize sticks skilfully and with deliberation, we can assume that Pithecanthropus was beginning to make some progress in the employment of objects which nature had manufactured for him.

The fact, too, that no tombs have been discovered is quite in keeping with the absence of tools. It indicates that Pithecanthropus did not bury the dead [7] which in its turn casts some light on his spiritual life, particularly his lack of the notions of past, present and future.

In spite of the minute examinations of the skull and the inferences drawn from it as to the probable structure of Pithecanthropus' brain not much can be said about his mental life, his thoughts and beliefs. We shall, therefore, resort to the procedure of comparison and interpolation [8] and read the past in the light of the present.[9]

PITHECANTHROPUS' BEHAVIOUR ANALYSED

Judging from the behaviour of their forerunners (animals) we can assume that just as the objects in their environment appeared to primeval people as hazy, ' impressionistic ' shapes, so their behavioural reactions formed integral wholes.

---

[1] Schmidt, l.c., p. 86.
[2] Keith, l.c., p. 420.
[3] De Pradenne, l.c., pp. 192-3.
[4] Moore, J. H. (1941). *Savage Survivals*. Watts & Co., London, p. 65. Tylor, *Anthropology*, I, p. 18.
[5] Lucretius. *De Rerum Natura*. Lib. v, 1282. Transl. by H. A. J. Munro.
[6] *Arma antiqua, manus, ungues, dentesque fuerunt, et lapides et item silvarum fragmina rami.*
[7] Keith, l.c., p. 425.
[8] See above, p. 18.
[9] Cf. Bailey and Weir, l.c., p. 247.

It does not suffice to say that they were wandering about, rummaging, picking up food, eating, climbing up trees, groping their way through the undergrowth, staving off noxious objects and animals and so on. Rather do we need to analyse out the elementary reactions involved in their diverse behavioural responses. Here we must needs resort to introspection and comparison.

Aldous Huxley has found felicitous terms for the description of, and the psychological reaction to, the setting of the scene. He speaks of the damp and stifling, tangled, prickly and venomous hothouse darkness of the jungle, through which one has to hack one's way laboriously, among the leeches and the malevolently tangled rattans. With regard to the emotions which this environment arouses, he uses words such as ' terrifying, profoundly sinister, appalling.' [1]

Thus far we have depicted the seamy side of Pithecanthropus' surround. The bright side is represented by the security he derived from life in packs, from the abundance of food, and from the relatively long period he devoted to the upbringing of his young.

In trying to translate the attitude towards danger into terms of behaviourism and neuro-physiology, we pose the question : How did primitive man meet the danger against life ? ' Slower than all winged and most four-footed animals, man isn't designed for flight ; nor for fighting, he's naturally unarmed . . . man's primary response to the approach of danger was the most universal one in the animal kingdom . . . a sudden crouching immobility, a statuesque stillness, which naturalists call " freezing ". '

' What is this mechanism that makes a timid animal lie still while his enemy passes by ? How does Nature—a convenient word for the resultant of the trial-and-error method over thousands of years—how does Nature accomplish this contradictory task ? By paralysing the sensorimotor nervous system and playing on the autonomic. " I can't trust you with your new apparatus, it would give you away. We must fall back on your old vegetative system." Thus emotion, the one connecting link between the higher centres and the autonomic, in crescendo waves of fear, melts the fuses, leaving the higher centres curiously detached and interested, while the autonomic plays the part of protector, the dilated pupils blurring the vision, the patching pallor blending with the shadows, the shallow breathing giving less movement, and so on.' . . .

---

[1] Huxley, Aldous (1936). *Do What You Will.* Watts & Co., London, pp. 90-102.

'When the danger is far away, or when the higher centres control the emotion so that it is less, then the ordinary alertness is merely increased, giving just enough stimulation to the thyroids to give increased awareness, just enough to the suprarenals to give an increase of blood-sugar in case it may be needed. If the danger is one that can be met by fighting, then after a period of suspense during which the autonomic gives a preparatory unloading of the viscera . . . then the mechanism goes into reverse, fear changes to anything between anger and eagerness, depending on whether the opponent is, say, a wild pig, or an examiner. But these are latter-day modifications; man's primary response to danger was "freezing," and this entailed a gradual decontrol of the voluntary nervous system and an opportunist playing on the autonomic.'[1]

Thus it is hard to picture them, as Dorothy Davison does, as 'very slow and clumsy' fellows.[2] On the contrary, that species of man which survived and whose offspring we are, had the ability to subsist in their environment probably more co-ordinately, efficiently and speedily than his animal forebears. The two latter adverbs are meant to refer to the peculiar mode, rather than form of action. We are referring to the postures from which actions started and to which they returned.

Everyone knows from his own experience what peculiar state of the musculature is meant by the word 'tension.' To understand the nature of tension we shall first of all give a brief account of the nerve mechanism concerned with the behaviour described on p. 46. The environmental stimuli evoking certain responses are sensed by an age-old mass of brain cells (ganglia), the *Thalamus*. It contains cells concerned with tactual, optic and olfactory sensations. Yet the thalamus is not a mere receptacle for primitive sense impressions. It plays a rather active role in that it continuously poses, as it were, the question 'What is to be done,' and so evaluates the situation. It then sends out messages to an equally hoary cell aggregate, the *Strio-pallidar System*. This executes the movements which the situation demands. It is possessed by an impetuous, and more or less, violent motive power. If uninhibited it brings about such primeval rhythmical movements as are still manifest in the baby's kicking and sucking, the leaps of joy or eagerness, laughing etc. As a rule, however, the thalamus holds the rein firmly, so ensuring a firm posture and steady action.[3]

---
[1] Lancet (1941), p. 58.   [2] Davison, l.c., pp. 40-41.
[3] Küppers, E. (1923). *Weiteres zur Lokalisation des Psychischen. Zeitschr. f.d. ges. Neurol. u. Psych.*, Vol. 83, pp. 263-276.

This power of the strio-thalamic self is manifest in the emotional attitude, the striving towards the source of pleasant stimuli, or away from unpleasant ones; the driving force which tinges the world with bright or gloomy colours of all shades. It is constantly subjected to environmental stimuli which either maintain the individual's balance and well-being, or bring about disquiet and discomposure. The task of the strio-thalamic self is to guide the individual in a world fraught with dangers of all kinds. No wonder that experiment and pathology have localized in the strio-thalamic system such emotional expressions as laughing, weeping, grimacing, the experience of pain (Sir Henry Head), and so forth.

Since the maintenance of a certain tension, and with it effective action is localized in that ancient part of the brain, the Strio-Pallidum, it can be assumed to have been even more powerful in Pithecanthropus in whom the cerebral hemispheres did not as yet exert such checking power as they do in modern man.

On a higher level of development the cortex of the cerebral hemispheres gains increasing control over the striatal system and grades the primary impulses, thereby integrating the thalamo-striatal, i.e., emotional ' self ' into a cortical, i.e., rational self. The better graded this process is, the more capable is the individual of ' thinking.' The struggle between conflicting impulses and the stoppage of one by the other made its impress on language at a relatively late evolutionary stage. (See pp. 186ff.)

We can, therefore, infer that the thalamic regulation of posture must have been influencing the physical qualities such as loudness, pitch and vigour of such utterances [1] as had been handed down to man from his animal forebears.[2] In the utterances of the animals the intensity, pitch, modulation, and the peculiar timbre of their voices obviously depends on and varies with the demands of the situation.

The peculiar modifications and degrees of tension are so powerful as to influence human language perpetually throughout its evolution. Here it may be anticipated that this is one of the characteristics which allow even the untrained listener to recognize a particular language, even if he does not understand the words, or if the native speaker is using words belonging to a foreign language. ' Not all

---

[1] Utterance is, throughout this book, regarded ' as the expenditure of bodily energy in muscular efforts, as a grouped pattern of bodily movements which can be heard, rather than as a string of sounds deliberately produced by a sequence of tongue positions and mouth movements.'
[2] Firth, J. R. (1937). *The Tongues of Men.* Watts & Co., London, p. 19.

languages require an equal expenditure of muscular force in the production of articulatory movements. In certain of them the effort is reduced to a negligible degree, speech flowing along in a continuous and easy fashion, with a sustained evenness of tone. In others, on the contrary, there is muscular vehemence which produces upon the ear an impression of violence, with abrupt stops, jerks and shocks.'[1]

THE RESPIRATORY AND ALIMENTARY TRACTS

Let us now consider in some detail the effector organs which carry out the tasks we have outlined.

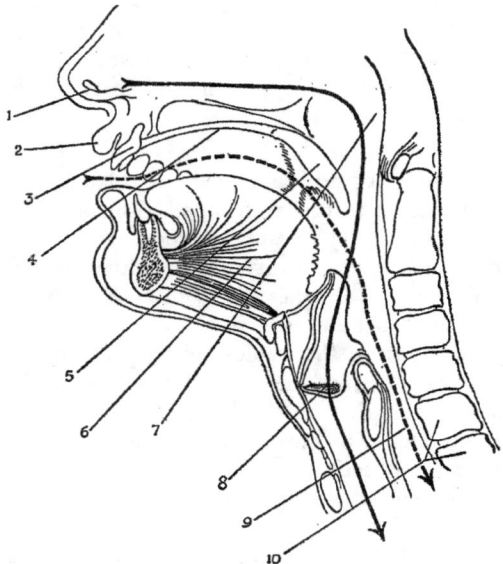

1. Nostril.
2. Upper Lip.
3. Upper Front Tooth.
4. Hard Palate.
5. Soft Palate.
6. Tongue.
7. Naso-Pharynx.
8. Larynx (Glottis).
9. Œsophagus.
10. Vertebræ.

FIG. 5 (After Grünwald)

The chemical interchanges essential for the maintenance of life, viz., eating and breathing, are ensured by the respiratory and digestive tracts. The functions of these tracts still form, even in the highest animals, the pivot of all their behaviour.[2] It is obvious that the organs of the respiratory and alimentary systems, such as

---

[1] Vendryes, l.c., p. 31.
[2] Douglas, L. C. (1932). *The Physical Mechanism of the Human Mind.* Livingstone, Edinburgh, p. 129 f.

the lungs, larynx, pharynx, tongue, lips, etc., are concerned with the activities involved in speech. It, therefore, becomes necessary to glance at some anatomical features of these two essential tracts.

Fig. 5 shows that a common pathway (the oral and pharyngeal cavities) serve both for the intake of food and of air. At the level of the fifth joint of the neck (cervical vertebra) the tract divides into two branches, one (windpipe and bronchi) giving access to the lungs, the other (œsophagus) leading into the stomach. It is obvious that the relative disposition of the two tracts constitutes a danger, namely, that of the intrusion of food into the respiratory tract, and of air in the alimentary tract.

In order to safeguard the proper functioning of both systems 'safety valves' have been developed within them. The upper orifice of the œsophagus is endowed with a muscular ring which keeps it closed during respiration so as to prevent air from entering the stomach.[1]

THE LARYNX

Far more complicated is the regulatory contrivance which guards the entrance to the windpipe. This safety-valve has to fulfil two obligations : (1) to prevent food from dropping into the bronchi and lungs ; (2) to prevent too sudden deflation of the lungs.

The device in question is the larynx (voice-box, Adam's apple). The usual definition of the larynx as the voice producing organ, is, however, from the evolutionist's point of view, incorrect. Everybody can see that the primary function of the hand, for instance, is that of grasping and holding. To declare that it is the 'writing organ' would be based on the assumption that writing is its original and main function, which is by no means the case. The following explanation will show that sound production was not the primary function of the larynx. Voice evolved, as it were, as a by-product of a biologically highly important function, in a manner analogous to that of the development of writing.

The various parts of the larynx evolved in early pre-human times, as is shown by the close resemblance between the structural patterns of the human larynx and the larynges of many animals, such as apes, cattle, dogs, and so forth.

The anatomical structure of the larynx still reveals that it once formed the uppermost part of the windpipe. It, like the windpipe, is a tube consisting of cartilaginous rings connected by

---

[1] Negus, V. E. (1920). *The Mechanism of the Larynx*. Heinemann, London, Chapter II.

membranes. The inner lining consists of a mucous membrane into which cartilages, connective tissue, muscles, and elastic tissue are inserted. Two aggregates of these tissues protruding into the larynx are known as the vocal cords. Their activities ensure maximum opening, and more or less firm closure. (See Figs. 6 and 7.) The vocal cords, which are almost constantly in action,

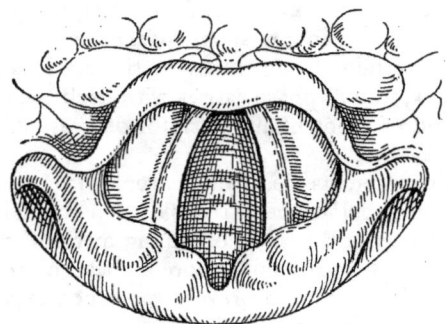

FIG. 6 (After Grünwald)

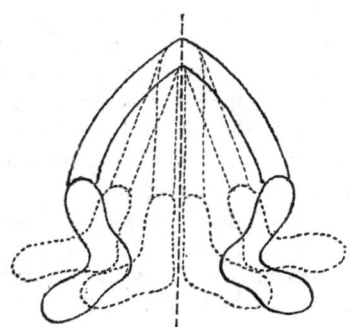

FIG. 7 (After Grünwald)
Showing the approximation of the vocal cords from respiration to phonation

can either approximate or separate from each other as the arytenoid cartilages glide towards or from each other and as their vocal processes turn inwards or outwards. The several muscles partaking in the movements of the vocal cords also ensure certain degrees of tension according to the 'meaning' of the response.

What then, are the nature, structure, offices and meanings of the diverse activities of the vocal cords? It needs no special elucidation to understand the action of the dilatators of the larynx, since obviously the intake of the optimum amount of air is vital to the individual's well-being. The vocal cords, therefore, diverge so as to ensure a maximum opening and to allow as much air as necessary to enter the lungs. Given normal conditions, inspiration is mute, since in the wide-open glottis no friction of air is possible.

The consumption of oxygen and the frequency of respiration naturally vary with the energy spent by the body. Yet, respiration also involves a certain derangement of the air balance within the chest. Every expiratory phase carries with itself the risk of deflation of the lungs and of a potentially harmful decrease of the tension of air in the blood.

The larynx counteracts this danger from within, which is, under normal conditions, below the threshold of perception. The vocal cords, acting as part of the *whole* breathing mechanism, and forming part of the integral body-mind, more or less narrow the passage between them (glottis) and so prevent too much expenditure of air, and safeguard the metabolic equilibrium.

The air which escapes from the lungs and passes through the glottis while the vocal cords are approximating, rubs against the edges of the vocal cords, or throws them into vibration when they have come to lie side by side. At an intermediate stage both friction and vibration may occur. Our hearing organ perceives the products of the interaction between the escaping air stream and those motor activities as *noises* of diverse kinds ranging from animal sounds such as barking, howling, mewing, cooing and so forth, to human sound such as crying, shouting, sighing, murmuring, humming, whispering, crooning, groaning, grunting, sobbing and so on.

So far as such noises consist of regular vibrations which make a more or less pleasant impression on us, they are said to constitute *voice*.

In subjecting the emission of sound to a closer examination, it will be convenient to deal separately with the initiation of voice, and with voice itself.

VOICE

The ability of man and of many animals and birds to produce vibrations in the respiratory tract, i.e., sound or voice, can be traced as far back as the fishes.

A number of them, such as some gurnards, the cod, the haddock, the horse-mackerel, numerous catfish, the sea-robin, the toadfish, and the sharp-snouted sea-horse, have an air-bladder endowed with musculature which the air, forced out, throws into vibration. A variety of growling, grunting, croaking, snoring, crooning, bellowing, purring, burring and whistling sounds can thus be produced.[1]

In the face of the biological facts Kant's interpretation of the cry of the new-born as a protest of the human spirit against its enslavement by the shackles of the senses can be understood.

If the analogy supplied by the Biogenetic Law hold good, early man's first vocal ejaculations may be assumed to have been like and to be represented by infantine noises described by Spencer as " severally long-drawn and nearly uniform from end to end . . . with little variation of quality between narrow limits." [2]

Many workers aver that the first utterance of man was the cry.[3]

There is reason to assume that the primeval vocal sound was soon used alongside with other modes of utterance. We shall later on have occasion to expound the importance and significance of those other sound patterns. Their existence must not make us underestimate the value of vocal sound. Floating mentally between states of ease and security, and states of fear and exertion, Pithecanthropus had constantly to alter the tension of the musculature in all parts of the body, and to regulate the expenditure of air through the larynx.[4] In this manner there arose vocal patterns characterized by diverse degrees of duration, intensity, frequency and resonance. Innumerable combinations of these characters are, of course, possible. They constitute the sonority, timbre, carrying power, pitch, modulation and other qualities of the voice.

Primitive man probably emitted all kinds of roaring, howling, yelling, hooting, screaming, squeaking, whining, moaning, groaning and other sounds in accordance with the given situation.

Such ejaculations or exclamations probably were among the earliest, i.e., lowest forms of speech embedded in the whole of man's behaviour. By virtue of the aforementioned properties they lent themselves particularly well to the conveyance of ever-varying emotional attitudes.[5]

The earliest vocal patterns may truly be said to have been

[1] Huxley, J., and Koch, L., l.c., p. 32.
[2] Spencer, H., l.c., p. 329.
[3] Cf. Regnaud, P. (1888). *Origine et Philosophie de Language.* Paris.
[4] Such adjustment can, of course, be achieved through other mechanisms too, but faithful to the Thucydidean precept, we are here singling out those which are relevant to the exposition.
[5] Cf. Spencer, H., l.c., p. 292.

emotional [1] as contrasted with rational activities in that their behavioural motor counterpart was inborn and hardly bridled. (See above, pp. 46 ff).

Those who coined the word ' *emotion* ' seem to have felt the nature of the psychic process, for the word is derived from the Latin verb *emovere*, literally ' to move out, to move away,' metaphorically ' to shake, to upheave.' The term thus stresses the motor counterpart of ' feeling.'

Vocal patterns were naturally interwoven into one indivisible set with other responses and sense impressions. On many occasions man's vocal utterances were embedded in the symphony played by the wild jungle orchestra. Pithecanthropus' ear may, at times, have found it difficult to make out the sense of that symphony, and to single out the part played by his fellows. Their ' solo part ' was ' masked ' by the orchestra's accompaniment. The conditions of daily life (bus-rides and the like) bring this masking effect home to us. When ' pricking up ' our ears we feel the mental and physical strain involved in the attempt at picking out and comprehending what is being said to us. This effort becomes particularly strenuous if we are not well acquainted with the language or if the trend of the conversation has partly escaped our attention.

Speech pathology demonstrates the difficulty of separating speech noises from other noises in cases which through brain diseases have regressed to an earlier, i.e., lower, evolutionary level. Patients who have recovered from Aphasia often state that during their illness speech was to them a bewildering mass of noises. Kehrer [2] described a patient who was word-deaf, i.e., could not apprehend words as linguistic wholes, although he was able to hear them ; at the same time his capacity to respond to non-linguistic noises of any kind and intensity was extinguished. The capacity to comprehend words returned, while the inability to heed extra-linguistic noises persisted.

We may assume that in Pithecanthropus' voice numerous shades of vowels were constantly bursting forth. They could, however, hardly have been stabilized, as their distinctive character mattered less to the listener than the fact that *some* sound indicating a certain emotional situation was emitted.

The normal speaker can with more or less facility distinguish between the finest shades of vowels. He perceives them as integral

---

[1] The same consideration applies to the clicks. See below, p. 70.
[2] Kehrer (1913). *Arch. f. Psychiatr.*

wholes, although musically each of them consists of a vast number of tones of diverse absolute and relative pitch and intensity.

The peculiar quality of a given speech sound is due to a group of overtones within a fixed range of pitch and intensity, superimposed on the fundamental tone whatever its pitch may be. These harmonics, as it were, ' form ' the speech sound and are therefore termed ' formants.'

Foreigners and the hard of hearing exemplify the difficulty which lies in perceiving those characteristic tones and giving them due prominence within the whole of the musical ' chord.'

Thus, Pithecanthropus may be assumed to have heeded to vocal patterns only as sets of tones, varied in pitch and intensity, possibly in a rhythmic manner, rather than to sounds in isolation, as only the whole pattern was emotionally significant. Even in our days we often lay more stress on the underlying speech melody or intonation than on the discernible speech sounds.

The fact that the foundation of voice was laid in animals which were in existence long before the genus ' homo ' developed, explains the high degree of automatization, the firm establishment of vocal sets and of the reactions to them.

Indeed every day experience supplies plenty of evidence.

1. The emotional meanings of vocal patterns are readily understood by human beings of all ages, and by many animals. The peculiar speech melody is to some extent dependent on the behavioural patterns involving increasing and decreasing tension. Here is an illustrative set of tones (Fig. 8).

FIG. 8
Infantile Cry (After T. Wilson. From Chamberlain)

2. Vocal patterns are to a great extent firmly linked with and hardly separate from the rest of the individual's behaviour. Actors tell us that they must really re-live the whole of a situation when they want to find the appropriate pattern of intonation. If they do not, the onlooker always more or less notices the artificiality of the performance.

3. When our fellow men give vent to their feelings of joy, sorrow,

regret, shame, commiseration, fright and so forth we can usually say whether their words correspond to their actual feelings.

So far we have described such features of voice itself as were, we believe, common to both Pithecanthropus and his precursors.

We now pass on to the discussion of the modes of initiation of voice as they can be observed in present-day man. We shall then return to the subject of voice itself and bring out the peculiarities of primordial human voice in contrast to animal voice.

VOCAL ATTACKS

Of the modes of setting the voice going there are three. These so-called *vocal attacks* are sound features accompanying the movements and positions of the vocal cords before they reach the middle line, thus closing the glottis and enabling the escaping air to throw them into vibration. The attacks are phonetically described as (1) aspirated, (2) soft, (3) hard.

ASPIRATED ATTACK OR SIGHING

If a considerable amount of air is escaping while the vocal cords are in the process of approximation and fairly near to each other a frictional noise, termed 'aspirated attack' precedes the voice. This acoustic phenomenon calls to mind and is, in fact, equal to that involved in the act of *sighing*, a behavioural whole which is observable both in animals and man soon after birth (Buffon [1]). A sigh may consist of the frictional noise only, or it may be followed by more or less deep, rough, nasal voice, or friction of air and vibrations of air may be interwoven.

SOFT ATTACK

If expiration sets in gently and increases steadily when the glottal aperture is closed, the escaping air throws the vocal cords into vibration, and the vocal attack, agreeable to the ear, is said to be soft.

The approximation of the vocal cords takes place in the same manner as in the aspirated attack, but at a greater speed. Thus the biological task of preventing too sudden deflation of the lungs is accomplished likewise. Dynamically and biologically there seems to be only a difference of degree between the aspirated and soft

---

[1] As quoted by Egger, E. (1903). *Beobachtungen und Betrachtungen über die Entwicklung der Intelligenz und der Sprache bei Kindern.* Wunderlich, Leipzig, p. 12.

attacks. Being otherwise alike they may be grouped in one class of modes of initiation which serve the function of safeguarding life against dangers from *within*. Seen from the psychological angle this natural reaction may be styled an expression of well-being. In the course of evolution it assumes the character of a *symbolic* (see p. 165) audible expression of pleasurable emotional states, such as relief, contentment, etc. In so far as they are activated by the urge to eject " bad air," and so to cope with a very primitive anxiety (suffocation), they symbolise equilibrium, independence and self-assertion.[1]

HARD ATTACK OR GLOTTAL STOP

The third type of attack, the hard attack or glottal stop, is an explosive noise produced by the air which under high pressure forces its way out through the tautly closed glottis.

Delving again into the history of the mammals we find that it is absent in such animals as cats, dogs, and so on. The reason for the comparatively recent appearance of the glottal stop lies in the arrangement and shape of the parts of the entire throat. There is a difference between the anatomical structures of the pharynx and its adjacent formations in the animals and in man, which is often overlooked. Most animals can breathe solely through the nose, whilst the mouth is reserved for the intake of food only. This is necessitated by the fact that the larynx is situated high up in the nasopharynx behind the posterior nostrils, and that the soft palate reaches far down to the level of the root of the tongue. In this manner the soft palate forms a barrier blocking the way from the mouth into the windpipe. (See Fig. 9.)

With the development of upright posture in the apes there begins the gradual descent of the larynx into the lower part of the pharynx. In man the laryngeal entrance is almost on the same level as that of the œsophagus. This novel anatomical arrangement is responsible for the taut and firm closure of the glottis which accompanies the act of swallowing, and is involved in the hard attack. Fig. 5, p. 49 shows that whenever a morsel is passing down the throat, there would arise the danger of its falling into the windpipe, were it not for the fact that the upper part of the latter has been transformed in such a way as to act as a safety valve reacting promptly to material danger from *without* by firm closure.

---

[1] Stein, L. (1948). A Note on the Treatment of Stammering. *British Journal of Med. Psychology*.

58 THE INFANCY OF SPEECH

This closure of the glottis and the glottal stop were thus originally a natural reaction to intruding foreign bodies.

It may be remarked in passing that the epiglottis was not designed —as is often assumed—as a protecting lid of the larynx, although it has incidentally assumed that role in man. 'In animals with a keen sense of smell the epiglottis is in contact with the soft palate in order to ensure that inspired air shall pass through the nose and thus keep up the activity of the olfactory sense. In animals which do not rely on the sense of smell this contact of epiglottis and soft

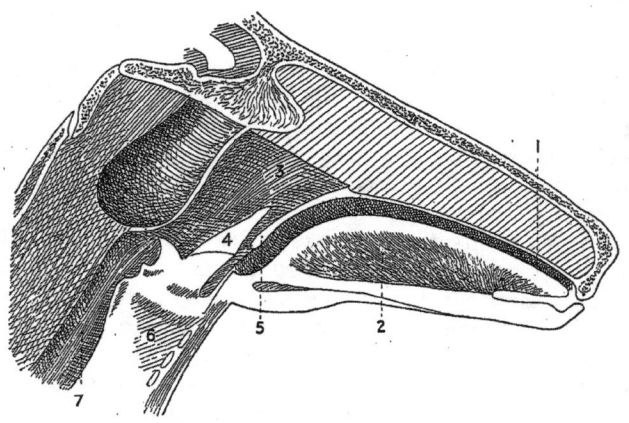

FIG. 9
Head of a horse. (After Chauveau)
1. Oral Cavity.
2. Tongue.
3. Cavum.
4. Epiglottis.
5. Soft Palate.
6. Larynx.
7. Pharynx.

palate is no longer required, and in Orang-utans (*Simia satyrus*), Chimpanzees (*Anthropopithecus troglodytes*), Gorillas and Man there is a gap of varying size between the two.'[1]

In summing up what has been said about the vocal attacks we have to guard against a fallacy. It is customary, as the adjective 'vocal' indicates, to regard the attacks as part and parcel of the vocalizing process. It goes without saying that vocalization must be initiated somehow, and therefore the term 'attack' is justified. For certain purposes the mode of initiation may be made the principle

[1] Negus, V. E. (1932). 'The Evolution of the Larynx and the Voice in Animals.' *Proceedings of the International Congress of Phonetic Sciences.* Amsterdam, p. 108.

of classification of phonation. On the other hand, it is undeniable that at least the aspirated and the hard attacks occur also as independent units. The former is, biologically speaking, the voiceless utterance of relief ; the latter may precede or terminate vocalization, but may also occur in isolation. It can be seen that these sets of activities performed by the larynx are primarily elicited by age-old vegetative stimuli, and as such are as yet ' extra-linguistic.'

They and other such vegetative reactions are among the earliest functions which have been subjected to the process of symbolization.

NASALITY

We can, by interpolation, attribute one more quality to primeval voice. It was in all probability *nasal*, at least in the early stages. It has been pointed out above (p. 57) that animals whose larynx is situated fairly high up in the throat can swallow safely although the nasopharynx remains open. (See Fig. 9.) There is therefore no vegetative urge to lift the soft palate during the emission of voice. The exhaled air which escapes through the nose, gives the voice its nasal timbre, provided, of course, the shape of the nasal spaces allows this peculiar resonance, i.e., components in the region 300 to 1,000 cycles [1] to arise.

On the assumption that Pithecanthropus' throat was somewhat ape-like we may imagine his voice to have been basically " nasal."

This propensity to nasal utterance is mirrored in evolutionary and pathological facts. It is well known that the languages, and particularly the songs of primitive races are often characterized by marked nasality. The same feature crops up after inflammation of the brain which may not have left any other traces of dissolution, i.e., signs or symptoms indicative of regression to lower, i.e., earlier levels of evolution. Relics of those earlier types of speech are still recognizable in archaic languages. Before the Indo-European mother-tongue had divided into the now known Indian, Iranian, Armenian, Greek, Albanian, Italic, Celtic, Slavonic and Germanic language families nasality must have been a common feature. Nasalization is met with in the Old Vedic language, e.g., *pursa> pumsa, paksa>punkha ; in Iranian, e.g., catanro against Sanskrit catasra, Avestan hazanhrem, vanhus, Sanskrit sahasra, vasu, and the

---

[1] Curry, R. (1940). *The Mechanism of the Human Voice.* Churchill, London, p. 116.

like.[1] This nasalization occurs either in conjunction with other consonants or intervocally. The process may be styled dissimilative in some cases, and compensatory in others. In dissimilative nasalization /j/ or /r/ or a semi-vowel in the ensuing syllable changes /j/, /r/, /v/ or such combinations as sibilant, spirant and semi-vowel, explosive (>spirant) and semi-vowel, semi-vowel and semi-vowel into a nasal.[2] As the result of compensation the nasal occurs when a vowel has been contracted with a sound following it (ei, eu, er, etc.), or it springs up before an intervocalic sibilant (/s/), sometimes owing to shortening of a long vowel. Both types are usually included in the class of spontaneous (autonomous) sound change.[3] The ornamental epithets indicate that the process arises from intrinsic tendencies, and is not produced by such external agencies as are at work in conditioned (heteronomous) sound change. If, for instance, Latin *gelu* /gelu/ ' frost ' changes into Italian *gelo* /dzelo/, it is obvious that in anticipating the articulation of the palatal vowel /e/ or [ie] the speaker has shifted the articulation of the pharyngeal /g/ forward, roughly in this manner : /ge/>/gje/> /dje/>/dʒe/.

In the case of Indo-European nasalization no such cogent reason can be detected. Moreover the question may be posed why the aforementioned spontaneous sound changes actually gave rise to nasalization, and not to any other changes such as lengthening of vowels, dipthongization and the like, processes which are often encountered in the history of languages. The evolutionist is inclined to see here the last relic of the dominance of an ancient speech pattern which was only gradually superseded by oral sound. The assumption is corroborated by the fact that in ancient Indo-Aryan nasalization is found pre-eminently in rustic speech which is usually more archaic than the accepted standard.

As regards the sibilants ([s] and kindred sounds) which are often involved in the process of nasalization, an, albeit tentative and by no means complete, explanation may be offered. There seems to exist a primordial association between the articulation of the tongue tip against the gums, and the elevation of the soft palate. The

---

[1] An asterisk * before a word indicates that it is an unrecorded earlier form inferred by comparison. The customary formulas A>B and A<B indicate that the word A has developed into B, or vice versa.

[2] It is customary to enclose in square brackets *phonetic* characters as opposed to those used in national orthography.

[3] Basu, G. C. (1944). ' Nasalization in Middle Indo-Aryan.' *Annals of the Bhandarkar Oriental Research Institute*, Vol. XXIV , pp. 175-90.

association of the two functions is biologically intelligible if it is recalled that the articulation of [s] is in all probability based on the motor pattern of sipping which would be impracticable without the closing of the nasal airway. Observation [1] reveals that if anything prevents the articulation of the tongue tip during speech (e.g., dental treatment, insertion of an artificial palate, inflammation of the gums) the fricative [s] becomes more or less blurred. Curiously enough the resulting sound is usually nasalized. In slovenly speech when the tip of the tongue is scarcely articulating there appears a nasal h [h̃] instead of [s] or [θ], e.g. [hænkju] for [θænkh̃u] ' thank you.' It seems, therefore, that, if the underlying sipping pattern is prevented from operating, the urge to lift the soft palate originally associated with it, ceases.

LINGUISTIC USE OF THE ATTACKS

The use of the different attacks, that is, biologically speaking, the employment of the two-way safety valve as a safeguard against either external or internal danger, has had far-reaching consequences, the import of which we shall exemplify briefly.

The sighing pattern has become differentiated into various vocal sounds. It can be said to form the foundation on which syllables beginning with [h] are based, the [h] representing the initial glottal fricative of the sighing pattern, the vowel being a modification of the laryngeal sound, brought about by peculiar shapes of mouth. If the glottis is narrow enough to permit the vocal cords to be thrown into vibration, or if the front part is closed and the hind part (between the arytenoid cartilages) open, the fricative noise originating in the latter, is interwoven with sound, and the [h] is voiced. This is, for instance, the case in some African languages, in Slavonic languages such as Ruthenian and Czech, in some Rumanian dialects, and other languages. That we find, for instance, in Old Czech *oko* besides *hoko*, ' eye,' Rumanian *ultui* besides *hultui* ' to graft ' illustrates the lability of vocal initiation. Latin [h] has disappeared in all Romance languages where it has given way to the soft attack, for example, Latin *habere*, Rumanian *aveá*, Italian *avere*, Provençal, Catalan *aver*, Spanish, Portuguese *haver* [aver], French *avoir*, Latin *hora*, Rumanian *oara*, Italian *ora*, French *heure* [œr], Provençal, Catalan *ora*, Spanish, Portuguese *hora* [ora]. The change from the aspirated to the soft attack can be

---
[1] Stein, L. (1918). Proceed. of the Oesterr. Ges. f. exper. Phonetik. Wien. med. Woch. No. 34.—*Speech and Voice* (1942). Methuen & Co., Ltd. p. 154.

ascertained in the historical development of many other languages. It has been setting in for some time in modern English, as is manifest in colloquial phrases like [it's gɔn]<' it has gone,' [aiv]<' I have,' etc. In Cockney the aspirated attack is tending to appear in the wrong places. Humorists use it to put their audience in good humour. The mere reference, for instance, to a newspaper man who had written ' sold hout ' on his blackboard is found funny.

Catullus in one of his epigrams (No. 84) derides a pompous Roman who from lowly rustic beginnings had reached a fairly high social standard. Yet he betrayed his upbringing by confusing the aspirated initiation of the vowels with the soft attack.

The soft attack is the standard initiation in many languages, especially in the Romance languages.

The glottal stop, having become part and parcel of linguistic communication, undergoes some modifications and is still more or less prevalent in various languages, where it usually initiates the vowels. In both vowels and consonants the hard attack is sometimes employed especially in states of anger or vexation. For instance ['nou][1] when it is meant not only to indicate negation, but also refusal, reluctance and anger. Under such conditions it may also occur at the end of a word. In Bari, spoken in the Anglo-Egyptian Sudan, the glottal stop is conventional at the end of many words, e.g., lio' ' my,' kwe' ' our,' but kwe ' head.' [2]

The glottal stop has assumed and is constantly assuming the role of a phoneme,[3] that is to say, ' a minimum unit of distinctive sound feature ' which has no cognitive meaning, but which in certain fixed arrangements makes up the meaningful forms that are uttered.[4]

In a number of languages of America and Africa consonants such as [p, t, k, s, j, ts, t, pf, tl, kl] can be accompanied by the glottal stop, for example, Hausa [k'ak'a] ' grandfather,' [kaka] ' harvest,' Zulu [k'ak'a] ' to encircle,' [khakha] ' to be acrid,' [ts'ɔbɔ] ' to smash,' [intl'ɔkɔ] ' head.' Such consonants are said to be ' ejective.'[5]

In German and other Indo-European languages vowels are as a rule initiated by the hard attack.

---

[1] ' indicates the glottal stop.
[2] Westermann, D., and Ward, I. C. (1933). *Practical Phonetics for Students of African Languages*. Oxford University Press, p. 60.
[3] Bloomfield. *Language*, p. 79.
[4] Bloomfield, L. (1939). *Linguistic Aspects of Science*. University of Chicago Press, p. 21.
[5] Westermann and Ward, l.c., pp. 96 ff.

Sievers[1] makes the interesting remark that the hard attack in Indo-European languages seems to be of rather modern origin. It is even doubtful whether it may be identified with the Greek *spiritus lenis*. Such doubts are founded especially on elision and contraction of neighbouring vowels, and on the fusion of words terminating in a consonant with an ensuing word. It appears that in ancient times the elisions and the contraction of neighbouring vowels, and the compounding of words terminating in a consonant with the following word, was more frequent than in comparatively recent centuries. It can, therefore, be assumed that the hard attack which would certainly have impeded this process, was absent, or at least less frequent at the time. Here are a few examples. Middle Dutch *geten<gi-eten, gint<geint, gonneert<geonneert*.[2] Old Gothlandic *gutnalþing<Gutnaalþing*, ' Law Assembly of the Good.' East and West Nordic (until the end of the Viking period, 800–1050 A.D.) *blán<bláan*, ' blue ' (Accus. Sing. Masc.).[3]

The relatively recent appearance of the glottal stop in the Indo-European languages at least casts a curious sidelight on the mentalities of the peoples concerned.

In some languages the glottal stop substitutes other oral stops. In the Slavonic dialect of Rosenthal in Corinthia [k] is replaced by the glottal stop [4]; in Danish the glottal stop terminates a word, formerly ending in [t], for instance, *hun'* ' dog,' German *Hund*, English *hound*; the same sound sequence without the glottal stop *hun* means ' she.' [5] In Cockney [t] changes into the glottal stop : bottle>bo'l, hot>o'. In the Bari language (Africa) [b] and [d] are sometimes weakened into the mere glottal stop, e.g., ['ayin] for ['bayin], ' nothing.'[6]

Pitch, too, has been conventionalized and has remained in close union with the vowels (vowel, Latin *vocalis*, i.e., that which is endowed with voice, the sounding).

In such languages as Cantonese, Chinese, Lithuanian, Serbian, Ancient Greek and in African languages, the pitch of a syllable or word is phonemic, i.e., determines its reference to objects or events,

---

[1] Sievers, E. (1901). *Phonetik. Grundriss der Germanischen Philologie.* Trübner, Strassburg. Vol. I, pp. 300–301.
[2] Te Winkel, J. (1901). *Geschichte der Niederländischen Sprache.* Ibid., Vol. I, p. 817.
[3] Noreen, A. (1901). *Geschichte der Nordischen Sprachen.* Ibid., Vol. I, p. 560.
[4] Mikkola, J. J. (1913). *Urslavische Grammatik.* Winter, Heidelberg, p. 27.
[5] Bloomfield. *Language*, p. 99.
[6] Westermann and Ward, l.c., p. 60.

and serves as a grammatical aid in the formation of sentences [1]; for instance : Efik (S. Nigeria), *akpa* [··] ' river,' [2] *akpa* [··] ' first,' *akpa* [·.] ' he dies ' ; *anam utom* [·...] ' he does work,' *anam utom* [.··.] ' a doer of work.' [3]

Pitch accentuation acts as a preserving force for syllables, and so long as pitch prevails the characters of the syllables and their vowels are largely maintained.

The accentuation of the early Greek language was—according to the Alexandrine grammarians—mainly one of pitch.[4] Its sister languages also employed the pitch accentuation, and some of them, for instance, Serbian, Latvian, Lithuanian, Slovenian,[5] are still preserving it to a greater or lesser extent.

Owing to the close interrelation between pitch, tonicity and vowel sound the former exerts a considerable influence on the peculiar sound and quantity of the latter.

Which part of an utterance originally bore more pitch and intensity, was probably determined by the emotional attitude of the speaker towards the situation as a whole, or, later on, towards a certain element of the utterance expressive of the situation. Rhythm may also have played its part. This can be inferred from facts in comparatively young languages. Ancient Greek, *phóros*, *gónos*, Ancient Indian, *bháras*, *jamas*, ' that which is borne ; birth, creature ' against Greek *phorós*, Ancient Indian *bharás*, Greek *gonós*, ' carrying, engendering,' where the place of stress refers to act, action and agent respectively.[6]

Examples from Slavonic languages also demonstrate the influence of intonation on the vowels. The resulting sound change is known as ' Ablaut ' or gradation: Lithuanian *tekù* ' I run,' *tākas* ' pavement.' [7]

The tendency in the Indo-European languages has been to substitute stress for pitch.

Along with this change unstressed syllables have been and are being mutilated, reduced to a minimum of sound, and finally shed.

We may assume that from hoary times there have always been

---
[1] Cf. Bloomfield. *Language*, pp. 116 f.
[2] The relative pitch of the syllables is indicated by the position of the dots within the square brackets.
[3] See Westermann and Ward, l.c., pp. 134 ff and 144.
[4] Atkinson, B. F. C. (1931). *The Greek Language*. Faber & Faber, London, p. 53.
[5] See Mikkola, J. J. (1913). *Urslavische Grammatik*. Winter, Heidelberg, pp. 116 ff.
[6] Mikkola, l.c., p. 117.
[7] *Ibid.*, p. 99.

changes in the character of the vowels which were ultimately caused by emotions bursting forth in intonation and rhythm.

Vocalic change in its turn influences the articulation of the surrounding consonants.[1]

Experimental phonetics has shown that the attacks have a definite influence on the flow of intonation. After a hard attack the pitch curve of the vowel tends to rise, whilst the pitch of a vowel following the aspirated attack is usually lowered. In vowels initiated by the soft attack the pitch is sometimes lowered, sometimes it remains steady.[2]

The important role which intonation and stress have been playing through the ages is still recognizable in the patterns, expressing questions, assertions, surprise, warnings and so forth.

These patterns, like the rather 'musical' calls of children on the street, hawkers and pedlars, tend to become more or less conventionalized. The various points which have been made mean to show why it is impossible to draw any inferences as to the specific words or sound patterns or, as it were, as to pre-historic grammars and vocabularies. (See above, p. 24.) Yet we maintain it is still possible to discern in all languages patterns indicative of certain perennial driving forces. (See also below, pp. 192.)

MOUTH AND THROAT

We now pass on to the description of the second system essential for the maintenance of life, viz., the digestive tract. Fig. 10 shows that the intake of food would seriously affect the nasal pathways if they were not protected by a safety valve, known as *Passavant's cushion*.[3] This is a fold brought about by the elevation of the pharyngeal mucous membrane. It protrudes into the nasopharynx and so meets the lifted soft palate half way, but is absent during respiration Fig. 10. This mechanism guarantees the widest possible aperture for breathing in and smelling, and the firmest possible closure to prevent food from intruding into the nose during the act of swallowing. Its presence during speech—where it is by no means *a priori* essential—is noteworthy as it is an indication of the role which the patterns involved in the intake of

---

[1] See below, p. 138.
[2] See *Tabulæ Biologicæ*. Ed. by Oppenheimer and Pincussen (1925). W. Funk, Berlin. Vol. II, p. 245.
[3] Stein, L. (1937). *Sprach und Stimmstörungen*. Weidmann, Vienna, Leipzig, Berne, pp. 104 ff. *Zur Frage des Passavantschen Wulstes*. Wien. Med. Woch., 1930, No. 35.

66 THE INFANCY OF SPEECH

food must have played in the origin of speech. From what has been said above (p. 5) it can be seen that Passavant's cushion cannot have been of any influence or importance prior to the descent of the larynx.

The alimentary tract of animals is capable of producing noises as accompaniments of ingestion. A fish, the Misgurnus, ' makes quite a loud noise by gulping air bubbles in at its mouth, swallowing them, and expelling them forcibly through its anus.' [1]

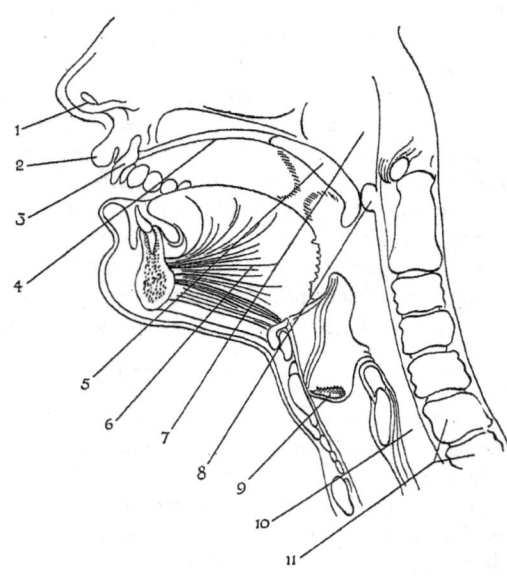

1. Nostril.
2. Upper Lip.
3. Upper Tooth.
4. Hard Palate.
5. Soft Palate.
6. Tongue.
7. Naso-Pharynx.
8. Passavant's Cushion.
9. Larynx.
10 Œsophagus.
11. Vertebræ.

FIG. 10
(After Stein)

Horses when irritated produce a more or less rhythmical noise by ejecting gas from the anus. This noise seems to have a highly emotional meaning which to all appearances it conveys to other horses. They in their turn respond by producing the same noise.

In man the upper part of the alimentary tract lends itself to the production of noises at two levels : (1) along the pathway from the lips down to the root of the tongue ; (2) at the entrance to the

---

[1] Huxley and Koch, l.c., p. 32.

THE HUMAN STOCK

œsophagus. The sound-producing agency is air either taken in or given out.

Sound making through the muscular ring around the upper orifice of the œsophagus is known as gulping and belching. The latter is a well-engrained capacity which in morbid conditions proves of the utmost value. The removal of the larynx because of malignant tumours, or shrinking scars in the larynx necessitates tracheotomy which in its turn renders phonation impossible. It is interesting to note that in such cases ancient evolutionary sound patterns are revived inasmuch as some patients spontaneously resort to the substitution of laryngeal sound by the noise accompanying the act of belching.

SUCKING

The most primitive type of ingestion performed along the pathway from the lips to the gullet is the act of sucking. It is ancient heritage and thus automatic, although certain movements involved (lips, tongue) can be subjected to the conscious will. Its highly complex mechanism and its further elaboration deserve our fullest attention.

Be it recalled that sucking requires a series of vacua in the mouth in order to cause the liquid to rise through the reduction of the atmospheric pressure weighing on it. To this end the mouth is divided into three chambers, the labial chamber, the palatal chamber, and the velar or laryngeal chamber. In these three chambers the air is rarefied by the closing and rounding of the lips, the curving of the tongue and the lowering of the jaw and the larynx.[1]

The new-born during its first weeks of life performs the act of sucking in complete silence, and displays the serenity and placidity correlated to the union with his mother who represents his ' world.'

The baby experiences his surround in his sucking reaction, he takes his mother in. It is not surprising that the verb ' to take in ' metaphorically indicates comprehension and intelligence. Children who were bottle-fed or in whom breast feeding was not satisfactory, often are unable to ' learn,' i.e., to take in what is presented to them, despite a fundamentally high intelligence.

---

[1] See Van Ginneken, J. (1939). ' Les clics, les consonnes et les voyelles dans l'histoire de l'humanité.' *Proceedings of the Third International Congress of Phonetic Sciences.* Laboratory of Phonetics of the University, Ghent, pp. 321 ff. De V. Pienaar, P., *Click Formation and Distribution. Ibid.*, pp. 344 ff.

IN THE BEGINNING WAS THE NEED[1]

The act of sucking performed by the human new-born does not essentially differ from that observed in every young mammal. Soon, however, the rarefaction of air necessary for the inflow of milk or its substitutes becomes accompanied by various noises, according to where and how their release takes place. The variety of sucking noises increases as the act of sucking itself is undergoing further specialization. The activities which involve these noises are described roughly as : lapping, sipping, sucking, quaffing, supping, swigging, smacking, swilling, etc. The noises themselves are termed ' clicks.'

Physically speaking, the noisiness of such acts of taking in food can be assigned to the vehemence with which this is achieved. The bio-psychological aspect is that of greed and avidity, which ' historically ' may be a later event. As clicking is undoubtedly genetically fixed, does it perhaps reflect the evolutionary changes brought about by the cooling down of the tropical or sub-tropical climate bringing about a scarcity of food in Pre-palæolithic times some 600,000 years ago ?

And does not the *playful* and joyful way in which the infant performs and listens to those noises, confirm the assumption ? We know that many other tendencies, predilections and plays of animals and human beings are the recapitulation of activities which their forbears developed.

The readiness with which the baby performs sucking movements as a specific reaction to the human voice from the third week of life [2] seems to bear out not only the antiquity of this reaction but also to indicate that early symbolization has thoroughly paved the way for ' listening ' as a preliminary to ' uttering.'

We have seen above (p. 32) that animals and especially apes, produce clicks, but their number is extremely small.

The progress, which babies exhibit and which we should like to postulate for Pithecanthropus,. consists in the vast extension of the clicking mechanism. Whereas every species of ape has only one or two clicks peculiar to it, the human infant produces them in great and fluctuating variety. If it be asked why apes did not acquire clicks when the earth was in the process of cooling down the reply

---

[1] Katz, D. (1937). *Animals and Man.* Longmans, Green & Co., London, pp. 159–60.
[2] Bühler, Ch. (1927). *Soziologische und psychologische Studien über das erste Lebensjahr.* Fischer, Vienna, p. 16.

THE HUMAN STOCK 69

must be that they, being physically better adapted to life (climbing, running and so forth), were not subject to the same degree of greed as was Pithecanthropus. The apes were thus prevented from advancing because ' Progress went with the creature which never set hard. . . . We are changing by preventing ourselves from becoming set.'[1] Apes did not advance in this respect because they did not *need* to. Pithecanthropus *was set hard* only in so far as he did not re-learn to climb for his food, and so forth.

In sucking and swallowing a very elaborate precision-mechanism is activated which requires the finest co-ordination of the muscles of the lips, tongue, jaw, pharynx, and larynx, innervated by the motor fibres of the Trigeminus, Hypoglossus, Glossopharyngeus, Vagus, Accessorius and Facial nerves. These motor nerves are stimulated by the sensory fibres of the Trigeminus (touch), Olfactorius (smell), Glossopharyngeus (taste), and Laryngeus Superior (touch) nerves.

The lowest centres of this mechanism and that of phonation, are situated in the spinal bulb.

The bulbar centre of phonation is in connection with the quadrigeminal bodies (*inferior colliculi*) where significantly the acoustic fibres end. Irritation of that area evokes sounds in dogs and apes.[2] (See Plate 8, B, 3.)

The cortical centre for the innervation of the vocal cords is situated in the lowermost part of the anterior central convolution of *both* hemispheres.[3] (See Fig. 2.)

Higher centres where gustatory stimuli elicit tasting, chewing and swallowing movements are situated in the thalamic area (see p. 47) and in the median, inferior surface of the temporal lobe, especially in the region of the *gyrus hippocampi* and the *uncus*.[4]

The centre from which the act of swallowing is elicited by will lies in the inferior part of the anterior central convolution in the region of the centre of mastication near that innervating the tongue and the larynx. It is connected with the *substantia nigra* which can thus be regarded as a subcortical centre.[5] (See Plate 8.)

The great antiquity and functional importance of the linkage

---

[1] Heard, Gerald (1934). *Science in the Making.* Faber & Faber, London, p. 199.
[2] Höber, R. (1919). *Lehrbuch der Physiologic.* Springer, Berlin, p. 359.
[3] Spiegel, E. A., and Sommer, I. (1931). *Ophthalmo- und Oto-Neurologie.* Springer, Vienna-Berlin, p. 315.
[4] Spiegel, E. A., and Sommer, I., l.c., pp. 69-70. Réthi, L. (1893). Das Rindenfeld des Kauens und Schluckens. *Proc. Akad. d. Wiss,* Vienna. Math.-nat. Kl., Vol. CII, III.
[5] Spiegel and Sommer. *Ibid.,* p. 313.

between olfactory and gustatory sensations, and movements of the lips and tongue is evidenced by the fact that the neopallium originated from the area where this relationship is effected.[1]

CLICKS

The habit of clicking can be found in every stage of language development, in every country and at all ages.

Children in the early babbling stage, and older imbeciles express their feelings and desires by them. Normal speakers all over the world use clicks more or less frequently as interjections with a conventional meaning. ' Some orientals think it polite to make hissing sounds by a rapid intake of air through the teeth.'[2] The French use [ʇ], i.e., a [t] 'sucked in' to express doubt or attract attention; an alveolar [t] reversed in the same manner signifies admiration or surprise; [ʃ] 'sipped in' sometimes conveys the 'satisfaction of the epicure and at other times a feeling of effort, or pain, either keenly or slightly experienced.'[3] English speakers use the repetitive click usually rendered ' *tut-tut* ' as an expression of shocking surprise, admiration, impatience, annoyance and similar emotional attitudes.

The number of clicks is infinitely greater than is illustrated by the above examples. The reader can, with some imagination, detect the counterpart of every consonant current in his standard language. Thus the source of English [p] would be the noise accompanying a kiss produced by the lips. If the tip of the tongue takes part in the kiss the resulting noises would be reminiscent of [pt].[4]

Our attempt at interpolation is facilitated by linguistic features still extant in some primitive peoples. There are many primitive languages in which, in spite of the very long history they have behind them, clicks are still preserved, for instance, in the sub-branches of Athapascan, Haida and Tlingit of the American Indian languages,[5] and in some African languages such as the Bushman,

---

[1] See Campion, G. G., and Elliot Smith, G. (1934). *The Neural Basis of Thought*. Kegan Paul, London, p. 26.

[2] Firth, J. R., l.c., pp. 33-34.

[3] See Vendryes, l.c., p. 33.

[4] For this reason and for the convenience of the reader clicks are in these pages represented by the inverted symbols for the consonants derived from them. The noises referred to above would accordingly be represented as [d] and [dʇ].

[5] Graff, W. L. (1932). *Language and Languages*. Appleton, New York-London, p. 430.

Hottentot, Sandawe, Bantu-Ngoni (Zulu, Xhosa, Swazi) and sporadically the Bantu-Sotho languages.¹

In the Namaqua language ' almost every word has an initial click, or has one in the middle of it, and some have two clicks.' They are produced by sticking the tongue against the palate and front teeth, or against the centre of the roof of the mouth, or far back in the mouth.² In view of the fact that these clicks seem to reflect the activities involved in sucking, we may assume ' beads ' of such rhythmic noises in the fashion of [ɖɪɖɪɖɪ ; ɖɪɣ, ɖɪɣ, ɖɪɣ ; ɖɖɖɖ ; ɲɲɲɲ] and similar ones on the one hand, and vocal sounds varying in shade, pitch, and intensity on the other, to have been the earliest types of human utterance.

Let us stop here for a while and consider the correlation between what is assumed to have been the socio-psychological background of earliest palæolithic man and his behavioural heritage.

Recalling that he lived more or less cheerfully " from hand to mouth " without aiming at securing the future,³ we may assume comparatively unstable, fluctuating utterances.

In trying to picture the possible state of speech of earliest man reference is often made to the deaf and dumb. What is generally emphasized is their power to communicate by gestures imitative or indicative of objects and events.

It is, however, equally important to stress that congenitally deaf persons are not really dumb in the strict sense of the word, i.e., absolutely without vocal sound and *audible* mouth gestures. In fact there is a remarkable stream of jerky vocal sounds continuously varying in pitch and loudness, at times intermingled with clicks.

These form one whole with grimaces and gestures. Within this whole the latter mime the event in question, whilst the sound-accompaniment supplies the emotional tuning. Paget⁴ and others believe that oral gestures too can depict events.

Besides voice and clicks there are observable in babies some few expulsory noises which accompany the acts of spitting, gargling,

---

¹ See Chatterji, S. K. (1939). ' Evolution in Speech Sounds.' *Third Intern. Congr. of Phonetic Sciences.* Laboratory of Phonetics of the University, Ghent. pp. 332 ff.
² Fraser, J. G. (1938). *The Native Races of Africa and Madagascar*, Humphries, London, p. 6.
³ Cf. Róheim, G. (1932). ' Psychoanalysis of Primitive Cultural Types.' *Intern. Journ. of Psycho-Analysis*, xiii.
⁴ Paget, R., l.c.

coughing and the like, all more or less indicative of rejection and distaste. We may include them in the sound table of primordial man. It will be seen below that these noises may have played their part in the further evolution of language. (See p. 115.)

So far our interpolation goes beyond the opinion of some linguists [1] and anthropologists in that we infer that the primordial patterns of utterance embraced not only emotional voicing but also clicking. These two patterns of sound were used side by side as independent units embedded in certain sets of gestures.

RHYTHM

The sucking and kicking movements of the baby are known to be rhythmical. The same is often said of standard speech when the rhythm of a person's speech is emphasized, and of certain pathological cases in which the impairment of the rhythm in speech is noticeable.

It is necessary, on this occasion, to point to the detrimental ambiguity which lies in the present-day usage of the word rhythm and its derivatives. According to Wyld's Universal English Dictionary, the term ' rhythm ' denotes a " movement characterized by regular recurrence and intermission, or by increase and decrease at regular intervals, of force, emphasis, stress, beat, loudness, cadence ; the essential quality of rhythm is to produce a sense of symmetry and regularity." [2]

Etymologists almost unanimously derive the Greek word *rhythmos* from the Greek base *rhy*, underlying the verb *rheo*, ' I flow.' They feel justified in doing so in view of such denotations of the word as the flow of an attire, harmony, accent, metre, etc., or its application to architecture, sculpture, a chain, a sentence and so forth. But Petersen [3] rightly points out the etymological difficulties [4] involved in this derivation. He therefore prefers Herodian's and Henri Etienne's derivation from the base *ery* or *Fry* " to draw, to pull," which entails the idea of activity. In this sense we speak of the rhythm of battle,[5] of a person's handwriting and the like.

---

[1] Van Ginneken, l.c., pp. 325–326, conjectures a primeval language without vowels. These he refers to a later evolutionary level. Others fall into the other extreme, holding that the cry was the only source of human language.
[2] Wyld, *Universal Dictionary of the English Language*. S.v. rhythm.
[3] Petersen, Eugen (1917). *Rhythmus*. Weidemann, Berlin.
[4] The suffix *-thmos*, for instance, was used to indicate doing rather than happening, as in *klauthmos*, ' endless crying,' *knyzethmos*, ' constant snarling,' and the like.
[5] The Military Correspondent of the *Evening Standard* (July 10, 1944) compares the rhythms of the battles in Normandy and those for the Baltic Republics.

THE HUMAN STOCK 73

Rhythmical happening can be said to be the fundamental character of all primitive movements in the material and animate world.[1] We need only think of the swinging pendulum, nystagmus, the scratching and stepping reflexes, breathing, the beating of the heart, and so forth.

Rhythm is a mode of movement which conspicuously pervades all life, nay, is the very essence of life ; the integration, disintegration and reintegration of the living matter takes place rhythmically. Rhythm thus pervades the activities of all living mechanisms from the jellyfish (medusa), which beats rhythmically,[2] to the drumming of one's heels, the clapping of the hands, the jumps of joy, dancing, marching, and, last but not least, musical and poetic patterns throughout their evolution.[3]

The sense of rhythm, i.e., the faculty to apprehend and appreciate rhythm, is innate. Being the essential mode of promoting life, its natural psychological aspect is that of a pleasurable emotion. The baby's behaviour seems to point to the pleasure he derives from being rocked in its cradle or from lullabies. Not only does he seem to enjoy the muscular sensation evoked in him by external forces, but he himself also cannot help executing his movements in a rhythmical way. Besides the kicking movements, sucking is performed reiteratively. Thus the clicks, too, are uttered in beads such as [ʇʇʇʇ, ɖʃʇsɖʃʇs].

In man rhythmical activity in the sense of involuntary reiteration of a motor pattern seems to be localized in the cerebral cortex. Brickner[4] reported on a patient who, when an area about three inches behind Broca's area on the mesial side of the left hemisphere was stimulated electrically, produced reiteration of speech sounds.[5]

---

[1] Howes, Frank (1926), *The Borderland of Music and Psychology*, Kegan Paul, London, p. 141, says : 'The rhythmic principle goes very deep and on it the whole universe seems to be run.'
[2] MacCurdy, J. T. (1928). *Common Principles in Psychology and Physiology*. Cambridge University Press, p. 146.
[3] 'By rhythm in language is meant any noticeable series of accents ; by metre is meant a series of accents which is not only noticeable, but also forms a definite repeating pattern.' Abercrombie, L. (1932). *Poetry*. Oxford University Press, pp. 16 ff.
[4] Brickner, R. M. (1940). 'A Human Cortical Area Producing Repetition Phenomena when Stimulated.' *Journ. of Neurophysiology*, Vol. III, No. 2, pp. 128 ff.
[5] Unfortunately this unique case was not investigated from the linguist's point of view. Only brief and cautious mention of it can therefore be made here.

74   THE INFANCY OF SPEECH

The early noises uttered by babies call to mind such *written* patterns as old Egyptian, *nhmhm*, ' to roar,' *ndddd*, ' to stay,' *ngsgs*, ' to overflow,' *ršrš*, ' to enjoy oneself.'[1] The ancient custom to omit the vowels in the visual representation of language seems to reflect the tendency to attribute significance to the noises rather than to vocal sound.

These facts corroborate our above assumption that in primordial language states of comfort were expressed, not only by certain vocal patterns, but also by rhythmical clicks. All the members of a group originally emitted the above-mentioned sounds and noises spontaneously, i.e., without *intentionally* trying to copy those of their mates. They were passing through the mimic stage well known from babies and animals. ' In gregarious animals, when a stimulus acts upon the group, each individual suffers from the impact of its reacting fellows, as well as directly from the stimulus, so that its fellows' reactions become linked to the stimulus and in future the individual responds to its fellows' reactions, even if it is not directly affected by the stimulus. These reactions become symbolic of the stimulus that causes them. Such reactions are mainly movements and sounds: in a group they become gesticulations and cries.'[2]

It should be noted, in summing up, that the noises (clicks) described, which are assumed to be the most elementary dynamic patterns involved in the formation of primordial utterance, are fundamentally expressions of the infant's pre-genital sexuality. The sucking of the mother's breast is, seen from the biological angle, an activity necessary for the maintenance of life; seen from the psychological angle it is a most potent erotic dynamism, symbolic of love, affection and tenderness, in other words of the incorporation of a good object such as a good mother or her substitute. It is known to everyone as the kiss. That such erotic patterns of action played a major role in the genesis of language is corroborated by the fact that, for instance, the English words, *kiss* and *quoth*, were, in all probability, derived from the same base.[3]

It probably needed some time to make sense impressions other than voice an adequate stimulus for utterance. For not until the

---

[1] Lach, R. (1920). ' Die Musik der turk-tatarischen, finnisch-ugrischen und Kaukasusvölker.' *Mitteil. d. Anthropol. Ges.* Vienna, Vol. L, pp. 31 f. Note the onomatopœic character. See below, pp. 161 ff.

[2] Dent, J. Y. (1936). *Reactions of the Human Machine.* Gollancz, London, p. 70.

[3] Wyld. Universal Dictionary of the English Language.

THE HUMAN STOCK

second month does the baby's voice become conditioned to the mere appearance of a person, known or unknown.[1]

In the following pages we shall quote chapter and verse in an endeavour to substantiate the above points. (See particularly the etymologies on pp. 130 f., 161 ff.

---

[1] Bühler, Ch., Hetzer, H., and Tudor-Hart, B. (1927). *Soziologische und psychologische Studien über das erste Lebensjahr.* Fischer, Jena, p. 17.

CHAPTER IV

UNFLEDGED LANGUAGE

THE THREE RUNGS OF MEANING

WE HAVE been unable to avoid correlating primordial utterances with certain psychological states, usually referred to as 'meaning.' Before passing on to the exact determination of primordial utterances we must consider what the term 'meaning' denotes. To keep off the slippery ground on our way, we must beware of confusing the protean 'meanings of meaning.'[1] We propose to base our deliberation on the fundamental space-time relationship between objects or events. In so far as we focus our attention on one of these we say with regard to other events that the one in the focus of attention has a '*meaning*.' Thus the area enclosed by a given circle in Fig. 11 comprises all the objects or events that are somehow related to the event thought to form the centre of the circle. It is

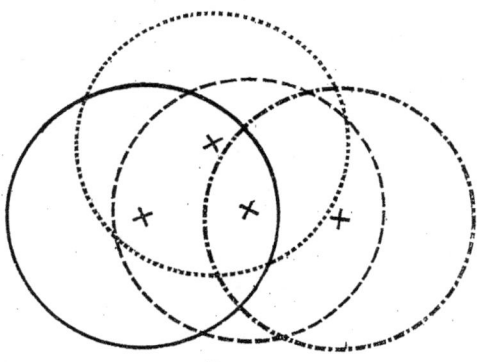

FIG. 11

obvious that the central event can itself be enclosed in several other circles (dotted lines, etc.) hinging on different centres. In relation to a given centre, the area of its circle shall be called the *field of reference*.

Thus the picture of a barometer in Fig. 12 refers to a multitude of events. The observer may pick out some of them, for instance,

---
[1] See Ogden, C. K. and Richards, I. A. (1923). *The Meaning of Meaning.* Kegan Paul, London.

Fig. 12

trains, ships, children, etc., and will readily comprehend what is said below.

The picture represents a certain stage in the contracting or expanding of a column of mercury which is said to be ' reacting ' to changes of air pressure. What the barometer shows or ' tells ' is correlated to other events indicated in the field of reference.

The same consideration applies to sense data other than visual, in particular to acoustic ones. For example, the ringing of a bell, the noise of thunder, the howling or barking of a dog, the singing of a bird, and the utterances of human beings ' mean ' something, in so far as such noises occur in a field containing other events.[1]

Thus, more or less complex bundles of sense data, commonly called objects or events, scientifically conceived as a total of reactions, have a meaning in so far as they refer to other perceptible objects or events.

The greater the power of perceiving objects in detail, of singling them out, and of correlating one occurrence to another, the *clearer* the meaning, i.e., the more differentiated the referential field.

We have so far described meaning as the *field of reference* in respect of the mere relatedness of one event to another, no matter whether that relationship is conceived as physical, mental or both, and without regard to ' truth ' or ' falsity.'

Having introduced the idea of reaction as a substitute for objects or events, we must now say a few words about the use of the term " reaction." Every occurrence in the world consists in a response of an object or being to an action or stimulus. Biologically it is inherent in the life process which consists in the continuous tendency to restore equilibrium more or less successfully after disturbances due to diverse stimuli. The psychological aspect of this process is the individual's affectivity or emotionality. We distinguish roughly two types of emotions : those of pleasure and those of displeasure, according as the individual strives towards or away from the stimulus.[2]

Such reactions constitute the ' *mode of reference*.' The greater the affectivity the more the referential mode overshadows the referential field.

Field and mode of reference are always co-existent, but their mutual relationship varies greatly according as affect or perception (cognition) prevails. It is this interrelation between field and mode

---

[1] Gardiner, l.c., p. 36, speaks of the ' area of meaning ' of a given word.
[2] Cf. Hobbes, *Leviathan*. I. 6.

of reference, i.e., emotional and cognitive meaning which we shall follow up in the growth of human utterance. It will be seen in the course of this inquiry that " meaning " is always a hierarchy,[1] that is to say, an utterance made at a given moment may convey to the actual or potential listener the notion of the fields and modes of reference which it has had during the speaker's life-time, and even in evolutionary time. Which particular field or mode of reference comes to the fore depends on the special circumstances associated with the development of utterance in individual life, tradition, and so forth.

It is convenient for the sake of exposition to throw into relief three rungs on the scale of referential development, and we now pass on to the discussion of the lowermost rung on to which Pithecanthropus may have climbed.

THE LOWERMOST RUNG OF MEANING

The kind of relatedness which existed between the primeval speaker and his surround [2] can best be viewed in the light of natural history as demonstrating the growth of the race, and that of babyhood as recapitulating evolution. This way of approach is advantageous as in both cases we have no immediate knowledge of the psychological counterpart of utterance. The mental aspect shall, nevertheless, be conjectured in so far as introspection and observation warrant inferences as to the psychological counterpart.

Let us recall that, viewed from the angle of behaviourism, the vocal attacks fall into two groups. One, comprising the hard attack, fundamentally contains in its referential field such events as threaten the individual from *without*. The referential mode is characterized by an action which upholds the individual's safety in the face of dangerous circumstances. The psychological correlate is fear in all its shades and degrees. The other, embracing the aspirated and soft attacks, is embedded in the field of such metabolic processes as occur while the equilibrium of the individual as a whole is being maintained. When life is threatened they bring safety from *within*. The mode of reference can therefore be described here as one of physio-psychological well-being, comfort, or pleasure. The vocal attacks are manifestations of the ' pleasure-pain ' principle (Freud).

---

[1] Blanshard, l.c., p. 216.
[2] Term coined by Sherrington for the Macrocosmus, i.e., the universe in so far as it is mirrored in man.

Voice itself too was a biological random event coupled with laryngeal activities safeguarding Pithecanthropus' ever-changing states of relative balance.

Interpolation under the guidance of what was said on p. 65, about the influence of stress, intonation and tonicity upon vowel sound, and of the development of vocal sound in babyhood, suggests increasing but unstable variety of vowels in conformity with the differentiation and variability of emotional response.

The vowels may have been nasalized at times. This assumption is warranted by the fact that infantile vowels during the first two months [1] are often nasal, that mild encephalitis sometimes leaves no other traces than nasal speech, and that many now living primitive tribes display a tendency towards nasal speech and song.

Consonants in the modern sense of the term, i.e., noises produced by expulsion of air, were probably non-existent. But as intermediates between nasal vowels and consonants, varieties of nasal sounds such as m, n, ḿ, ń,[2] were perhaps produced. The child, ' giving itself to a sort of tasting,' utters them as early as the first four weeks.[3]

Pithecanthropus and his nearest relative, Sinanthropus, probably uttered a variety of clicks which through their very nature and origin referred, as they still do, to events which contribute to and enhance the vitality of the individual. They are both physically and psychologically antagonistic to the attacks in that they invite such events as further the security of the individual from *without*. Thus they may be regarded as expressive of the sense of care and love, social feelings which may have reached a fairly high degree of development in Sinanthropus.[4] (See pp. 83 ff.)

The performance of these two behavioural functions, if we may guess from the first few months of babyhood during which the two activities remain detached, may have been the sole modes of utterance for the first three hundred thousands of years of man's existence on earth. The clicks readily lend themselves to symbolization. Valentine, for instance, reports sucking noises at the age of one year when a drink is wanted [5] and ' kissing noises ' as

---

[1] Garbini, A. (1892). *Evoluzione della voce nell' infanzia*. Verona, p. 53. Quot. by Chamberlain, The Child, p. 91.
[2] ' Signifies palatalization, i.e., the raising of the front part of the tongue towards the palate while a consonant is being articulated.
[3] Allaire, Dr. (1884). ' Des premiers rudiments du langage infantin.' *Bull. Soc. d'Anthr. de Paris*, p. 485. Quot. by Chamberlain, The Child, p. 96.
[4] Cf. Schmidt's chart, l.c., p. 228.
[5] Valentine, l.c., p. 401.

expressive of 'request.'[1] At the age of one year and four months the sucking noise became a label for water.[2]

The above reference to 'kissing' noises invites digression into the etymologies of the English words *kiss* and *buss*. They are probably cognate and can both be traced back to an Indo-European base which is still surviving in the word *quoth*.[3] That the same sound sequence has given rise to terms denoting 'speaking' as well as 'kissing' betrays the wisdom of our ancestral name-givers. The modern phonetician brings out with telling effect the fundamental relationship between kissing, i.e., clicking, and speaking, when he defines the kiss as a 'labial velaric click,'[4] i.e., a click made by the lips and the soft palate.

It will be pointed out explicitly that the referential field 'existed' in Pithecanthropus' mind only as a scarcely differentiated whole. This included also the noises which he produced and which as soon as they had been emitted figured amidst other sense data.

The surround was experienced *in* the individual's reactions. Pithecanthropus' world consisted of objects and persons in so far as they made him voice and click. The latter being the activity of sucking was thus the absorption of that which elicited it, and helped to keep the individual in touch (contact) with others.[5] Thus the above-described utterances of Pithecanthropus expressed the mode rather than the field of reference.

This seems to be borne out by the baby in his first month, for whom, Charlotte Bühler [6] surmises, no " somebody " exists as yet.

The clicking noise as an accompaniment of the act of incorporation, can easily be discovered in the more or less loud kiss, where it patently indicates modes rather than field of reference.

Psycho-analytical interpretation of the behaviour of primitive tribes reveals the psychological significance of sucking. In Central Australia, for instance, ' no woman who has milk or even merely a breast to play with will refuse a child, and thus not only is frustration unknown but the child starts life in a happy state of communal

---

[1] Valentine, l.c., p. 213.
[2] *Ibid.*, p. 413.
[3] See Wyld, *Universal English Dictionary*.
[4] Beach, D. M. (1938). *The Phonetics of the Hottentot Language*. Heffer, Cambridge.
[5] See Bühler, Ch., l.c., p. 36. Révész, l.c., p. 165, has from other premises arrived at similar conclusions. He is inclined to think that the need for contact (Kontakt-bedürfnis) engendered speech.
[6] Bühler, Ch., l.c., p. 17.

motherhood. He can always get the nipple when he wants it and he is never weaned until he weans himself.'[1]

From this we may infer that in ancient epochs the somato-psychic union was upheld a comparatively long time and should thus have promoted and facilitated the transmission of the sucking, i.e., clicking attitude. The very gradual transition from milk to other food strengthened—as it still does—the libidinous influence of the oral zone and gave rise to variegated symbolisms within a strong bond of tribal solidarity. Ambroise Paré [2] may here be cited as one who recognized the significance of the alimentary canal for all human development when he quoted Persius as saying : ' *Magister artis ingenique largitor venter, negatas artifex sequi voces.*' (' The stomach, i.e., hunger, is the maker of art and the dispenser of genius, skilful to supply an eloquence which nature had denied.')

The assumption that the mode of reference rather than the field of reference were the sum and substance of Pithecanthropus' walks of life allows of the further conjecture that vocal sound of everchanging variety played a prominent part in expression, whilst articulatory movements had not yet acquired the power of signifying objects and ideas. The later stages in the development of language reveal that articulatory noises lend themselves particularly well to this task. This could only be facilitated by a further refinement of the selective activity of ' listening,' i.e., singling out specific sounds from the multisonous orchestra which surrounded Pithecanthropus. This capacity must have developed much later. In the baby the faculty of listening becomes noticeable only during the second or third month, and reaches its maturity much later.[3] From the evolutionary point of view it seems significant that the baby responds to natural sounds and noises earlier than it does to the human voice.[4]

Although we are only on nodding terms with the conformation of Pithecanthropus' brain we can well believe that he was capable of impulsive gestures, some of them productive of sounds and noises correlated to the fundamental emotions of love, hunger and fear. Such reactions are mainly controlled by subcortical layers which in view of the relatively small brain must be assumed to have been dominant. But according to Elliot Smith ' a brain must reach a

---

[1] Róheim, l.c., p. 75.
[2] Quot. by Chamberlain, *The Child*, p. 96.
[3] See the tabulated survey in Hetzer, H., and Tudor-Hart, Beatrix. ' Die frühesten Reaktionen auf die menschliche Stimme.' In Bühler, Ch., l.c., p. 112.
[4] Hetzer and Tudor-Hart. *Ibid.*, p. 112–3.

weight of 950 grammes (about 1,000 c.c. in volume) before it can serve the ordinary needs of a human existence—before it can become the seat of even a low form of human intelligence. . . . In this respect Pithecanthropus . . . falls below the human limit.'[1]

Considering all the characteristics enumerated above we can picture Pithecanthropus as a being in whom ' the inner life of the soul and external environment formed, biologically, an undivided whole, wherein the individual was one with his surroundings.'[2] The division into individual and surround, into subject and object was not yet, or only to a very small extent, achieved.

That mental wholeness was manifest in the gestures and utterances we have elucidated. Gesture-utterance of the Pithecanthropus age thus ' meant,' i.e., referred to, a compact union of the individual with his surround; its mode of reference can be said to have been proto-emotional.

The field of reference was homogeneous, very little differentiated, inasmuch as detailed perceptions were rather scanty. The continuity between the speakers and their surround was upheld in so far as space was bridged by the sounding air common to all speakers.

It may be felt that in assigning to Pithecanthropus a more or less clear-cut type of language we have abused the licence conceded to the story-teller. The same objection may be raised as to the linguistic behaviours we are going to attribute to the ensuing races. There would remain no alternative but to put the matter in highly abstract terms. The narrator shudders at this thought, since he, ' in emptying his sentences of all imagery, also empties them of all meaning.'[3] Proto-human creatures and their behaviour are here introduced as it were, as fabulous specimens in which the inquirer's ideas, and, most probably, the hierarchy of oral attitudes underlying his own speech are personified. Analysing these and correlating them with successive types of human ancestry the narrator does not introduce his forebears as actual representatives of peculiar types of language, but rather as illustrative of certain linguistic tendencies. The story shall serve as a framework to aid the arrangement of such types, and our understanding.

SINANTHROPUS

Only a fairly short period of comparative well-being was allotted to the Pithecanthropus race. Having been enjoying a warm and

---
[1] Elliott Smith, as quoted by Keith, l.c., pp. 603-4.
[2] Schmidt, l.c., p. 87.
[3] Jagger, J. H. (1940). *English in the Future.* Nelson & Sons, London, p. 37.

fruitful world for several millennia, they were stricken by the first (Günz) glaciation in the late Pliocene age. Only few of them may have endured the years of extreme cold.

The offspring of those who could adapt themselves reached the First Interglacial period and again enjoyed a more genial climate for about 75,000 years.[1] The First Interglacial Period ended approximately 480,000 B.C. In geological layers dating back to that time the remains of a human type, *Sinanthropus* or Pekin man, were found in a cave near Pei-Ping in China.

No considerable advance in spiritual life and its expression can be assigned to that period. Yet although ' a paradise under a tropical sun would not awaken new-born Man out of his dawn-state to a higher degree of evolution ' [2] it may have facilitated the stabilization and transmission of such abilities as Pithecanthropus had acquired.

Among them the power of ' articulating,' i.e., of sound and noise making was handed down to the offspring but the utterances so produced were not or were hardly ' articulate ' as they did not consist of stable parts each of which was meaningful in its own right. There was transmission of loud mouth-gestures, but no tradition. In other words, language was a kaleidoscopic set of sound patterns which formed one genetically fixed whole with certain preponderantly emotional attitudes. The ability to produce these linguistic patterns was not, however, due to miming the models of the older generation, nor was there any idea of aiming at such traditional conventions.

The high antiquity of such utterances explains the tenacity with which they are still used by modern man, children, adults, normal and mentally deficient alike.

With the oncoming of the subsequent period (about 475,000 B.C.) the conditions of life changed considerably as the earth was cooling down again. So much so that vast areas of Europe and North America were covered with ice, which had flown from the North at the rate of about a quarter of a mile per annum.[3]

In Europe, creatures such as the sabre-toothed tiger, the ancestor of the horse (*Equus stenonis*), two species of elephants, the mammoth, the hippopotamus, the woolly rhinoceros and several species of deer were still surviving from the Pliocene age and were competing

---

[1] Osborn, H. Fairfield (1916). *Man of the Old Stone Age*. As quoted by Keith, l.c., p. 303, footnote.
[2] Schmidt, R. R., l.c., p. 45.
[3] Childe, V. G. *What Happened in History*, p. 25.

UNFLEDGED LANGUAGE 85

with newer varieties which eventually replaced them.[1] In America, horses and camels were common. It is noteworthy that among the tools found in Sinanthropus' cave ' none can be regarded as a *specialized* [2] weapon of the chase. Indeed they are so shapeless that it is impossible to say exactly what they were used for.'[3]

Under such hard living conditions human beings could hardly multiply considerably. They were relatively rare creatures living probably in small isolated groups which had a difficult stand in the face of the then living animals, particularly as they did not understand how to build homes or defence works.

Sinanthropus, one of Pithecanthropus' near relatives, lived up to early Pleistocene times, perhaps because he was able to use fire, and perhaps to take shelter in caves, as did such coeval animals as the cave bear, cave lion and cave hyena.

The implements he may have used were just bones or clubs, stones he picked up and threw away immediately after use. Some archæologists claim, however, that even in times prior to the first Ice Age people may have used pieces of flint that appear to be intelligently chipped, but such ' tools ' probably served a variety of purposes, such as those of a knife, chopper, scraper, roasting utensil, battle-axe, splitting tool, and so on.[4]

As a creature which had learnt how to increase its own power by some, if very crude, implements, and how to protect itself by using and making fire, the Sinanthropus race can be said to have made a first timid attempt at crossing the boundary-line between beasts and manlike creatures inasmuch as purposive care for the maintenance of life was budding in them.[5]

In this respect Sinanthropus is intermediate in type between Pithecanthropus and the Piltdown Man,[6] who will presently enter the stage.

Miss Davison surmises that ' one of the greatest benefits fire conferred on man was the stimulus it gave to family and . . . social life, and the occupation of the caves still further encouraged this. Even language must have received a fresh impetus. The long dark nights and cold wintry days, when there was little to do but gather

[1] Childe, V. G. *What Happened in History*, pp. 25-6. Bailey, E. B. and Weir, I., l.c., p. 477. Sollas, l.c., p. 161.
[2] My italics.
[3] Childe, V. G. (1944). *Progress and Archæology*. Watts & Co., London, p. 13.
[4] Childe, V. G. (1941). *Man Makes Himself*. Watts & Co., London, p. 48. Schmidt, R. R., l.c., p. 96.
[5] See Schmidt, R. R., l.c., pp. 44, 89-90.
[6] Smith, G. Elliott (1931). *Early Man*. Benn, London, p. 14.

round the fire, encouraged conversation and the exchange of ideas.[1]

It has yet to be made clear, however, what sort of ' conversation ' they may have carried on, what ' ideas ' they may have possessed, and how, perhaps, they may have exchanged them. To this end we must first consider the setting. It seems safe to believe that with the camp fire ' the density of a primeval forest is no longer the only refuge of man ; with this new life-preserving weapon he extends his territory to the regions of the North.'[2] And so in the first Interglacial Period, some four to five hundred thousand years ago, many parts of Europe, Africa, and India were populated by diverse species of Man who had been able to withstand the hardships of the first glaciation.[3]

The world of the lower Pleistocene period was very different from what it is now. ' For instance, during part of the Pleistocene Britain was joined to the continent of Europe. Much of what is now the North Sea must have been dry land, and men could have followed the equivalent of the Thames till it joined an early Rhine. Though the chief mountain ranges had already been uplifted before the first " men " began to make tools, they lived to see quite important hills thrown up by the folding of the earth's crust. . . . Catastrophic changes in climate undoubtedly affected the whole earth ; three or four Ice Ages followed one another in high latitudes, and were accompanied by periods of torrential rain in now arid sub-tropical zones.[4] (See Chronological Survey, Table 13, page 87.)

Some 600,000 years ago the human stem divided into two main branches, the members of which apparently acquired slightly better adaptation to an ever changing surround. But they too underwent several variations which, with one exception, namely the ancestors of the now living races, were doomed to extinction.

PILTDOWN MAN

One representative of the surviving race was Piltdown Man or Eoanthropus (*eōs* ' dawn '), whose fossils were found in Piltdown (Sussex). (See Fig. 3.) He struggled along for another 100,000 years and possibly evolved some capacities perpetuated up to modern man.

His face was much more massive than that of modern man, his jaw more ape-like (Boule) and the muscles of mastication did not

---
[1] Davison, l.c., pp. 63-4.
[2] Schmidt, l.c., pp. 91-2.
[3] Davison, l.c., p. 49 f.
[4] Childe, *What Happened in History*, pp. 24 f.

work exactly as in modern man. As in the apes the sides of his otherwise human head sloped inwards. The palate was large, the ratio between it and the brain being about 1 : 30, whilst in modern British skulls the ratio is 1 : 59.6. (See Table 14.) The capacity of the brain was about 1200–1400 c.cm., which places it in the middle of the small-headed group.[1]

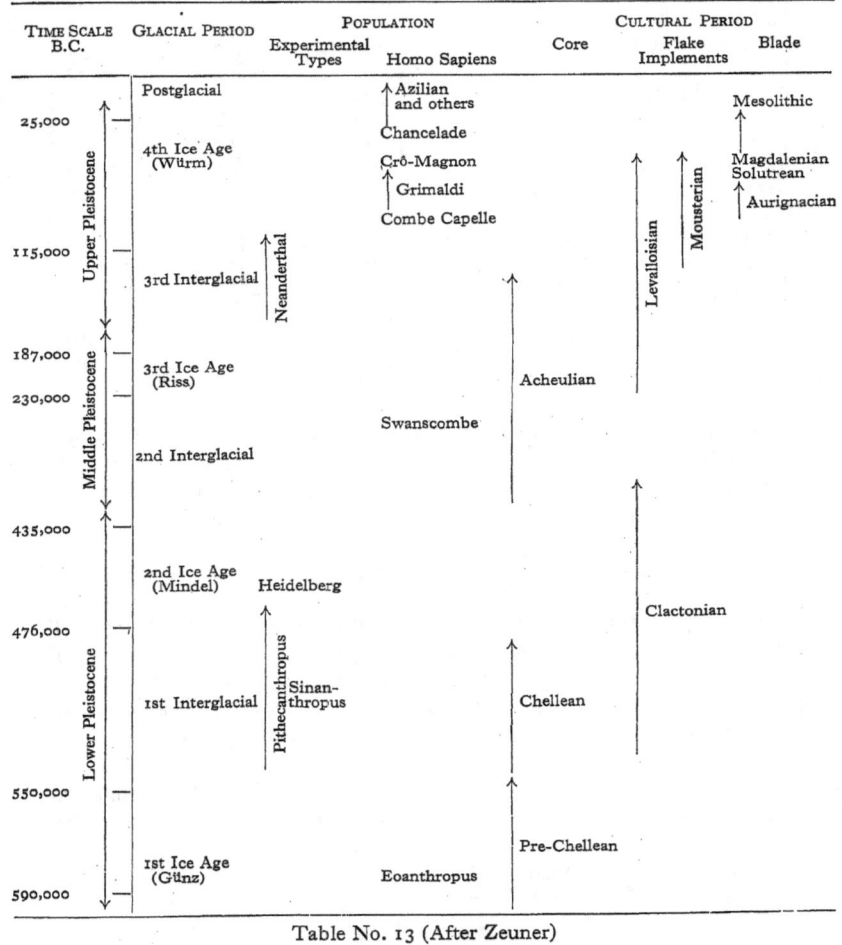

Table No. 13 (After Zeuner)

---

[1] Keith, l.c., pp. 527, 528–530, 532, 604.

	Palatal area in cm.²	Cranial capacity in cm.³	Ratio
Gorilla (male)	65·00	578	1 : 7·9
Chimpanzee (female)	36·50	320	8·7
Piltdown skull (Keith's reconstruction)	42·00	1400	33·3
Gibraltar skull	31·60	1200	38
La Chapelle skull	39·00	1620	41·5
Rhodesian skull	41·00	1300	31·7
Talgai skull	40·00	1300	32·3
Wadjak skull I	35·00	1550	44·3
,, ,, II	41·00	1650	40·2
Tasmanian skull	36·70	1350	36·7
[1]Australian aborigine skulls	31·60	1290	40·8
[1]Negro (West Coast) skulls	29·00	1350	44·4
[1]Chinese skulls	26·50	1470	55·6
[1]British skulls	25·00	1490	59·6
[1]Ancient Egyptian skulls	25·00	1380	55
[2]Skulls of natives of Punjab	28·60	1375	48
[2]Bushman skulls	24·70	1250	50
Child at birth (European)	6·50	300	46
Child at 3½ years (European)	9·00	1050	116

Table No. 14 (After Keith, l.c., p. 659)

The speech area in the third frontal convolution is well marked [3] while the convolutions of the central region [4] (sensation and movement) and of the frontal lobe [5] as a whole are not sharply indicated in the brain cast of Piltdown Man.

HEIDELBERG MAN

Remains of another, probably later variety (of Early Pleistocene time, approximately 450,000 [6]) of the hominid stem, Heidelberg Man, were found at Mauer, near Heidelberg, Tanbach, Ehringsdorf (Germany) and at Krapina (Jugoslavia). Here again, ' anatomists have been struck by the apparent discrepancy between the " humanity " of the teeth and the massive power—almost bestiality of the jaw itself ' [7] which shows no trace of a chin. A comparison shows that Heidelberg Man's jaw stands midway between the

---

[1] Mean measurement of ten skulls.
[2] Mean measurement of five skulls.
[3] Keith, l.c., p. 609.
[4] Keith, l.c., p. 620.
[5] Keith, l.c., p. 636.
[6] Zeuner, l.c.
[7] Keith, l.c., p. 327.

anthropoid apes and man, and is reminiscent of that of the Australian native. Those creatures lived in the preglacial forest together with the lion (*Felis leo fossilis*), a leopard, an extinct form of wild cat, a dog (*Canis neschersensis*), two forms of bear, the forerunners of the cave-bear, a boar, a species of bison, an early Pleistocene form of horse, the beaver, an early form of rhinoceros (*R. etruscus*) and an elephant (*E. antiquus*).[1]

It stands to reason that the people of this period, having to rely for a living on the vicissitudes of their hunting and fishing, and on the gathering of wild berries, roots, eggs, grubs, slugs and shell-fish, could not multiply to any considerable extent.[2]

Europe's 'few inhabitants had to struggle hard merely to hold their own'[3] during that period.

CHELLEAN CULTURE

Piltdown Man and his relative, Heidelberg Man (genus Palæonthropus [4]) can be said to have developed a 'culture' in that they 'conceived the need' for tools, and knew how to manufacture them.[5] It is doubtful whether Piltdown people actually chipped flint implements, but it is known for certain that they shaped elephants' thigh bones into tools perhaps of an all-round purpose.

Here we have for the first time a chance to cast a glance at man's achievements and so to draw some inferences as to his psychosomatic character. Since 'the works of man's hands are his embodied thought,'[6] they may well cast light on his speech. We shall try to put to good use the analysis of such achievements in all subsequent cultural periods, and to arrive at some conclusions as to the types of speech peculiar to those epochs.

Remains of a stone-culture known as Chellean [7] have been excavated from early Pleistocene layers in Chelles (France)[8] (500,000–400,000 B.C.).[9] Here various tools in the form of scrapers, piercing instruments, and knives with coarse, broad retouches with

---

[1] Keith, l.c., pp. 320-324.—Sollas, l.c., p. 174.
[2] Childe, G. *Man Makes Himself*, p. 35.
[3] Keith, l.c., p. 251.
[4] Baily and Weir, l.c., p. 350.
[5] Keith, l.c., p. 605.
[6] Sollas, l.c., p. 63.
[7] For convenience the obsolete term Chellean is here retained, although the writer is well aware of its ambiguity and of the controversy now raging. See Van Riet Lowe, C. (1946). Some Observations on the 'Tumbian' Culture. *Man*, XLVI, 3. Chellean culture is now usually referred to as Abbevillian.
[8] Fallaize, E. N. (1928). *The Origins of Civilization*. Benn, London, p. 27.
[9] Tilney, F. (1930). *The Master of Destiny*. Heinemann, London, p. 66.

marked concavities, made of flint were found.[1] They were 'not hafted but held in the hand and were designed to increase the efficiency of the hand or fist'[2] (French coup-de-poing, English hand-axe, 'boucher' [Sollas], hand-stone [Osborn], fist-flint [Brown]). (See Fig. 15.) Chellean industry was also discovered in Portugal, Spain, Africa near Thever, Luxor and Assiut)[3], Rhodesia, in the Cape region, in Arabia, Palestine, the Tigris and Euphrates valleys, India, in the Malay Archipelago, and in North America.[4]

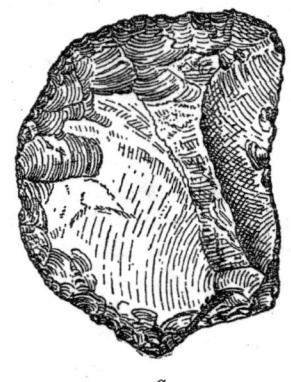
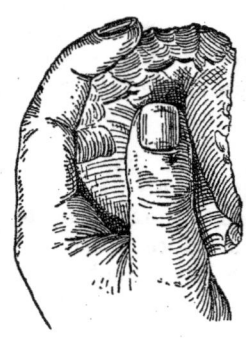

a   *b*
FIG. 15
a, Chellean scraper.   b, the same, showing how it was held in the hand. (After Comment. From Sollas)

With the use of the flint mankind entered the first stage of its cultural history : the Stone Age.

For the sake of clarity we append a tabulated survey of the respective divisions and subdivisions after Burkitt.[5] (Table No. 16)

The enormous advance which the use of tools represents is obvious from the facility with which even the simplest and crudest tool helps to master the surround. It is the first prehistoric evidence we have of the awakening of intelligence in so far as it is manifest in the utilization of substitutes.[6] True, when apes, for

---

[1] Sollas, l.c., pp. 165, 513, footnote.
[2] Brown, G. Baldwin (1928). *The Art of the Cave Dweller*. Murray, London, p. 38.
[3] De Pradenne, l.c., p. 143.
[4] De Pradenne, l.c., p. 230. Sollas, l.c., pp. 165 ff.
[5] Burkitt, M. C. (1933). *The Old Stone Age*. Univ. Press, Cambridge, p. 25. The table is to be read from bottom to top.
[6] MacCurdy, l.c., p. 64.

UNFLEDGED LANGUAGE 91

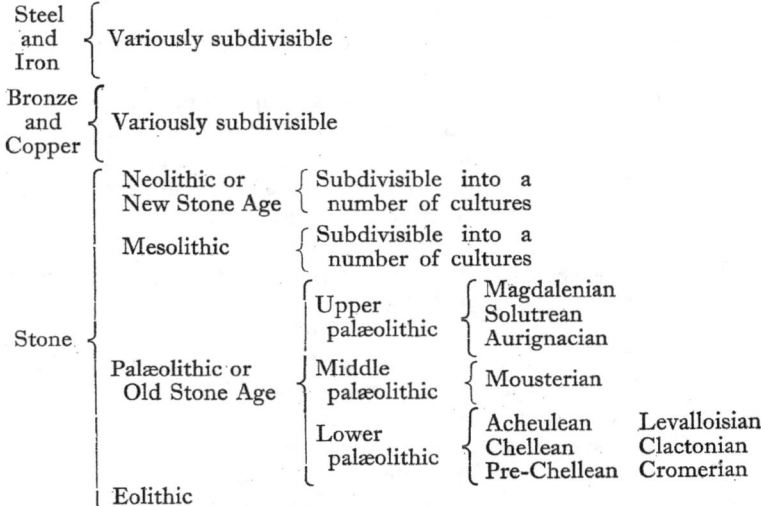

Table No. 16 (After Burkitt)

instance, pick up a stick in order to reach a banana outside the cage they show this ability in the bud; but in the Early Stone Age we encounter a manufactured, literally ' *hand-made* ' substitute. All progress during the Lower Palæolithic period pivots round the elaboration of tools of the *coup de poing* type.[1] The use of tools is prophetic of many achievements of *homo sapiens*, as the '. . . analysis of *qualities* in the most advanced human sense is, perhaps, having its rudimentary beginning with the utilization of substitutes.' [2]

The awakening of ideas about life and its continuance after death is indicated by the fact that Chellean people buried their dead.[3]

CHELLEAN LANGUAGE

What may the speech of these early people have been like? It will be profitable to scrutinize first some of the views held by eminent historians and archæologists. H. G. Wells [4] does not think that Heidelberg Man could have had articulate speech, because his " quasi-human jaw-bone " was " a clumsy jaw-bone,

[1] Burkitt, l.c., p. 56.
[2] MacCurdy, l.c., p. 63.
[3] Keith, l.c., p. 258.
[4] Wells, l.c., p. 30.

absolutely chinless, far heavier than a true human jaw-bone and narrower, so that it is improbable that the creature's tongue could have moved about."

Fallaize also opines that ' Certain ape-like appearances on the inside of the jaw, connected with the muscular structure of the tongue make it improbable that this being . . .' (viz., Heidelberg Man) ' could use his tongue for the purpose of talking, even though it was probable that Pithecanthropus had some powers of rudimentary speech.'[1]

Dorothy Davison on the other side surmises that although apish, the jaw of the Heidelberg Man allowed its owner to speak.[2]

Sir Arthur Keith lays weight on the fact that ' In the Heidelberg mandible, and to some degree in that from Spy, the lower part of the symphysis encroaches, as in the ape . . . on the floor of the mouth. Yet, in spite of this ape-like feature we must grant the possibility of speech to the Heidelberg Man.[3]

Keith Henderson also attributes ' some kind of coherent speech ' to all hominid types we have so far encountered.[4] He believes that Piltdown Man was capable of some rude kind of articulate speech so far as the rather simple brain convolutions in his fairly well developed forehead warranted it.

Some comment must be made, however, on the above statements before we can conjecture anything as to the speech of those still ' experimental ' types of man.

First of all it is well known that a rather primitive conformation of the jaw, the palate and the tongue does not prevent utterance. Parrots furnish an instinctive example of the ability to ' talk ' in the sense of emitting some, albeit harsh and meaningless sound sequences. Every such utterance is articulated, i.e., produced by certain more or less co-ordinated movements of the speech organs.

Articulation may, of course, be hampered to some extent (seen from the angle of ' modern ' language) by the malformation of the speech apparatus. It may render the formation of certain sounds impossible. The pathology of speech furnishes us with evidence which, however, corroborates what was said on p. 85, namely, that malformations of the oral cavity by no means prevent coherent, meaningful speech of some sort.

---

[1] Fallaize, l.c., p. 25.
[2] Davison, D., l.c., p. 52.
[3] Keith, l.c., p. 331.
[4] Henderson, l.c., p. 36.

Last, but not least, we must bear in mind that a morphologically intermediate skull does not warrant the assumption that its bearer had a mentally intermediate character,[1] though this may not be improbable.

We shall therefore proceed with the utmost possible caution in our interpolation. From all we know about their world we may with some confidence infer that the gregarious instinct of Chellean people was, in view of the dangers which surrounded them, further developed than in their forebears. Considering the behaviour of apes at one end of the scale, and that of subsequent human types at the other, we may, by interpolation, infer that Chellean people had a strong emotional linkage, and a budding idea of mutual aid. This may at times have been manifest in hunting calls, cries of warning, clamours of indignation (Keith Henderson), ejaculations of love, tenderness, panic, and so forth, all of which accompanied the gestures peculiar to, or symbolic of, a given situation.

Perhaps it dawned on them that the great forests, the vast masses of vegetation, were fundamentally and utterly inimical to them, that they were aliens in the midst of an innumerable throng of hostile beings. Our own behaviour, and that of every young living being, tells us ' that the world is bottomlessly strange; alien even when it is kind and beautiful; having innumerable modes of being that are not our modes; always mysteriously not personal, not conscious, not moral; often hostile and sinister; sometimes even unimaginably, because inhumanly, evil.' [2]

It may have been this feeling of being different, of being an intruder, a weakling, which gave rise to an increase in the stoppage of impulses, which brings about the integration of function correlated with planning thought.

So far we have not been able to infer more than that early man's utterances [3] were not much different from the cries and screams and from the sucking noises in animals and babies. They formed patterns independent and isolated from one another within the whole set of behavioural reactions.

So far as the evidence from children with retarded maturation goes we may with some justification assert that the two types of

---

[1] De Pradenne, l.c., pp. 23-4.
[2] Huxley, Aldous, l.c., pp. 91-94.
[3] Throughout this book the term ' utterance ' refers to the mere emission of sound, as distinct from expression which indicates more or less intentional and purposive utterance. See the definition on p. 48, note 1.

noises were for many thousands of years merely coexisting and not interconnected.

The two primeval types of non-integrated, chiefly vegetative and slightly symbolized language is represented, on the one hand, by a speech disorder, rightly or wrongly termed *Hottentotism*. In this disorder the observer cannot fail to recognize the intonation pattern of a sentence which the patient has imitated. The vowels are more or less correct, but the almost complete absence of consonants is equally striking.

In normal infants we can, on the other hand, find the prevalence of jaw-breaking aggregates of consonants such as *mk-mk* for ' smacked,' [1] even when at the age of 1,6 imitation is well under way.

We shall now make the assumption that the eoanthropic race made some progress in speech in a way analogous to that manifested in the utilization of tools, i.e., substitutes. The advance must thus have been in the direction of an increased range of things that were to be mastered.

At this juncture we have to recall a peculiarity so common and firmly engrained in all existing primitive races that it seems fair to presume that Chellean people possessed it in even greater measure.

Modern man has arrived at perceptions and their reproduction in the mind (images) through disregarding the impulses, desires, inclinations and actions in which the notion is embedded.

In the primitive mind the mental pictures of things are not yet dissociated from the other mental processes (emotions) but form one *integral* whole with them.

Such mental pictures (images) have been termed by Lévy-Brühl ' collective representations.' [2]

The primitive usually acquires such mental pictures—as is only natural—in situations of a highly emotional character.

His mental patterns therefore are and remain wholes in which peculiar feelings (fear, hope, love, desire, expectation and so on) and attitudes (aggression, flight) bear more weight than the cognitive element. They are not only pre-logical, but even pre-magical. (See below, p. 161.)

To resume the argument, primitive man succeeded in extending the range of things to be mastered, by the intermediary of a tool. In other words it was his hand that had to be made more capable

---

[1] Valentine, l.c., p. 423.
[2] Lévy-Brühl, L. *Les fonctions mentales dans les sociétés inférieures.* Germ. transl. by W. Jerusalem (1921). *Das Denken der Naturvölker.* Braumüller, Vienna. Chapter I.

of working, and handling objects. Indeed, R. R. Schmidt has reasons to surmise that the earliest flint implements may have been manufactured " in the image of the hand." [1] (See Fig. 17.)

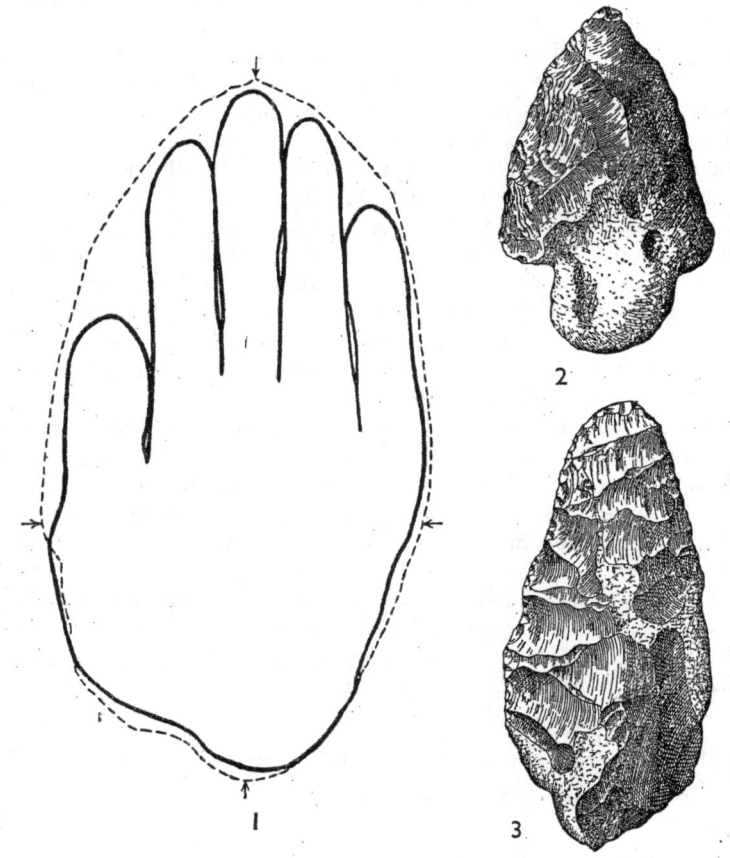

FIG. 17
Early Palæolithic Implements, formed in the image of the hand
1. Outline of the hand superposed on the contour of a flint implement from St. Acheul.
2. Chellean implement.
3. Acheulian implement.
(After R. R. Schmidt)

If the ' intake ' of the main objects of primitive man's desires was to be helped by an intermediary analogous to the hand, surely

---
[1] Schmidt, R. R., l.c.

the utilization of the sucking noises as preliminary reactions to that end must have presented itself to the mind. That those noises were coeval with other means of ' taking in ' is corroborated by the fact that sucking and grasping automatisms reappear in pathological cases with increasing clouding of consciousness, thus unveiling the ascent and dominance of formerly powerful tendencies which in modern adult man are overridden and bridled by higher levels of consciousness. This is paralleled by Stern's and Dix' observations that even in the latter part of the first quarter of the first year the mouth still participates in grasping movements of the hands.[1]

Furthermore, J. LeRoy Conel has demonstrated that during the first month of life those cortical layers concerned with the movement of the hands and the co-ordinated movements of the eyes necessary for vision show definite advance in maturation. Broca's area shows little advance, but the receptive area of the parietal lobe and of the occipital lobe are better developed.[2]

Babies from the fourth or fifth months of life take heed of visual impressions more than of audible ones.[3]

Thus—we may infer—in hoary evolutionary ages and certainly in Chellean times things seen for a time outweighed things heard. This attitude towards vision led to a more fruitful appreciation of the surround. In conjunction with the well-developed grasping and holding movements it helped in the manufacture of, albeit crude, tools.

Simultaneously the firm and ancient union of grasping and clicking encouraged the employment of these noises as tools. In this manner the referential field (see p. 76), embracing noises and ' handling,' began to differentiate. (See p. 104.)

---

[1] Stern, W., l.c., p. 72.
[2] LeRoy Conel, J. (1941). *The Postnatal Development of the Human Cortex.* Oxford University Press.
[3] Hetzer and Tudor Hart, l.c., p. 115.

CHAPTER V

NEW-FLEDGED LANGUAGE

AMALGAMATION OF SUCKING AND VOICING

FOR SOME time noises accompanying sucking and vocal sounds may have continued to exist side by side. As each of these functions is performed at a different anatomical level (mouth and larynx) there exists the a priori possibility of their simultaneous occurrence.

With the changing conditions of life these two biologically diverse and physically antagonistic activities merged into each other. Looking at this process of amalgamation in retrospect one cannot help styling it a happy marriage of sucking and voicing. It is the first step towards the integration of speech through 'emergent evolution.' Two hitherto independent integers are beginning to merge into one another in such a way as to display new features unknown in the constituents. The naive adult is prone to regard the units which he isolates, such as vowels, consonants, syllables, etc., as elementary. It is only with the help of the evolutionist that he can recognize these apparently ' simple ' units as more complex than other bigger wholes embedded in more ancient evolutionary layers.

We can follow up the unfurling of these patterns in the speech of both children and the still extant primitive races.

THE STAGES OF BABBLING

Let us imagine, for instance, that the first phase of the sucking activity, viz., the lip movement is given prominence and that this hallucination of taking or seeking the nipple is occurring while voice as an expression of well-being is being emitted. Fig. 18 demonstrates the process of amalgamation in a kind of musical notation.

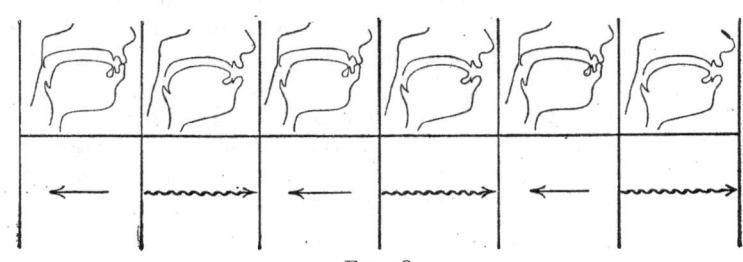

FIG. 18
(After Stein)

98   THE INFANCY OF SPEECH

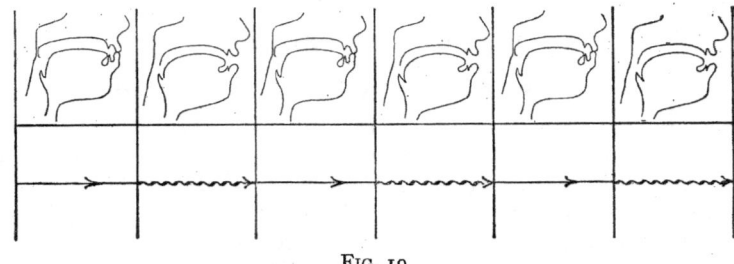

FIG. 19
(After Stein)

It appears that the continuous stream of voice becomes intersected by rhythmical clicks. The new whole so arising gives the impression of a sequence of syllables each consisting of the same sound and noise elements.[1]

It goes without saying that any vowel shade and any click can partake in this uniting process. So far as the activities of babies go, several phases of the sucking process may intersect the voice stream and so bestow more variety on the result, whilst the vowels show more or less uniformity.

The analytic mind of the adult listener who has learned to write and read, usually conceives sequences of the type [d∧d∧d∧] as combinations of the sound units [d] and [∧]. At best, they are regarded as juxtapositions of the ' syllable ']d∧]. To describe them as ' reiterated syllables ' as is often done, would lead us, however, into a trap laid by the very terms used.

The foregoing observations demonstrate clearly that neither single sounds nor isolated single syllables can be assumed to have been the original speech units. Rather does it appear that what is now termed a sequence of reiterated syllables is, genetically, the result of emergent evolution in as much as two diverse integers, namely a stream of voice (sighs, groans, etc.) and rhythmical clicks, have been welded together into one indivisible dynamic whole of considerable size.

We will reserve the term ' reiteration ' for the process involved in the above examples to distinguish it from reduplication,[2] a process derived from what is here called ' reiteration.' (See below, p. 125.) The term ' juxtaposition ' shall denote the more or less

---
[1] Stein, L. (1942). *Speech and Voice*, pp. 31 f.
[2] Graff, l.c., p. 81, uses the term ' reduplication ' for ' the process by which a sound combination is used twice or several times in juxtaposition within the same word.'

deliberate repetition of an already well established sound-unit or single syllable.

The linguistic feature brought about by the unification of voicing and sucking as displayed by the baby is termed ' *babbling*.' Through the integration of two physically different and antagonistic, but bio-psychologically kindred, impulses primitive man had unwittingly solved the problem of passing from *interjectional* utterances to articulated language, in so far as the term ' articulation ' here refers to the act of putting together, or to the junction between two parts.[1] We shall see on several occasions, how this accomplishment leads to increasingly high degrees of *articulateness*.[2]

Containing elements that are highly pleasurable, babbling is sometimes retained as late as the age of two or three years. Even when he understands and is able to say quite a number of adult words, the child still likes to insert babbles such as French *dodo* for *dormir* ' to sleep,' English *din-din* for ' dinner ' (M. M. Lewis). Valentine records *ba-ba-ba* for ' bath,' *par-k par-k par-k* for ' park ' at the age of 1 ; 4, *book book book* for ' book ' at the age of 1 ; 5, *go-go* ' Gordon,' *Ki-ki* ' dirty ' 1 ; 8, ' *at wawa choo-choo* ' for ' I (want to put the) dog (to) bed ' at the age of 2, and " repeated babbling " of " nonsense syllables " as late as 2 ; 3.[3]

In the company of other babblers of the same linguistic stage the child readily throws overboard the conventional language which he has so far mastered and employs his natural language instead. And the children claim to understand each other perfectly ! We may well believe them since they obviously employ an international language as opposed to the national language spoken by their elders.

Another peculiarity of primitive speech owes its origin to the primordial sequence of sucking movements.

It is well known that infants can and do produce innumerable ' jaw and tongue breaking,' ' unspeakable ' sequences of consonants, defying every attempt of phonetic notation,[4] particularly during the second quarter of the first year.[5]

The ornamental epithets used above are to denote our conviction that they are hard to pronounce. And why do we say so ? Because,

[1] See Wyld's *Universal Dictionary*.
[2] See below, pp. 171ff.
[3] Valentine, l.c., p. 418.
[4] We are here using the term ' consonant ' for *all* classes of noises, in contrast to *vocalic elements*.
[5] See Valentine, l.c., p. 395.—Lewis, M. M. (1936). *Infant Speech*. Kegan Paul, London, p. 239 ff.

having 'consummated the marriage,' we are essentially different from the babbler, and do no longer produce consonants qua successive noises involved in and arising from the act of sucking, such as [ptk], [pts], etc. (See above, Fig. 19.) In accordance with the Biogenetic Law we may assume that the process of amalgamation just described, which appears genetically fixed in every baby, recapitulates occurrences of by-gone ages.

Thus we can assume the language of the Chellean races to have consisted of long, more or less stable sequences of shades of vowel and clusters of clicks, such as, to mention comparatively simple ones overheard in small children's talk: [ꭰeꭲeꭹꭺꭰꭰꭲeꭹv . . .], [ꭲꭰꭲuꭹ ꭲꭰꭲuꭹ . . .], [ꭰꭲꭲoqꭰꭲ ꭰꭲꭲoqꭰꭲ].

Evidence from such primitive languages as North American Indian languages suggests even longer and more varied sequences. In our days the parts of such sequences possess a definite grammatical, syntactical, or lexicographical significance. We shall conjecture below how these small units may have attained their meaning. (See pp. 155ff.)

A relic from the time when only the insertion of noises into the stream of voice as a whole, and not the position of each in a given expression was significant, seems to be persisting in the Balta language of Sumatra. It is the comparative freedom from significance of the position of consonants in the vocalic stream, which is manifest in the synonymous *lab-a* and *bal-a*, *der-em* and *red-em*, *lap-is* and *alp-is* ; *talgang* and *tangal*. Similar examples occur in other languages, such as that spoken in Samoa.[1]

The salient features may have been—so far as we can guess from primitive languages—rhythmical recurrences of certain units ; great length of the ' beads ' ; specific intonation and the use of the vocal attacks expressive of the emotional background ; enormous variability.

Paul [2] assumed that the number of primordial sounds was a comparatively small one. Steinthal opposed this view and pointed out that in primordial man every clear-cut and individual perception was reflected in a particular sound. Every observer of infant speech will be inclined to agree with Steinthal, when he recalls the vast number of sound variations the infant produces during one day. Gesell has recorded as many as 75 diverse sound patterns in one day, a figure which is likely to be an understatement.[3]

[1] Meyer-Rinteln, W. (1905). *Die Schöpfung der Sprache*, p. 245.
[2] Paul, H. *Prinzipien der Sprachgeschichte*. As quoted by Marty, l.c., p. 202.
[3] Gesell, A. (1925). *The Mental Growth of the Pre-School Child*. MacMillan, New York.

Thus primeval utterances were probably most multiform and 'irregular' in conformity with the ever-changing conditions of life. Jespersen arrived at the same conclusion from other premises.[1] 'Entirely free sound combinations' formed the accompaniment of early man's activities. The organization and more elaborate symbolization of these utterances was reserved till a much later stage of evolution. To Graff 'it does not even seem essential that when man first began to speak, he should have grouped his manifold non-linguistic experiences in the structural and categorical moulding of his speech material. Entirely free sound combinations may have served for the symbolization of all he wanted to say. It seems rather more probable that the instinctive process of organization began only after the making of language had set in and after the free material had become too cumbersome to manage.'[2]

We become awake to the primeval character of language if we consider the multifariousness of some still primitive offshoots. Graff[3] emphasizes the poor vocalism, but extremely rich and varied consonantism of some North-East Caucasian languages. (The European is astonished by the thirty declensional cases of the noun in Awar, and by the six nominal genders in Chechen. In this language almost every noun and many of its verbs are "irregular.")

The languages of China (except Corean), Japan, Central and South Africa (except Swahili), Burma and some Indian languages have conventionalized the vocal attacks. In these languages 'the meaning of a speech sound depends not only on the articulation, but also on the type of laryngeal sound by which the articulation is energized.' (See Attacks, pp. 61ff.)

This primitive state is, to some extent, reflected in the diversity of language among native tribes. 'The aboriginal Australians, estimated as some 200,000 in all, spoke no less than five hundred languages.' In the 150,000 square miles of California Kroeber distinguishes thirty-one families of languages and at least 135 dialects.[4]

The multiformity of the still existing primitive languages is, of course, also due to isolation and to several other factors of a higher psychological order (magic, tabooism and the like) to which we shall refer at a later juncture. (See pp. 141ff.)

In fact the supporters of magical beliefs not only allowed the

---
[1] Jespersen, O. (1922). *Language*, pp. 412 ff.
[2] Graff, l.c., p. 200.
[3] Graff, l.c., p. 413.
[4] Childe, V. G. *What Happened in History*, p. 19.

unsettled sound table to subsist, but used its infinite variations to express the most delicate shades of meaning.

THE MEANING OF BABBLING

We have noted that the original sequence of 'syllables' arose when the outflowing stream of voice was being interspersed by noises due to the antagonistic process of rarefaction of air in the mouth. This intersection of the breath stream seems to be well engrained. So much so that certain aphasiacs who cannot enunciate a word or phrase referring to a given notion are still able to make as many efforts of expiration as there are syllables in the utterance concerned.

In the light of our previous remarks (see pp. 79ff) on the biological import of voicing and sucking, and the inferences as to their psychological counterpart, we can now formulate the significance of the event just described. Two entirely diverse phonetic functions have been united by reason of one salient quality which they have in common. Both voice and clicks accompany processes *safeguarding* the individual's balance. The former occurs in response to stimuli arising *within* the organism, the latter in response to stimuli coming from *without*. Being derived from sucking the mother's breast clicking implies more than the mere intake of food. For if we look at it as a bio-psychological whole it can be regarded as the fundamental link in the chain formed by mother and child, the archetype of a 'group.' And therein lies the germ of its future erotic and social significance. Casting our minds back to the referential levels hitherto encountered, we recall that the two audible accompaniments of primitive speech behaviour referred to the maintenance of the individual's balance and to its restoration when being endangered from either *without* or *within*. The mingling of these two tendencies is to be considered from the angle of the baby and from that of early man.

The fact that for some months voicing and clicking remain independent from one another in the babe, seems to signify that the problem of reconciling the need for emancipation and autonomy so recently expressed by the act of birth, with the persistent desire to remain united with the mother is as yet unresolved. This floating between two antagonistic tendencies may well reflect what was happening in primeval man. On the assumption that outward expression runs parallel with mental processes we can now pass on to the interpretation of those inner events. The terms ' from within ' and ' from without ' used above refer to the *direction* of the speech functions under investigation. Those terms pertaining to the technical language of physics and physiology, or behaviour, must now be translated into terms contained in the vocabulary of the psychologist.

Love (Greek *erōs*) is the idea which crops up when the flow of psychic energy connecting or relating two or more mental beings to one another is contemplated. It is commonly defined as the feeling of being drawn towards, of being attracted by, of striving for, or tending towards a person or object. ' Love is the force which both preserves and develops the individual, and at the same time defines his attitude towards others. Love is the urge towards all co-operation, synthesis and growth.'[1]

Such striving ends when the loving person has united himself with or has absorbed the beloved person or object. (Hence the use of the same word for both ' hunger ' and ' love ' in some primitive languages, and in poetic diction.) Manifold grasping and holding activities are executed by several parts of the motor system, which co-operate as a whole in the fulfilment of the desire for unification. Since utterance is only part of that behavioural mechanism it is no wonder that the organs concerned with it, such as lips, tongue and so on, besides the limbs, participate in the action. And indeed some of the earliest natural sound sequences, such as [ɖaɖaɖa], [ɿəɿəɿə], [ɿɿə ɿɿə ɿɿə], [ɖɿɿ ɖɿɿ ɖɿɿ], [ɿɿəʋ ɿɿəɿa ɿɿəɿa . . .], are accompanied by *grasping* movements which may be interpreted as ' aiming ' at the fulfilment of the desire to be united with the beloved person or object. Anyone acquainted with erotic speech behaviour will note in it the babbling tendency embedded in the grasping attitude.

The earliest form of utterance emerging out of the unification of voicing and clicking represents the coming to grips of two antagonistic psychological principles. The former can be styled individualistic, the latter social.

In the light of individual development we can with some probability reconstruct more fully the significance of early babbling in Chellean people. We can vividly picture the homely babble which linked them when at ease around the camp-fire after a day of struggle which had demanded strong efforts in a strange and inimical

---

[1]Howe, G. (1931). *Motives and Mechanisms of the Mind.* Lancet, Ltd., London, p. 96.

world. (See Davison's suggestion, p. 85.) They exchanged feelings of connectedness, experiences of the day past, perhaps accompanied by miming, but they hardly conveyed to one another ' concepts ' in the modern sense of the word. Speech did not as yet communicate ' ideas.' This conjecture is borne out by Piaget's observations on children. According to him the child's language is, up to the age of about six, ' egocentric.' The child ' talks either for himself or for the pleasure of associating anyone who happens to be there with the activity of the moment. . . . He feels no desire to influence his hearer or to tell him anything.'[1] The child's remarks ' evoke no reaction adapted to them on the part of anyone to whom they may chance to be addressed.'[2] The society in which he lives is one ' in which strictly speaking, individual and social life are not differentiated.'[3] This explains why children ' are perpetually under the impression that people can read their thoughts, and in extreme cases, can steal their thoughts away,'[4] an idea not uncommon among primitive races.

Elementary babbling thus expresses also the earliest (lowest) level of meaning, as it is still recognizable in the etymology of the term ' meaning.' (See p. 162f.) Babbled sequences have, of course, their referential field, inasmuch as they are reactions to such stimuli as our analytic mind perceives as persons, animals, trees, fruits, and so forth. Babbling hardly refers to these objects as such. Rather is it the peculiar *mode* of relatedness between the speaker and his surround, which is expressed. In view of the emotional attitudes just described its mode of reference can be styled *erotic*.

We shall presently correlate that coming to birth of the individual out of the primitive group with the aforementioned newly gained mode of linguistic expression, and see how the growth of individuality manifests itself in speech.

RHODESIAN MAN

In early Pleistocene times, round about 500,000 B.C., the human stock had split into several types such as those represented by Heidelberg and Piltdown Man already referred to.

From their more ' *modern* ' stem also sprang a new species of man represented by *Rhodesian* Man (Broken Hill, Rhodesia) who

[1] Piaget, J. (1928): *The Language and Thought of the Child*. Kegan Paul, London, p. 9.
[2] Piaget, l.c., p. 35.
[3] Piaget, l.c., p. 41.
[4] Piaget, l.c., p. 101.

lived with elephant, hippopotamus, rhinoceros, zebra, antelope, lion, leopard and hyena.[1]

Rhodesian Man's skull and stature are more ape-like than those of any living or extinct type,[2] but they are also quite distinct from those of the Bushmen and other now existing races.[3]

This creature, like Neanderthal Man and the Australian aborigines, still displayed enormous ridges over the eyes ' needed to complete a facial skeleton which is subject to forces generated by powerful muscles of mastication,'[4] another indication of the role which the mouth activities played in those days.

The Rhodesian brain was small and primitive ' in the form and size of its convolutionary areas,[5] especially the temporal lobe, and the anterior and posterior central gyri. (See Fig. 2.) ' The brain outfit of Rhodesian Man was less in volume and simpler in pattern than in Piltdown Man . . . it scarcely reaches the lowest level of the Australian aborigine. Yet it ' was many rungs higher than that of the Java Man; this in turn was many steps higher than that of the gorilla.'[6]

Rhodesian man, although on a lower rung than the Australian aborigines, the most primitive living race, was by no means a beast-like creature. We learn from him that a rudimentary mental structure was sufficient to enable him to fashion knives and scrapers and to paint as the Bushman still does.[7]

Excavations at Boskop and T'zitzikama seem to show a steady evolution of race and culture along Chellean, Acheulean and Mousterian lines up to the Bushmen civilization. This supports a certain parallel development in Europe, Asia and Africa.[8]

Both Rhodesian Man and Boskop Man have some resemblance with Neanderthal Man ; Boskop Man also calls to mind Crô-Magnon and negroid types.[9] (See below, pp. 144ff.)

Another remarkable human type, which also is assumed by some to be ancestral to the Australian on the ground of certain resemblances, is represented by ' the primitive Talgai Skull found in

[1] Keith, l.c., p. 378.—Sollas, l.c., p. 495 ff.
[2] Keith, l.c., p. 386.
[3] Sollas, l.c., p. 497.
[4] Keith, l.c., p. 404.
[5] Keith, l.c., pp. 390–3.
[6] Keith, l.c., p. 621.
[7] Keith, l.c., pp. 378–9.
[8] See Henderson, l.c., p. 80.
[9] De Pradenne, l.c., p. 182.

Pleistocene deposits in Australia and the skull from Wadjak in Java which is described as Proto-Australian.[1]

NEGROES

A more successful experiment in evolving *homo sapiens* resulted in a type of human beings, the *negroes*, who very probably were fully evolved in early Pleistocene times [2] and whose offspring so far as they are still surviving in conditions somewhat comparable to early palæolithic ones, may furnish valuable parallels.

The negro race of Africa divides into four main classes : (1) the true negro ; (2) the Bantu ; (3) the Bushman-Hottentot ; (4) the Negrito (Negrillo).[3]

The 'true negro' inhabits West Africa and is known under the names of his subspecies : Senegalese, Sudanese, Nigeria and Dahomey negroes, Ashanti Mundingo, Kru, Mossi and Walof negroes.

The Bantus (Zulus, Kaffirs, Ubangi) are included in one class on linguistic grounds, but represent a mixture of various physical types.

The Negritos are pygmies living in the forests of Central Africa.

The Bushmen used to populate South Africa but are now confined to the northern part of South West Africa, and to central and northern districts of the Kalahari desert.

The Hottentots, kindred to the Bushmen, now inhabit South West Africa north of the Orange River.[4]

Although the languages of these races have now reached a fairly high standard they still exhibit certain archaic features which will aid our efforts at interpolation.

MOUSTERIAN MAN
(Homo Primigenius)

Several scores of thousands of years had elapsed when the most successful branch of the Pleistocene race, that of Mousterian or Neanderthal Man was populating the world.[5]

His remains were found in Upper Pleistocene strata corresponding

---

[1] Fallaize, l.c., p. 27.
[2] Keith, l.c., p. 355.
[3] Lewis, J. H. (1942). *The Biology of the Negro*. The University of Chicago Press, p. 19.
[4] Lewis, J. H., l.c., pp. 20–22.
[5] Elliott Smith (1916). *Proc. Brit. Acad.*—(1924.) 'The Evolution of Man.' p. 69.

to the Last Interglacial Period (from about 180,000 B.C.),[1] at Gibraltar, Neanderthal, Taubach, Weimar, Ehringsdorf Steinheim on the Murr (Germany), La Naulette, Spy (Belgium), Malarnaud, La Chappelle aux Saints, Le Moustier, La Ferassie, La Quina Pech d'Aze, Saint-Brelade (France) Malta, Jersey, Banolas (Spain) Rome, Sipka, Ochos (Moravia), Krapina (Croatia), Tabiha (Galilee) Palestine, Broken Hill (South Africa), and in Ordos (China). (See Fig. 3.c.)

Neanderthal people entered Western Europe from the East probably twice. The first invasion took place long before the cave period, i.e., perhaps in the Second Interglacial Period.

The warm interval between the Riss and the Würm glaciations in Europe probably attracted a second invasion [2] of Neanderthal people who were possibly the offspring of the same stock which had generated Heidelberg, Rhodesian and Piltdown Man in the Middle Pleistocene Age. The belief that Neanderthal Man stood on a higher evolutionary rung than his precursors is confirmed by the traces of his activities. Whether he was the direct descendant of that stock or that of an extinct species is of minor interest here.

Neanderthal Man was—according to Boule—' a loose-limbed fellow with an easy shuffling gait—knee and hip joints slightly bent,' of upright, but low posture (5 feet 1 inch to 5 feet 5 inches)[3] and a stooping attitude of the trunk.[4]

His face was characterized by the distinctly projecting brow ridge which is only remotely approached by that of the Australian native;[5] the nose was flat, the muzzle consisted of thick, slightly mobile lips, the heavy massive and powerful jaw contained large teeth which did not overlap in front, but met edge to edge, the neck was powerful, thick and muscular. The big head, the base of which was straight and simian in conformation (Gibraltar skull) was as a whole thrust forward.[6]

In respect of both the form and the size of the palate, and the form of the molars, Neanderthal Man had diverged from the simian type. The teeth were, to all appearance, adapted to the grinding of rough vegetable diet.[7]

---

[1] Zeuner, l.c.
[2] Schmidt, R. R., l.c., p. 22.
[3] Keith l.c., p. 221.
[4] Schmidt, R. R., l.c., pp. 46–7.
[5] Sollas, l.c., p. 233.
[6] Fallaize, l.c., p. 29.—Schmidt, *ibid.*—Keith, l.c., pp. 157, 185–6, 182.
[7] Keith, l.c., pp. 211–15.

The ratio of brain to palate is 38 c.cm. to 1 cm. (Gibraltar palate).[1] The size of the brain is equal to that of the modern Australian native, and of the Bushman (cf. table on p. 88), but in respect of its general conformation and its simple and broad convolutions it is more ape-like.[2] The third frontal gyrus, where the motor speech patterns are localized, is imperfectly developed.[3] As a whole, Mousterian Man must have given the impression of muscular rather than intellectual strength.

Mousterian people probably lived on berries and other wild fruits, nuts, hazel nuts, leaves, etc.[4] like their forbears. Although there were many animals which—we might think—were their hunting prey, the afore-mentioned shape of the teeth does not support that they were preponderantly hunters.

Up to the fourth glaciation they may have led a relatively easy life which can hardly have encouraged novel activities. For—

> ' It is not learning, grace nor gear,
> Nor easy meat and drink,
> But bitter pinch of pain and fear
> That makes creation think.' [5]

In strata related to the last Ice Age (120,000–20,000 B.C.)[6] we find Neanderthal fossils alongside with lion, leopard and hyena, which survived in Europe up to historic times. The rest of the fauna consisted of ' two forms of elephants, lemming, voles, saiga-antelope, a Pleistocene form of horse, the cave hyena, the Alpine marmot, the boar, the ibex, the bison, the reindeer, the mammoth and a form nearly allied to the African elephant (*E. antiquus*); three forms of the rhinoceros; the musk ox, the arctic fox, the arctic hare, and other mammalian species associated with a cold climate.' [7]

' With the change in climate to intense cold, Neanderthal Man took shelter in the caves. And for almost the whole of the remainder of the Palæolithic period man was predominantly a cave dweller.' [8]

It is difficult to imagine the walks of life of Neanderthal Man,

---
[1] Keith, l.c., p. 215.
[2] Keith, l.c., p. 202.—Schmidt, l.c., p. 48.
[3] Schmidt, l.c., p. 50.
[4] Henderson, l.c., p. 52.
[5] Kipling, R. *Verse.* ' The Benefactors.' Hodder & Stoughton, London, p. 391.
[6] Zeuner, l.c.
[7] Keith, l.c., pp. 164–65.—Sollas, l.c., pp. 214 ff.
[8] Fallaize, l.c., p. 28.

because even the very lowest of present-day peoples, such as the Yahgans of Tierra del Fuego who are living under the hardest conditions, are probably superior to him.[1]

It can, nevertheless, be presumed that he was, to a limited extent, an artisan though the working of flint had not yet become a 'specialty' of a certain class of craftsmen. ' When in lower, or on a modern view only in early middle pleistocene times unmistakable tools, stones patently shaped in an intelligent and purposeful way, do appear, their use is still uncertain. Probably each had many uses ; tools were not yet specialized as with us to specific ends, but the same roughly chipped flint served all purposes from dispatching a tiger to scraping the hairs off his hide or digging up roots.'[2]

If it be true that the ' first shaped tool is proportioned to its prototype, the human hand,'[3] as the bone-knife of the Eskimos still is,[4] it would indicate the very first, crude attempt at singling out the ' quality ' of ' form.' It would also show that the need for an extension of human limbs first seen in the apes, was now given a further and more purposeful expression—a noteworthy advance in the utilization of substitutes. (See pp. 111ff.)

No doubt those people had to expend a certain amount of effort to find their food. Yet, it seems that in spite of the constant preoccupation with their food, they had not acquired any degree of foresight. They were universally improvident.[5] They ' acted on the spur of the moment ' rather ' than after careful reflection '[6] as the Central Australian aborigines still do.[7]

All that speaks for Neanderthal Man's ' wisdom ' or ' skill ' is the fact that he did have tools, that he had fire at his command and that he not only buried his dead children and relatives, but also provided them with food and tools.[8]

Round about the time of the fourth glaciation traces of the Neanderthal race fade out. The reason ' is unknown. Terrible wars of extermination exist only in the imagination of writers '[9] who,

---

[1] Fallaize, l.c., p. 36.
[2] Childe, *What Happened in History*, p. 28.
[3] Schmidt, l.c., p. 96.
[4] Werkmeister, W. H. (1939). ' Languages as Cultural Indices.' *Philosophy of Science*. VI 3, p. 359.
[5] Elliott Smith, Human History, p. 261.
[6] Davison, l.c., p. 60.
[7] Róheim, l.c.
[8] Keith, l.c., pp. 189, 223.
[9] Davison, l.c., p. 83.

it must be admitted, feel that such exterminations were the inevitable result of a struggle between more brutish and more human species,[1] for

" when in this world's unpleasing youth
our god-like race began,
the longest arm, the sharpest tooth
gave man control of man." [2]

' Neanderthal is a distinct species which branched off from the human tree at some early date, but which, owing to its failure to adapt itself to changing conditions, died out entirely before the intrusion of the modern type, better equipped in mind and body, which appeared in Europe at the end of the Ice Age. Others . . . are not entirely convinced that the Neanderthal people became entirely extinct, and see in some of the skulls of a later period in Eastern Europe a survival of Neanderthal character, while others would also find survivals in some of the modern population of the sea-coast of Frisia and in Northern Germany,' [3] as well as in Africa where Rhodesian Man survived, until towards the end of the Palæolithic Period conditions became unfavourable to his special adjustment.[4] Schmidt believes that ' groups of the ancient Neanderthal form retreated, at the beginning of the last glaciation, perhaps along with the retreating warmth-loving animals, into the hot regions on the border of the inhabited world ; and that there they found it possible to survive the Ice Age, although excluded from contemporary advances in civilization (in Europe). We may conjecture, though insecurely, that the Neanderthal race there developed into the primitive races of prehistoric Africa.   Africa, however, was not their only retreat ; it is probable that a second and later migration moved eastward.' [5]

Be this as it may, it strikes the anthropologist that in the regions of the Pacific a people was found by the European settlers which resembled the Neanderthal race and the anthropoids : the Tasmanians of Australia (since extinct). They lived on hunting, fishing and fruit-gathering. Their tools of Mousterian or

---

[1] Henderson, l.c., p. 59.
[2] Kipling. ' The Benefactors.'
[3] Fallaize, l.c., p. 27.
[4] Fallaize, l.c., p. 31.—Peake and Fleure. *Hunters and Artists*. Clarendon Press, Oxford, p. 39.
[5] Schmidt, R. R., l.c., p. 59.

Aurignacian type were held in the hand without a heft. Their weapons were of wood (mace, throwing stick, spear, javelin).

ACHEULEAN AND MOUSTERIAN CULTURES

Long after the time of the major glaciation [1] the peoples of the Neanderthal species developed successive cultures known as Acheulean and Mousterian, named after St. Acheul near Amiens (Somme) and Le Moustier in France, where the respective remains and implements were first found. In England, Acheulean skeletons were found at Bury St. Edmunds (with the remains of the mammoth, *Elephas primigenius*).[2] Acheulean people manufactured, cut and pointed wooden stakes, spears [3] and flint tools.

It is noteworthy that ' the flint workings ' of the Acheulean period (approximately 450,000 B.C.)[4] (Caddington Hill) ' seem more extensive than the needs of a local family or even a local tribe would demand; we seem here to have struck a factory for the manufacture and export of Acheulean implements.'

Acheulean tools have been discovered at a higher level than that of the Chellean industry of Thebes, Luçor and Assiut [5] (see above, p. 90) in deposits near Madras, and in the basins of the Kistna and Godoveri.[6]

They differ from the Chellean type in that they betray finer workmanship. The flake tools and especially the lanceolate points and borers are not only better finished, more elegant and regular, display narrower, longer and finer retouches, but are also more efficient.[7]

The age of the Mousterian culture commenced at about 200,000 B.C.[8] In the early phase of that period ' Europe had a warmer climate than it has now ; by the time this culture had evolved into another phase, the temperature had so fallen that the Arctic conditions of the Würm glaciation spread southwards as far as the Thames valley.'[9]

---

[1] Keith, l.c., p. 182.
[2] Keith, l.c., p. 239.—Sollas, l.c., p. 196.
[3] S. Hazzeldine Warren (1911). *Quarterl. Journ. Geolog. Soc.* LXVII. *Proceedings,* p. xcix ; *Essex Naturalist* (1912), xvii, p. 15. *Prehistor. Soc. East Anglia* (1922). III.
[4] Zeuner, l.c.
[5] De Pradenne, l.c., p. 143.
[6] De Pradenne, l.c., p. 208.
[7] De Pradenne, l.c., p. 104.
[8] Cf. Zeuner, l.c., p. 284.
[9] Keith, l.c., p. 156.

The implements of this period show a certain progress in technique inasmuch as they appear to have been adapted to diverse and more special purposes. Among early tools the cordiform type of coup de poing prevails (Africa, Palestine, Transjordania, South-East India, Western Europe, Spain, Central Italy); it was followed by the Levalloisian type, and later by side-scrapers, discs, etc.[1]

From the distribution of the implements Burkitt [2] concludes that the early coup-de-poing industry in Europe was of African origin, whilst the flake tool civilization had spread from Asia. Remains of the latter industry have been unearthed in Central Europe (Tanbach, Ehringsdorf, Weimar) and as far East as Alfontova-bar near Krasnoiarsk (Siberia) and on the Yenisei.[3]

If it is permissible to regard Mousterian tools as the result of a deliberate co-ordination of useful qualities found both in core and flake tools,[4] this accomplishment must cast sufficient light on the mentality of those artisans to allow certain general inferences.

The progress of technique would in the first place suggest that Neanderthal people were steadily developing more and more power of concentrated observation and of recognition of detail, not to forget the budding sense of form.[5]

Lastly, we must not overlook the fact that the species who finally developed the Mousterian culture was able to hold their own for many thousand years, up to about 100,000 B.C. Their survival for a comparatively long evolutionary period suggests that they must have attained to a high degree of integration, specialization, if not over-specialization, manifest in a more highly evolved mode of consciousness in the direction of a less impulsive, more purposeful, self-asserting individuality.

Having outlined the nature of their behaviour, we will now pass on to considering the linguistic segment of that behaviour.

MOUSTERIAN LANGUAGE

Only vague hints have been dropped as to Neanderthal Man's speech. Miss Davison opines that his 'speech centres were sufficiently developed to enable him, in a simple and limited way, to talk.' She stresses, however, that 'with such a brain, having

[1] Burkitt, l.c., pp. 116 ff.
[2] Burkitt, l.c., pp. 120 ff.
[3] De Pradenne, l.c., p. 191.
[4] See Hawkes, Jacquetta and Christopher (1943). *Prehistoric Britain*. Penguin Books, p. 20.
[5] Schmidt, R. R., l.c., pp. 224-9.

only simple and coarse convolutions, he would not have many ideas to express.'[1]

Others have been less felicitous both in the choice of their premises and in their inferences.

Sir Arthur Keith points out that ' in order to secure free movement of the tongue and easy, articulate speech, it is highly advantageous to have the floor of the mouth opened out. In anthropoids the lower border of the mandible encroaches on, and diminishes the area of, the floor of the mouth. In the most highly evolved forms of men the lower border of the mandible is widened or opened out. . . . In Neanderthal Man the expansion of the lower border of the mandible is less complete than in man of the modern type.'[2]

Schmidt thinks that ' the budding mental powers loosened the human tongue. With the chin-formation, the muscles of speech and the cerebral speech centre, the mechanism for the consummation of onomatopœic speech was made perfect.'[3]

Yet, Keith Henderson feels that the Mousterians did ' not talk much, or at least not very coherently ' because ' their jaws are scarcely made for talking.'[4]

If articulateness means a quality of speech recognizable by the division of an utterance into distinct and significant parts,[5] then we can fathom in early babbling the first origins of articulate speech inasmuch as the primary stream of voice is broken by noises other than vowels. Considering the great variety of clicks and the modifications they can undergo, we can realize the enormous prospects which the amalgamation of voicing and clicking opens up. Millions of combinations are possible which provide vehicles for communication. Yet mankind in Pliocene times had not acquired the conceptual material which could form a cargo. Tremendous upheavals and strenuous efforts were necessary to achieve this end which was probably denied to all the afore-mentioned racial and cultural types.

One branch of the hominid family seems to have been far more successful in the advance of thinking : the Neanderthal race. In view of their accomplishments in the tool-making technique we may attribute to them, and particularly to the Mousterians, the power to

---

[1] Davison, l.c., p. 60.
[2] Keith, l.c., pp. 209–10.
[3] Schmidt, l.c., pp. 101–2.
[4] Henderson, l.c., p. 45.
[5] The *Shorter Oxford Dictionary* gives this meaning as dated 1594.

use the babble already available to them as a purposeful means of communication.

We have seen above (p. 97) how a new unit, totally different in appearance, emerged. We shall now expound how mankind elaborated that early type of speech. As regards the first step in the refinement of primeval babbling, we gain valuable information from both baby-talk and primitive languages.

In the first place it should be borne in mind that during the sometimes rather prolonged period of babbling (up to about the third year) the child gradually detaches himself, as it were, from the mental cord which links him with the mother ; he is becoming an individual, an ' I ' as opposed to the original, integral ' we,' and a subject as opposed to an object.

We have seen the young baby in relation to his surround as a being affected by and forcibly responding to it. What perhaps stands out in his dim experience is the way in which he is influenced, and what matters most is the greater or lesser ease with which he can take in and assimilate the ' things ' surrounding him.

With the awakening of the self, the ' ego,' this attitude comes to be somewhat reversed. Response to an outside event is changing into a primary action which makes the environment react. What was first ' moved out,' i.e., was subjected to ' emotion ' (Lat. *emovere* ' to remove, to shake, to upheave '), is now moving, i.e., is making other people do something. Thus the mode of relatedness is changing its *direction*. The self viewed as the ' centre ' into which the ' forces ' from the surround once streamed in, is now sending out forces into the surround. Centripetal attitude is gradually changing into a centrifugal one.

Thus we can imagine Mousterian people floating between taking in and giving out, a struggle between the social we-ness and the growing me-ness.

HALF-CLICKED SOUNDS

We have seen above (p. 102) that the preservation of the ' self ' is manifest in the expulsion of air. This in its turn is involved in the production of voice. Self-assertion, then, gives birth to the analytic mind with its power to see, apprehend and respond to factual diversities, without, as yet, conceiving ' universals,' i.e., general concepts.

It may be surmised that the emergence of the ' person ' as opposed to ' objects ' should be reflected in the articulatory changes which elementary babbling, inherent in all small children's constitutional behaviour, soon undergoes.

In accordance with the Biogenetic Law we assume that, with the development from we-ness to me-ness and the dawning of the Self, phonetic patterns expressive of the social attachment, i.e., the clicks, were gradually losing their essential property ; while the sucking movements remained the same, the rarefaction of air in the mouth necessary for incorporation was superseded by greater or lesser compression as a preliminary to expulsion of air from within. In other words, influx was giving way to efflux of air.[1] (Fig. 19.)

This process may have been aided by co-existing expulsory noises, e.g., the ' contented ' gurgling noises (from the tenth day) which seem to account for the guttural r [R], observed by Valentine as early as the thirty-eighth day,[2] spitting and coughing.[3]

That the giving up of the tendency to rarefy the air in the mouth was a comparatively recent process indicative of an immense struggle between the primeval level of undivided social unity and the overriding stratum of the Self, is confirmed by the fact that some primitive races still adhere to such phonetic patterns. In the languages quoted above (p. 70) clicks still are conventionalized constituents of words.

The era of the clicks was probably followed by one characterized by semi-clicks. In some languages of South Africa and of the Caucasus a timid, but significant step toward closer integration of voicing and clicking has been made inasmuch as the first part of a click is still rarefactory whilst the second part has become explosive, i.e., consonantal. Such sounds have, of course, been conventionalized throughout the ages and so nowadays form stable elements of the sound table. They can be followed either by a vowel or a consonant.[4]

Some African languages have still preserved a type of speech sound which seems to shed light upon the articulatory advance from sucking to the clicks and to the consonants as we know them. It is an essential feature of the African clicks that they are always articulated at *two* points. In all of them the back of the tongue articulates against the soft palate while the main articulation is

---

[1] See Beach, l.c.
[2] Valentine, l.c., pp. 98, 395.
[3] Aston, W. G. (1894). ' Japanese Onomatopes.' *Journ. Anthropol. Institute*, London, XXIII, pp. 352–362. Quot. by Chamberlain, *The Child*, p. 115.
[4] Van Ginneken, l.c., p. 323.

I

taking place at some other point of the mouth.[1] (See Fig. 20, a, b, c.). This phonetic pattern is indeed strongly reminiscent of the act of sucking.

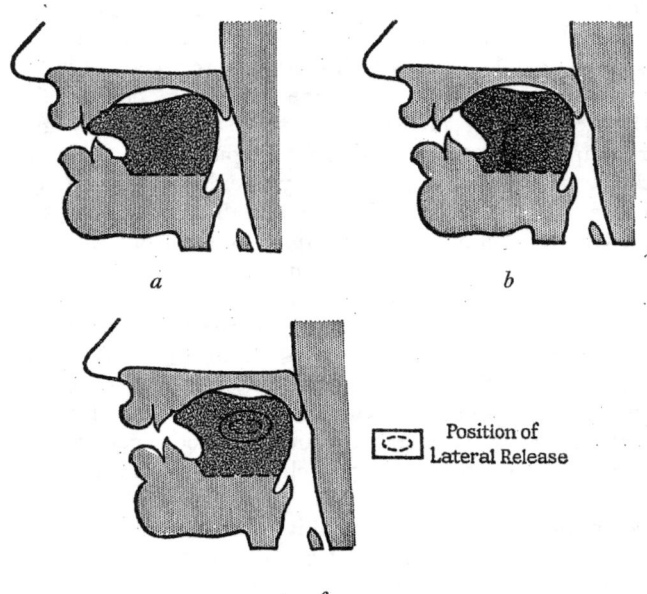

FIG. 20
Clicks (After Westermann and Ward)
a, Dental Click. b, Palato-alveolar Click.
c, Lateral Click.

In some sounds of such African languages as Ibo (S. Nigeria), however, the velar articulation has been abolished and the inflow of air is brought about by lowering the larynx while the speech organs are in position for the stop. In this manner the chamber between the point of articulation and the larynx becomes larger and causes the air to flow in on the release of the stop.[2]

Other African languages like Noho (Cameroons) show a tendency towards a reduction of the vigour of pronunciation so that only a small quantity of air is drawn in.[3] Such sounds may have led the way to the consonants, i.e., noises produced by the outgoing air.

[1] Westermann and Ward, l.c., pp. 78 ff.
[2] Westermann and Ward, l.c., pp. 92 ff.
[3] Westermann and Ward, l.c., p. 93 f.

It may be remarked in passing that the Bushmen, in making each kind of animal speak its own language, systematically transmute clicks into consonants. In the Tortoise's language, for instance, the labial element is given prominence, in the Ichneumon's language more palatals, dentals and sibilants occur.[1]

CONSONANTS

With the fading away of the antagonism between expelled voice and drawn-in noises, the final stage of integration was reached. In children's babbling its accomplishment can be observed up to approximately three years of age. All the stages of babbling deserve the epithet "*prelinguistic.*" By this term I mean to indicate that sequences like]d∧d∨d∧], [*pipipi*], [*pətɒk*∧ *pətək*∧], [m∧m∧m∧], [*plu plu plu*] are still mere utterances, i.e., they are unintentional and aimless accompaniments of the speaker's motor behaviour; they are not intended to be verbal statements; rather are they expressive of the emotional oneness with the surround. (Cf. Fig. 18 with Fig. 19.)

There were probably thousands of small variations of loudness, pitch, vowel-shades, and other noises in accord with the vicissitudes of daily life.[2]

Utterances were as little ' specialized ' as were the flint tools of early Pleistocene times.

There is no need for us to explain variation as characteristic of biological occurrences. Rather shall we have to demonstrate and elucidate the growth of simplicity, uniformity and stability of utterance.

The conversion of clicks into ' consonants ' was gradually leading to the modern sound table, a process which is, as some primitive languages show, by no means completed. Every click is as it were a ' mother sound ' which, if it comes into happy union with the ' father sound,' i.e., voice, brings forth a fricative or explosive consonant in place of it.

Be it noted that in case of retarded maturation or of psychosomatic regression the individual often fails to achieve syllables. To the condition known as Hottentotism (see above, p. 94) we can now add certain cases of imbecility, senile dementia and a type of

---

[1] Sollas, l.c., p. 475.
[2] Steinthal, H. (1871). *Abriss der Sprachwissenschaft.* Dümmler, Berlin. I. 405. ' Dem Urmenschen ergab sich aus jeder scharf und individuell aufgefassten Wahrnehmung ein individueller Lautreflex.'

stammering in which the patient, owing to anxiety, unconsciously reverts to the sucking stage and so replaces consonants by clicks. He can release these but fails to release or to join them with the vowel. He unconsciously wishes to remain a suckling and therefore cannot achieve the unification which results in a syllable.

It can also be seen that the bud of articulate, syllabic speech is not comparable to an autogamous, i.e., self-fertilizing flower. Autogenesis of syllabic speech is as unthinkable as is parthenogenesis in human beings. Only when combinations of consonants and vowels and ' liquids ' [m, n, l, r] have come into being, has the happy marriage (see above, p. 97) been fruitful.

Viewed from this angle the advice given by a Welsh clergyman to the English Bishop of his diocese : " You must put the tip of your Right Reverend tongue against the roof of your Right Reverend mouth, and hiss like a goose," [1] if you wish to learn the Welsh ' *ll*,' betrays to those in the know the wisdom, or at least the evolutionary intuition of the adviser.

We must not underestimate the immense potentialities entailed in the introduction of sucking noises into the voice, or ' babbling.' Looked upon from the phonetic angle it appears that innumerable combinations and permutations of vocal sound, i.e., vowel shades and consonantal elements of enormous variety, are possible. They are capable of expressing many diverse situations once man avails himself of them.

Variability inherent in the process of amalgamation of voicing and clicking accounts for certain linguistic features. In some cases, for instance in the Romance languages of Southern Europe, the preponderance of voice may be so great as to give the effect of conspicuous vocalism, while in others, such as the Germanic and Slavonic languages of Northern Europe, the ' consonantal ' element with preponderant noise clusters may stand out. Whether one or the other will come into appearance depends originally on the existence of those mental states which are manifest in voice and in clicks or semi-clicks. In later stages of a given language other rules of sound change come into play. It is for the sociologically-minded philologist to explain them by considering the changing mental attitudes of the speakers.

Considering the immense number of shapes possible in the mouth with organs as flexible as the lips, tongue and pharynx walls, we cannot help agreeing with Seth and Guthrie on " infantile babbling

---

[1] Poulton (1937). *History of Evolution*. Watts & Co., London, p. 25.

being a random activity."[1] In fact, if we were able to resolve the random babbles into well determined linguistic occurrences, we might hope to have found the clue to almost the whole problem of phonetic change and of linguistic diversity.

We can, however, derive some insight into what might have happened in times of yore from the ontogenetic development of human utterance.

Certain predilections can be detected in the suckling which seem to account for the prevalence of certain sounds peculiar to his later babbling. Every infant seems to have his pet clicks, and the first ' word ' which he will later on pick out of the many which may have reached his ear, will largely depend on those pet clicks. One mother was wondering why her baby had chosen just the word ' hallo ' as his first target of imitation, until it was recalled that [ʇ-ʇ], genetically a kind of loud sipping, was the favoured click.

In another case it was reported that the first standard word uttered was Germ. ' Apotheker ' ' dispensing chemist ' a word which was often used by the girl's father who was a doctor. We need not wonder at this seemingly considerable achievement, if we recall that many infants delight in retaining the sequence [ɖʇɣ] which actually reflects the *whole* of the sucking process.

We may, at this juncture, deal with the oft-heard question as to why certain speech sounds occur more frequently than others. Marty[2] quotes Johannes Müller as pointing out that on the average in all languages the " easiest " sound combinations are the most frequent ones, whilst the harder ones appear only spasmodically. This conception, still held by some, is erroneous and cannot be too strongly opposed. In actual fact, all speech sounds are equally easy to the minds of those who are capable of pronouncing them. As regards babies, they find those sounds ' easy,' i.e., will tend to use first those sounds which can be based on their favourite clicks. Before copying sounds heard, infants begin to single out certain parts of the sequence of sucking noises ; they then go on uttering strings of isolated clicks in a rhythmical manner, e.g., [ɖɖɖɖ], [ʇʇʇʇ], nasal sounds [m̩ m m̩], liquids [ʃʃʃʃ], and so on.[1] (For the phonetic rendering, see p. 70.) At the age of seven months the play with newly acquired sounds is marked. With regard to the playful and apparently enjoyable handling of sounds the human baby differs

---

[1] Seth G., and Guthrie, D. (1935). *Speech in Childhood*. Oxford University Press, p. 86.
[2] Marty, l.c., p. 225.

distinctly from the baby-ape inasmuch as the latter does not play with sounds, even if brought up in the company of a human baby.[1]

Once the speaker has adapted his natural language to conventional sound patterns these latter become gradually canalized, whilst others disappear through disuse. If in later life the speaker is forced to adopt a foreign language, he finds those sounds ' hard ' which do not happen to occur in his own, consolidated, national language. Let us, then, imagine how man may have come to stabilize and conventionalize certain sound patterns so that the primeval world language split into group languages.

Considering that in a fertile district hunting life requires 100 square miles to support 300 people[2] we may believe that primeval man lived in small communities which formed, as it were, oases within vast spaces full of awe and danger. This mode of life may have invited the idea of uniformity of behaviour. It is obvious in animal life, where it is described as ' herd instinct.' Primitive races still dread novelty and originality. Everything must be kept in its place, nothing must be altered, lest it involve danger and mischief. This attitude is still recapitulated in most small children whose adoption of neatness and accuracy their parents admire. It is in reality nothing but a vestigial fearful behaviour. Small children also exhibit a noteworthy memory for the wording of stories and strongly object to even slight alterations. It thus seems permissible to infer that all members of a primordial group partook of the same experiences, their picture-thinking and attitudes were alike, and their multiform utterances were common to them all. Casting a glance at our ancestors' primeval utterances so far as our fantasy has urged us to build up their patterns out of the still existing relics, we do not feel any longer that—as Vendryes says—' it is impossible to say in what form human speech first took shape.' Nor can we agree that in an ' endeavour to determine the conditions which made speech possible '[3] we must confine ourselves to a consideration of psychological and social factors. Primordial speech was not engendered solely by these.[3]

Although those original speech patterns arose in some form of social community, and should, therefore, be *conceived* as psychological phenomena, it is convenient to *describe* the beginnings of utterance in biological rather than in psychological terms.

---

[1] Kellogg, W. N. and L. A. (1933). *The Ape and The Child.* New York, p. 281. As quot. by Valentine, l.c., p. 398.
[2] Sollas, l.c., p. 290.
[3] Vendryes, p. 7.

We also feel that the alternative question as to ' whether language is an acquired fact resulting from education or, on the other hand, instinctive and spontaneous ' is inappropriately posed by Vendryes. His view is that ' normal children can teach us nothing on this point ' because ' from birth they are aware of the exterior world. Before emitting sounds they are brought into relation with their environment by their hearing, and from the moment they speak they find themselves part of the warp and woof of social interchange.'[1]

Observation of small children reveals that the peculiar features of early utterance are by no means due to corresponding external linguistic stimuli. The babbles of congenitally deaf and blind children corroborate this in so far as they produce clicks, groans and babbles, although to them the models are virtually non-existent. The tendency to babble and the activities involved in it are to a high degree genetically fixed in all human beings. In this sense, and only in this sense, can we understand why " St. Basil was charged by Eunomius with atheism for holding the view that babies ' learn ' to talk." [2] Biological evolution has furnished the raw material for eloquent speech. Man has been able to preserve and utilize its plasticity. The further handling of the articulatory material depends, in the main, on another faculty of great evolutionary age and import : *imitation*, and its sub-form *onomatopœia*. Before passing on to this subject we shall follow up the development of babbling up to relatively late linguistic stages.

As regards the peculiar relatedness of the last stage of prelinguistic babbling with the behavioural context, it seems safe to say that babbled utterances such as [ʌpʌkv-ʌpʌkʌ], [bulʌbulʌ] and the like, are purely emotional, integral units, corresponding to and concomitant with other behavioural wholes (gestures).

The discarding of the component of air rarefaction seems to indicate the concealment of the purely erotic meaning; although such utterances as [dadada], [mamama] and the like, still carry with themselves the primary meaning of *social* we-ness, they have now adopted a more *personal* meaning. Utterance has changed its direction : the clicks denoted ' intake,' the consonants are ' outgoing.' A new pattern : that of a ' tool ' which can conjure up a delightful, if partly hallucinatory surround, living or non-living, is gradually emerging.

---
[1] Vendryes, l.c., p. 9.
[2] Briffault, Robert. *The Mothers*. (1927). Allen & Unwin, London. Vol. I, p. 23.—Gregory of Nyssa, *Contra Eunomium*, i, xii, pars altera, in Migne, Patrologiæ coursus completus. Series græca, Vol. xiv, cols. 258, 999.

Children between the ages of five and twelve months begin to use reiterated utterances like [*bababa, dadada, nanan*] in this 'manipulative' (M. M. Lewis) manner. Such sequences are expressive of more or less differentiated feelings of joy, gratification and so on, and, significantly, are the only ones that arouse smiles and kindred gestures when interspersed in a series of words spoken by adults.[1] They may in such cases, with some licence, be styled the 'emotional copula.' (See p. 6.) Psychoanalysts have long recognized that children of both 'natural' and civilized peoples begin their mental development from a purely libidinous, imaginary state. Only such features are picked out from the impressionistic whole, with more or less distinction, as serve the gratification of their desires.[2] This is *their* emotional world, in contrast to the *cognitive* concept, of which, rightly or wrongly, we pride ourselves.

Similarly primitive man was linked with his mates by reiterative utterances which were undergoing constant change. A continuous prattling, accompanying gestures, was going on—entirely free sound combinations and sequences, the *parts* of which had no conventional meaning in themselves. Primitive utterance probably consisted of long 'beads' of still uninhibited, emotionally tuned, reiterative sound complexes. They were hardly expressive of definite and detailed cognition. It probably did not matter what particular sound sequence was uttered, so long as the libidinous interrelation and union of the individual with others was upheld.

The 'ejection' of noises was about to become an instrument of man's 'will.' This was in keeping with the state of mind which we may presuppose in Acheulean and Mousterian people. In contrast to their early precursors who, in picking up a stone or club, were still rather dominated by what happened to be at hand, Mousterian people adjusted what they found to their specific purposes and so imposed their will on the objects of the environment. Thus in contrast to the former feeling of identity with the group achieved by 'taking in,' the 'self' with budding awareness forces its acts on the surroundings. Yet, it is not the environment of modern civilization. It is a hunter's world in which 'the endless struggle with nature calls the huntsman to constant readiness. . . . For the hunter, sleep is like the slumber of the beasts : he rests on the threshold of wakefulness, ever ready to spring with activity into the

---

[1] Cf. Valentine, l.c., pp. 404-419.
[2] Cf. Ferenczi, S. (1916). Contributions to Psychoanalysis. Badger, Boston, pp. 181 ff. As to the ignoring and repressing of the unsatisfactory reality, see below, p. 179.

clear day. Dream and the waking life are here the same—*one reality.*'[1] . . . 'The uncivilized man knows but one world, embracing all experience; his apprehension of it resembles that of our young children. For him, the outward and visible world is one and the same reality with the world of imagination, including the life of dreams. His outlook sees but one plane, compounded of his adventures in both these regions.'[2] It has been assumed by some that totemism, i.e., the belief in a close and mystic union between a person or group and some natural object, such as an animal, fire, red ochre, season of the year, etc., dates from this remote time.[3]

We have surmised that it was not so much the sum total of sounds in a sequence which at first gave primitive utterance its character as the peculiar form which emerged when the whole of voice as the carrier of expression was interspersed with noises and thus intersected into smaller wholes. Being of hoary age this tendency towards rhythmical repetition must have exerted its influence ever since the ' happy marriage ' was consummated. We may now add that in the utilization of the aforementioned sound sequences the totemistic outlook may have played a prominent role. The primitive hunter of our days expresses the relationship between himself and, say, a crow, by stating that he *is* the crow, that *he possesses* the crow, that the crow *possesses him*, that he and the crow are of the same flesh, or that the crow is his elder brother.[4] Such statements are by no means felt as incompatible with one another. Thus reiterative utterances may conceivably have been the outward expression of the emotional oneness prevailing in the speaker in relation to all those in his field of reference.

We can agree with Vendryes when he says that ' the languages of uncivilised peoples may supply us with useful information about the relations between language and thought,' but must reject his assertion that they cannot enlighten us ' on what was the original form of language.'[5] In fact the study of primitive languages in itself, and especially if taken up with a view to comparing them with other modes of utterance, allows us to extricate the germinating core and brings us rather near some of the possible, and perhaps probable, original patterns of language.

---
[1] Schmidt, R. R., l.c., p. 167.
[2] Schmidt, R. R., l.c., pp. 3-4.
[3] Sollas, l.c., p. 284.
[4] Sollas, l.c., p. 284 ff.
[5] Vendryes, l.c., p. 6.

Like the embryologist, the philologist must set himself the task 'to decide in any given case whether a particular feature is ancient and ancestral, or modern and adaptive.'[1] On the following pages this will be carried out.

REITERATION

The manner in which reiterative utterance has further developed illustrates the deep significance of the amalgamation of voicing and clicking.

Steinthal reported the case of a girl, aged eighteen months, who, seeing barrels being rolled from a barge to the shore, uttered: [lululu]. A fortnight later [bululu] was used to depict the rolling of the auxiliary legs of a table. After another fortnight the play with a rolling coin was referred to by [dullrullul]. More than two weeks later the girl said [lululu] again, meaning to report that she had been given marbles. Even at the age of four she automatically uttered the same sequence of sounds when her father was winding up a clock, although she had otherwise acquired full command over her mother tongue.[2]

In the first place it is to be remarked that the girl's utterance was by no means stabilized in its details. Rather was it the general reiterative feature which remained constant for the relatively long period of four years. In such wise this unsophisticated, unpremeditated example lays bare the thoroughgoing and persisting power which emanates from the primeval rhythmical tendency. It creates patterns which at the outset refer to occurrences as wholes. The notions of agent, action, modality, tense, and so forth, have not been singled out, and are not denoted as yet.

In view of the domineering part which reiterative patterns play in childhood the chances are in favour of a successful search for their evolutionary analogon. Indeed the pleasurable urge to reiterate is clearly borne out by what Margaret Mead tells us about the aborigines of New Guinea. 'There is no belief that it is necessary to give a child a formal teaching; rather chance adult play devices are enlisted. One of these is the delight in repetition. Melanesian languages very frequently use repetition to give an intensity to speech. To go far is expressed by " go go go," to be very large by " big big big." So an ordinary anecdote runs: " So the man went went went. After a while it was dark dark

---

[1] Kerr, l.c., p. 18.
[2] Steinthal, H. (1881). *Abriss der Sprachwissenschaft*. Dümmler, Berlin. Vol. I, pp. 382–3.

night. So he stopped stopped stopped stopped stopped. In the morning he awoke. His throat was dry dry dry. He looked looked for water. But he found none. Then his belly was angry angry, etc. . . ." Although strictly speaking these repetitions should all have a function in expressing duration or intensity, very often the mere habit of repetition runs away with the narrator and soon he will be saying, " Now he met a woman. Her name was Sain Sain Sain," or, even repeating a preposition or particle. . . . . A crowd also has a tendency to pick up a phrase and repeat it or turn it into a low monotonous song. . . .'[1]

In Central Australia two boys would go on enumerating each other's lovers for hours and hours, old men chant the same two or three words of a long song for hours.[2]

The languages of primitive tribes abound in reiterative words the meaning of which does not suggest that reiteration is used for any grammatical purpose. Words from the various languages quoted at random may illustrate this type of word formation: *Apooapoo* ' dumb,' *kookoo* ' yes,' *mooromouroo* ' disabled, deformed,' *nillanilla* ' mirage,' *ooroo-ooroo* ' hard, tough, strong,' *kaka* ' mother's brother,' *mura-mura* ' mythical gods,' *oobi-oobi* (name of mountains) (Dieyerie language of Southern Australia),[3] *wiliwili* " Hawaiian light cork-like wood," [4] *kaya-kaya* " Nigerian method of fishing." [5]

Linguistic records from a comparatively late historical period provide similar examples. In Ethiopian, for instance, we find *adlaqlaq* ' he has staggered ' (or ' he has caused to stagger '), *ahmalmala* ' it has been verdant.' In Old Egyptian, *chc* ' to stand,' *nhn* ' to be young,' *grg* ' to set a trap, *shs* ' ' to run ' [6] (vowels are not represented in Old Egyptian spelling).

In magic formulæ, such as those contained in the collection of Triads by Kuno Meyer in the Royal Irish Academy, Todd Lecture Series, vol. viii, pp. 12 sqq, the threefold repetition of a word plays a great part,[7] and in the popular songs of many peoples the refrain is a regular feature.

Mephistopheles, having knocked at the door of Faust's study, is

---

[1] Mead, Margaret (1942). *Growing up in New Guinea*. Pelican Books, pp. 26–7.
[2] Róheim, l.c., p. 74.
[3] Curr, E. M. (1896). *The Australian Race*. Melbourne. II, p. 89. Quot. by Chamberlain, *The Child*, p. 116.—Sollas, l.c., pp. 298, 324.
[4] Hornell, J. (1942). ' Floats.' *Journ. R. Anthropol. Inst.* LXXII, p. 34.
[5] Harris, P. G. (1942). ' The Kebbi Fishermen.' *Journ. R. Anthropol. Inst.* LXXII, p. 30.
[6] Lach, R., l.c., pp. 31–32.
[7] Weise, O. (1909). *Language and Character of the Roman People*. Kegan Paul, London, p. 69.

asked in by Faust's 'Come in.' Yet he admonishes Faust that 'Thrice be the words expressed,' if he is to cross the threshold.[1] In these examples the emotional value of reiteration is still preponderant if not overwhelming.

The primary tendency towards reiteration of the same sound has left its traces in the poetic devices known as alliteration and assonance. Considering what has been said about the origin of reiterative utterance we can understand why passages, such as the opening of Piers Plowman,

In a summer season when soft was the sun,
I shope me into shrouds, as I a shepherd were,
In habit as a hermit, unholy of works,
Went wide in this world, wonders to hear ;

or Swinburne's

The full streams feed on flowers of rushes,
Ripe grasses trammel a travelling foot,
The faint fresh, flame of the young year flushes
From leaf to flower and flower to fruit.[2]

appeal so much to our sentiments, and influence us like music which makes most extensive use of the recurrence of motifs. In considering these devices one cannot help recalling the onomatopœic representation of events in the babble of the girl described by Steinthal (see p. 124). It has been reported by reliable witnesses that poets sometimes to try to re-live the babbling stage in order to get fresh inspiration. The babbles which then spring up soon turn into beautiful verses. These not only reveal deep-seated sentiments but are also full of alliterations.

Reiteration has, throughout the ages, proved to be a valuable aid to the creation of grammatical forms. Reiterative patterns readily lend themselves to the expression of (1) intensity or intensification ; (2) multitude ; (3) degree ; (4) duration and/or completion of an action ; (5) diminution ; (6) instrumentality and causation ; (7) negation ; and (8) tense. Here are some examples : Old Armenian *medsadeds* ' very big,' *caracar* ' very evil,' *hoids-hoids* ' very much,' [3] Papuan *dika* ' bad,' *dikadika* ' very bad,' [4] Indonesian (Mentaway)

[1] Goethe, J. W. *Faust*. Transl. by Anna Warwick (1892). Bell & Sons, London, p. 50.
[2] Quot. by Abercrombie, l.c., pp. 33, 38.
[3] Lach, l.c., p. 31.
[4] Capell, A. (1937-39). Word-building and Agglutination in South-Eastern Papua. *Bulletin of the School of Oriental Studies*, Vol. IX, pp. 769-75.

igi-igi-igi-igi ' more numerous than anything imaginable,' Old Javanese *angin* ' wind,' *angin-angin* ' tempest,' [1] Chinese *liao* ' alone,' *liao-liao* ' very much alone ' ; *li₃²-ti₃¹* ' lonely,' *li₃¹-ni₃²* ' to exhort.' [2] In the Luritja language (Central Australia) *tjipa-tjipa* means ' happy, being in a state of rapturous delight, ecstasy, as, for instance, in coitus ' [3] a possibly cognate word is *tjitjipanga-tjitjipa* ' a game with leaves and sticks foreshadowing what will happen when the little girl becomes a married woman.' The corresponding game of playing at being grown up for boys is called *kapata-kapata*.[4]

Malay *orang* ' human being,' *orang-orang* ' human beings.' Japanese *tabi* ' time,' *tabi-tabi* ' many times, *tokoro* ' place,' *tokorotokoro* ' places,' Chinese *jên* ' human being,' *jên-jên* ' everybody ' ; [5] Papuan *hua* ' banana,' *huahua* ' fruit in general.' [6]

Old Egyptian *snfḥfḥ* ' to loosen,' *sdɛdɛ* ' to tremble,' *wɛdɛd* ' to be greenish ' (*wɛd* ' to be green '), *r̈sr̈s* ' to enjoy oneself,' *gbgb* ' to be weak.'[7]

English *murmur*, French *cricri* ' cricket ' (see also below, p. 129). Papuan *kadarakadara* ' to continue playing.' [8]

Sanskrit *pac̆* ' to cook,' *papac̆* ' I have cooked ' ;[9] Greek *tetheka* ' I have put,' Old High German *teta*, Anglo-Saxon *dide*, English *did* ;[10] Greek *ni-ns-jomai>nissomai* ' to come, to go ' ; Old Slavonic *deždja<de-d-jŏ* ; [11] Latin *tutudi<tudtudi* ' I have beaten,' *peperci< parcparci* ' I have saved,' Greek *leipo* ' I leave,' *leloipa<liploipa* ' I have left ;' Papuan *bur* ' to break,' *to-bubur* ' broken.' [12]

Papuan *pinimina* ' fragment,' *pinipinimina* ' crumb,' *mwata* ' snake,' *mwatamwata* ' worm.' [13]

Quechuan (South American Indian) *palla* ' to collect,' *palla-palla* ' collector,' Duke of York Island language *kili* ' to dig,' *kili-kili* ' spade,' *aki* ' to break,' *akak* ' hammer,' *akari* ' to bewitch,' *akakaṛa* ' spell,' *balui* ' to recompense,' *babalu* ' recompense ' ; [14] Papuan *wose* ' to do,' *wosewosena* ' doer,' *abagibugibu* ' frying pan,' *metani*

---

[1] Graff, l.c., pp. 424, 155.
[2] Finck, F. N. (1910). *Haupttypen des Sprachbaus*, p. 18.
[3] Róheim, l.c., p. 52.
[4] Róheim, l.c., p. 32 f.
[5] Graff, l.c., p. 155.
[6] Capell, l.c.
[7] Lach, l.c., p. 32.
[8] Capell, l.c.
[9] Lach, l.c., p. 32.
[10] Whitney, l.c., p. 267. This interpretation of English *did* is, however, doubtful.
[11] Kluge, l.c., p. 433.
[12] Capell, l.c.
[13] Capell, l.c.
[14] Graff, l.c., p. 155.

'to plait,' *metametamnina* 'the warp of a cloth.'[1] Latin *gingiva* 'gum' represents a reiterative form of the base which has furnished the English verb *to chew*, German *kauen*, and Old Slavonic *živati*, 'to chew.'[2]

Papuan (Dobu) *lotolotō* ' not taste.'[3]

In Germanic the formation of the present tense by means of reiteration (cf. Latin *bibo*, Sanskrit *pibami* ' I drink ' ; Latin *gigno* ' I beget ' ; Greek *mimno* <*mi-menō* ' I remain ' ; Latin *se-r-o*, *si-st-o*) was lost with the exception of Old High German *wiummen*< *wi-wm-jan*.[4] Some forms became so petrified as to finally grow into new stems : Old High German *biben*, past tense *bibeta* is derived from the reduplicated present tense *bi-be-m*, *bi-be-s*, *bi-bai-d*= Sanskrit *bibhe-mi*, etc. (stem *bhi*).[5]

If we may believe in the accuracy of the observations recorded in 1857 by Schlegel and others, it would appear that in those days the reiterative tendency was even more marked than the above examples indicate. Here are some reiterative words as quoted by Schleicher :[6] Hawaian *lo-a*, *lolo-a*, ' long,' *lololo-a*, ' very long,' *lelelele*, ' to run away often '; Ewe *didīdī*, *didīdīdī*, ' very old,' *gadagadagada*, word denoting heat, *kankankan*, word denoting brightness, *lililili*, word denoting keen scent.

Reiteration has not ceased to influence word formation nor has it lost its original emotional power which engendered the abovementioned purely grammatical systematized forms. If an Italian says *pian-piano*, *molto-molto*[1] instead of *pianissimo*, *assai molto* (very quiet, very much), if the Frenchman says *c'est beau, beau, il est gros, gros* instead of *tres beau, tres gros*, or if a Greek says *zestá, zestá kollouria* ' piping hot jam rolls,' *eisai pollý pollý kakós* ' you are exceedingly naughty,'[7] ; if an Englishman say ' he talks and talks ' instead of ' he keeps on talking;'[8] ' goody-goody ' for ' very good ' ; he works and works ; it's a cold, cold day[9] or if King Lear reiterates " never, never, never . . ." it is not so much the repeated action or the intensity which the speaker expresses, but rather his

---
[1] Capell, l.c.
[2] Wyld. Universal English Dictionary.
[3] Capell, l.c.
[4] The customary formulæ A>B and A<B indicate that the word A has developed into B, or vice versa.
[5] Kluge, F. (1901). Vorgeschichte der Altgermanischen Dialekte. Paul's *Grundriss der Germanischen Philologie*. Trübner. Strassburg. I/1, pp. 432–34.
[6] Schleicher, A. (1861). *Sprachliche Curiosa*. Beiträge zur vergleichenden Sprachforschung. Berlin. Vol. ii, p. 392.
[7] Vendryes, l.c., p. 152.
[8] Graff, l.c., p. 205.
[9] Graff, l.c., pp. 154–5.

peculiar sometimes paroxysmal, emotional attitude such as amazement, bewilderment, even anger and the like. Shakespeare's Mistress Quickly tends to reiterate a phrase as present day Cockneys still do. When she is excited she says ' I have borne, and borne, and borne, and have been fubbed off, and fubbed off,' or ' do me, do me, do me your offices.'[1]

Interesting examples of reiteration have been mentioned by Bloomfield. They show that reiteration as a grammatical form can attach to any part of a sound sequence, and that it may precede the isolation of significant parts. ' In Tagalog, the underlying form ' [ta : wa] ' ' a laugh ' appears reiterated in the derivative [ta : ' ta : wa] ' one who will laugh ' ; this form, in turn, underlies a derivative with the infix [-um] namely [tuma : 'ta : wa] ' one who is laughing.' On the other hand the form [pi : lit] ' effort ' *first* takes the infix [-um-], giving [pu'mi : lit] ' one who is compelled,' and is *then* reiterated, giving [pu : pu'mi : lit], which underlies [nag-pu : pu'mi : lit] ' one who makes an extreme effort.'[2]

Onomatopœia, too, makes use of reiteration in word forming, for instance, *ulambulambu*, name of a bird ;[3] *tjutalpi-tjutalpa* ' bird dance '[4] (Luritja language). Turkish *bül-bül* ' nightingale ' ; English (dialectal) *dang-swang* ' vigorously,' *dee-gee* ' kind of dance,' *dibber-dabber* ' wrangle,' *diddy* ' female breast with milk in it, *dimmy-simmy* ' languishing,' *dixie-fixie* ' emprisoned,' *drill-drolls* ' trailing plants, wild convolvulus,' *driggle-draggle* ' untidy dress, untidy women,' *drippity-droppity* ' the game of drop the handkerchief,' *fid-fad* ' fastidious person,' *fidge-fadge* ' slow, easy pace in walking,' *fic-fac*, *fix-fax* ' the tendonous parts of meat, *ligamentum nuchæ*,' *giff-gaff* ' mutual obligation,' *ping-pong* ' game resembling lawn-tennis,' and many others.[5]

In Hebrew, where word-stems consist mostly of three consonants, we originally find all of them reiterated, e.g., *sechar-sechar* ' to move fast,' whilst in later stages only the second, accentuated part remains reiterative : *sechar-char*. Significantly, this archaic mode of expression preponderates in literary Hebrew of an emotional character, for instance, in hymns, *bəzifzuf, məzafzef, jəsalsalu, jəzalzalu, məsagseg, məchalkel, bəzilselei* ;[6] these examples, taken at

---

[1] Matthews, W. (1938). *Cockney, Past and Present*. Routledge, London, p. 116.
[2] Bloomfield, *Language*, p. 222.
[3] Róheim, l.c., p. 61.
[4] Róheim, l.c., p. 33.
[5] See *English Dialect Dictionary*. Ed. by J. Wright. Oxford, 1903.
[6] Psalm 103.

random, could easily be multiplied. In Indo-European languages the same process can be observed. (See above, p. 127.) Although the history of language shows a tendency to inhibit reiteration, the vocabulary is constantly enriched by reiterative words intruding from baby-talk, a fact which demonstrates the all-pervading power of babbling.

The most familiar examples are the ' names ' of the parents, such as *mama, papa, dada,* which are found in hundreds of languages up to recent historical times.

Pirson,[1] for instance, mentions *tata* for ' pater ' in Gallic inscriptions. Family members other than parents are similarly named, e.g., *iti-iti* ' unborn child ' (Luritja language).[2] Even in modern Chinese which is preponderantly monosyllabic, family relation is expressed by reduplications, e.g., [*ko ko*] ' elder brother,' [*mej*[4] *mej*[4]] ' younger sister,' [*tsje*[3] *tsje*[3]] ' elder sister.' [3] (The figures indicate varieties of musical pitch.)

Both [papa], [mama], and other similar forms occur in the sense of ' breast ' in many languages, e.g., Chinese nai^3-nai^3 ' young women, young mother,' literally ' milk ' ; tsa^1-tsa^1-r ' breast.' [4] In English, especially in dialects, the former has survived in the archaic form *pap* and *pappy* [paːpi] ' infant feeding,' ' nipple of breast,' ' soft infant food,' ' a mother's milk ' ; ' the projection of the mouth ' ; *pap o' the hass* ' uvula ' ; *pap-mouth* ' soft, effeminate man, childish boy or girl.' [5] Prof. Orr of Edinburgh has drawn my attention to French *poupée* ' doll,' assumed to be derived from an hypothetical Latin word *pŭppa*. The Romance derivatives, French *poupard* ' suckling,' Italian *poppa* ' mother's breast,' North Italian *poppa* ' doll,' Old Italian *poppina* ' eye, bud,' French *poupe,* Provencal *popa,* Italian (Milan, Ferrara) *poppa* ' nipple,' Italian *poppar,* Provençal, Catalan *popar* ' to suck,' Rumanian *pup* ' kiss,' [6] as well as English *puppet, puppy,* and *pup* strongly suggest that these words owe their origin to a babble containing *p*. This in its turn probably sprang from the primordial rhythmical sequence of labial sucking noises.

---

[1] Pirson, L. (190). *La langue des inscriptions latines de la Gaule,* pp. 219 ff. As quoted by Ettmayer, K. (1910). Characteristik des Altfranzösischen. Freiburg, p. 23.
[2] Róheim, l.c., p. 104.
[3] Bloomfield, *Language,* pp. 278-9.
[4] Finck, l.c., p. 18.
[5] The English Dialect Dictionary.
[6] Meyer-Lübke, *Romanisches Etymologisches Wörterbuch,* No. 6854.

According to Weekley, who in one of his books devotes a chapter to Baby's Contribution to Speech, 'we may suppose that baby, as his consciousness developed (the present writer would interpolate Man in the Making) shortened his two favourite reduplications into *pa* and *ma*, and that these two syllables went into the melting-pot of speech, acquired terminations, became eventually Greek *pater* and *meter*, Latin *pater*, *mater*, and in the Teutonic branch of the Aryan languages went through consonantal changes resulting for us in *father*, *mother*.'[1]

The reiterative tendency is also manifest in well-established conventional words of the class in question. Thus, Latin *amita* ' aunt ' became first French *ante*, and was then ' distorted ' into the babbled word ' *tante* ' which is now standard.[2]

In some cases such reiterative baby-words as are normally said to denote ' mother ' acquire a different meaning. In the Luritja language of Central Australia the word *mama* means ' wound,' but significantly enough it is a children's word for ' vagina.'[3] In Latin it means ' breast,' in German *Muhme*, Middle High German *muome*, Old High German *muoma* it denotes ' mother-sister,'[4] in baby-talk it sometimes means ' food,' ' eating,' ' sweets', ' kissing ', ' desire ', and so on.

The word thus reflects the scale of differentiation from the primordial compound ME-MY MOTHER to object love and sexual love.[5]

This development of meaning was engendered by a primitive attitude comparable to the phase in the development of the child ' when before the first teeth appeared he imbibed his mother's milk in an essentially passive attitude. In this phase of development the erotic function of the mouth may be compared to the part played by the vagina in coition, while the flow of milk corresponds to the seminal fluid.'[6] The original meaning surges forward with primitive, libidinous vigour in the following passage from a ' Song ' by Audrey Beecham :[7]

---

[1] Weekley, Ernest (1930). *Adjectives and other Words*. Murray, London, p. 88.
[2] Canello, Arch. Glottal. III, 341, l. As quot. by Meyer-Lübke, W. (1913). *Historische Grammatik der Französischen Sprache*. Winter, Heidelberg, p. 50.
[3] Róheim, l.c., p. 29.
[4] R. Much, as quot. by Lach, l.c., p. 31.
[5] Cf. the instructive diagram in Howe, l.c., p. 84.
[6] Róheim, G. (1930). *Animism, Magic and the Divine King*. Kegan Paul, London, p. 96.
[7] *Poetry in Wartime* (1942). Ed. by M. J. Tambimuttu. Faber & Faber, London, pp. 25-6.

Setting out or turning back,
The old wound split in new strife,
A new wound is a new eye
A festering wound a womb of different life.
Where shall we hide but in the wound ?

The original, emotional, mode of reference is reflected on the one side in such alliterative and assonantic, almost ' poetic ' words as *flipflap, helter-skelter, fiddle-faddle, fingle-fangle, wishy-washy, sing-song, roly-poly, shilly-shally, riff-raff* ; Cockney *pishery-pashery, gibble-gabble, tittle-tattle, slip-slop* ' soft drink,' *hobbadyboody* ' country fool,' *fish-fosh* ' kedgeree,' *cag-mag* ' rough meat,' Mistress Quickly's *tilly-folly*,[1] Americanisms such as *bang-spang, sneakins-meakins, willopus-wollopus*,[2] Middle English *guegoe*, Modern English *gewgaw*, etc. ; on the other side in pet names and nicknames such as *Mimi, Koko, Pipi*, Italian *Gigi* for *Luigi, Peppe* for *Giuseppe* ; *Harty-Tarty* (the Victorian Lord Hartington), *Cribbley-Crabbley*,[3] *namby-pamby* (formed in ridicule from the name of Ambrose Philips, author of feeble pastoral poems, died 1749) ; [4] Princess Elizabeth is to her parents *Lilibet*, i.e., *lili* + *bet*.

English dialects contain a fair number (roughly three per thousand) of reiterative words, many of them onomatopœic, of which only an arbitrary selection may be presented : [5] *pip-pop* ' swing gate, kissing gate,' *pinny-ninny* ' Christmas game played with pins,' *marly-scrarly, mawl-scrawl* ' the common green caterpillar, a small shrivelled apple,' *mickmick* ' the green woodpecker,' *midge-madge, ming-mang, mish-mash, mixty-maxty, miz-maze, muxter-maxter* ' confusion,' *mingledy-pingledy, higgledy-piggledy, mingle-mangle* ' confused,' *mimpsy-pimsy, mink-mimp* ' affected, fanciful,' *miminy-piminy* ' meaningless expression used by children in their games,' *minniminny-monifeet* ' centipede,' *mousey-pousey* ' a child's name for the mouth,' *nivvy-nivvy-nick-nack* ' a guessing game or method of casting lots,' *nibble-nabble* ' to do anything by pieces,' *nibby-gibby* ' a touch and go,' *nickle-nackle* ' a tangle,' *canny-nanny* ' a small stingless humble-bee,' *bee-bee* ' lullaby,' *bibble-babble* ' idle childish talk,' *bit-bat* ' bat,' *blish-blash, tittle-tattle* ' idle talk,' *blitter-blatter* ' rattling irregular noise,' *bobaw* ' don't touch, don't meddle,' *brittle-brattle* ' hurried motion causing a clattering noise,' *catty-watty*

---
[1] Matthews, l.c., pp. 111, 119, 122, 124, 141, 153.
[2] Wentworth, H. (1944). *American Dialect Dictionary*. Thomas Y. Crowell Co.
[3] Andersen, H. The Drop of Water.
[4] Wyld. Universal English Dictionary.
[5] See English Dialect Dictionary.

'rubbish, balderdash,' *chim-cham* 'to beat about the bush,' *chiff-chaff* 'chaffinch, willow-wren,' *chitchat* 'mountain ash' (*Pyrus aucuparia*), *chitter-chatter* 'foolish talk, chattering of the teeth from cold,' *niggly-naggly*, 'dull, gnawing (pain)' *clichity-clachity* 'shaky (of machinery),' *cling-clang* 'in confederacy,' *clip-a-clap* 'with a clattering noise, foolish talk,' *clish-clash* 'idle talk,' *clitter-clatter* 'rattling noise,' etc.

Recent word coinage shows how much alive the old tendency of reiteration still is. The fact, for instance, that the verbs 'to talk' and 'to walk' sound almost alike has invited the formation of the word *walkie-talkie*, which most vividly depicts the army men who directed naval gunfire by radio in the battle of Normandy.

We have so far been endeavouring to retrace the possible evolution of language under the guidance of such records or observations as furnish cross-sections of human behaviour, which we can arrange on a time scale. Our guides have been archæology, anthropology and child psychology. Pathological conditions, too, allow a further verification of what has hitherto been said, insofar as speech disorders often result from regression to earlier stages of evolution. Here the most cogent evidence is furnished by stammering. This disorder is brought about by such conditions (mental or physical shock, concussion, sunstroke, mild inflammation of the cerebral cortex, intoxication, post-morbid conditions, retarded maturation, etc.), as impair the highest level of speech at which the ideas and feelings are transformed into verbal expressions. It is now a well ascertained fact that in its initial phase Stammering is characterized by reiterative utterances, for instance, *tha tha, thank you, far far far farther afield*.[1]

Mankind must have remained in its 'babbling stage' for many thousands of years, since the babbling tendency is now entirely innate in all babies. So great is the power of the tendency towards reiteration that, according to Dr. M. M. Lewis, 46 per cent. of the earliest six words of 27 children of six different nationalities were found to be reiterative.

If it be objected that babbling utterances may just as well be interpreted as the child's futile attempts to copy our language, or as its automatic response to audible stimuli, the argument can easily be refuted by the fact that babbling can be observed even in congenitally deaf and blind children who cannot possibly have been subjected to such stimuli.

---

[1] Stein, L. (1942). *Speech and Voice*. Methuen, London, pp. 112 ff.

In the structure of early babbling the phonetician notes the emergence of an entirely *new* feature, viz., the clear-cut *division* of the stream of voice into smaller, easily perceptible units. Voice is here degraded to a mere vehicle whilst the consonantal elements assume the role of communication between at least two self-asserting individuals. Consonants are more communicative than vowels in spite of their lesser carrying power, because they perpetually carry with them all the elements of social linkage derived from sucking and the superimposed individualistic element involved in the expulsion of air, not to forget their intrinsic value as elements which divide the stream of voice into distinct parts.

It is thus perhaps not chance that in old linguistic records which already employ the spelling method, such as in Old Egyptian writing of Menes' epoch (4400 B.C.), the vowels are not represented.[1]

The earliest Ethiopian and Hebrew texts adhere to this rule which was in force as late as the 6th and 7th centuries A.D., when symbols for vowels were introduced in order to preserve the traditional pronunciation of the Holy Scripture.[2]

The foregoing examples have furnished sufficient grounds for the conjecture that sequences of reiterated syllables were at the outset purely expressive of comfort. They did not refer mainly to particular ' objects ' of the external world, all of which (including acoustic phenomena), we may assume, appeared to the children of nature in an impressionistic manner, as it were in a haze. Rather were they expressive of the aura of emotions emanating from those objects.

LALLING

Talking for the mere sake of emotional linkage rather than for the purpose of communicating definitive ideas entails that the novel linguistic tendency emerging out of the integration of voicing and clicking is given more or less free play. Thus it is not surprising to find constant variation, i.e., ' the inherent instability characteristic of all living matter, '[3] also manifest in language.

A continuous tendency towards certain sound changes can be observed both in the speech development of children of all countries and in the history of languages. A comparison of these linguistic changes reveals certain rules which suggest their great antiquity, universality and potency. The striving after greater or lesser

---
[1] Childe, *Man Makes Himself*, p. 134.
[2] Strack, H. L. (1907). Hebräische Grammatik. Beck, Munich, p. 4.
[3] Kerr, l.c., p. 88.

stability of speech patterns is due to factors which operate on a higher (later) evolutionary level.

Egger [1] was one of the first workers who with philological and biological acuity investigated the speech of infancy. He collected many parallels between the development of the child and the evolution of the human race. W. Ament, who approached the subject from the same point of view, emphasized the feelings of pleasure which are expressed by the overwhelming multitude of finely nuanced sounds in baby-talk.[2]

This enormous variability of the child's articulations is usually referred to as *lalling*, German *lallen*, Latin *lallare*, Greek *lalein*. It may be remarked in passing that the meaning of the onomatopœic stem has undergone many changes. Its Greek derivative means 'to mumble,' 'to babble,' 'to prattle,' 'to jabber,' 'to chat,' also 'to twitter.' It then adopted the meaning of 'talking' in general. In archaic Greek it also meant 'to say,' 'to enunciate,' 'to announce,' 'to teach,' 'to praise.' A cognate word is Greek *alalá* 'battle-cry,' metaphorically 'army,' 'confused shrieking,' 'woeful screams,' 'loud acclamations,' 'jubilation over a victory.' A similar Greek word is *eleleū* 'war cry.' The Latin stem yielded Rumanian *lălĭu*, Lorrainese *lalá*, Provençal *lalo*, Spanish *lelo* 'simple-minded,' 'simpleton,' 'idiot'; Old Italian *lellare*, Montalesian (Pistoja) *lillare* 'to lark about.'[3]

In Old Dutch, *lollen, lullen* meant 'to talk twaddle.' If it has nowadays become an obscene word,[4] it is probably because its archaic erotic connotations have come to the fore.

It was thought for a long time that the sounds and sound sequences of baby-talk represented a real chaos owing to the child's inability to imitate adult speech. Ament and others [5] have demonstrated that the child's utterances are not mere futile attempts at

---

[1] Egger, Emile (1879). *Observations et réflections sur le developpement de l'intelligence et du langage chez les enfants.* Picard, Paris. German translation of the fifth edition (1887) by H. Gassner, with introduction by W. Ament (1903). Wunderlich, Leipzig.

[2] Ament, W. (1899). *Die Entwicklung von Sprechen und Denken beim Kinde.* Wunderlich, Leipzig, p. 34.

[3] Meyer-Lübke, *Romanisches Etymologisches Wörterbuch*, No. 4860.

[4] See Te Winkel, Jan (1901). *Geschichte der Niederländischen Sprache.* Paul's Grundriss der Germanischen Philogie. Trübner, Strassburg. I/6, p. 884.

[5] See Humphreys, H. F. (1880). 'A Contribution to Infantile Linguistics.' *Transactions of the American Philological Association.* XI.—Oltuszewski, *Die Entwicklung der Sprache beim Kinde.*—Lewis, M. M. (1936). *Infant Speech.* Kegan Paul, London.—Stein, L. (1925). 'Das universelle Stammeln im Lichte der vergleichenden Sprachwissenschaft.' *Zeitschr. f. d. ges. Neurol. u. Psych.*, XCV, pp. 100 ff.

imitation of adult speech, but are determined by the same laws of sound change as operate in the evolution of normal language. The little child often possesses a sound table which contains an enormous number of sounds, including those spoken by those around him. In due course the child has to adapt his language to that heard in his group, and so has to curtail the number of his own sound varieties. The successful adjustment hinges largely on the child's readiness to fit himself into his social group.

In some cases of impaired maturation and asociality the natural (individualistic) tendencies gain the upper hand in the struggle with rules imposed by the social group. The ensuing lack of social adaptation is manifest in a speech disorder known as Dyslalia. In severe cases the disorder may make the impression of ' gibberish,' owing to the many deviating sounds which render the child's utterances more or less unintelligible.[1] A few examples will illustrate this point. The little child's sound table contains, in the main, the same vowels as that of his elders. Some sound changes, however, such as [a] > [ä] (as in Swedish), [i] > [e] as in German *benden* for *binden* ' to bind,' *spetz* for *spitz* ' a species of dog,' *bete* for *Bitte* ' request,' *mella* for *Kamilla*, [u] > [o] as in *ompfen* for *Strumpf* ' stocking.[2] English [ef], [a], [wel], [oi], [mel], [mei] for *if, out, will, I, mill, me* are reminiscent of similar changes in various languages. In Late Latin inscriptions from the second century onwards, for instance, short [i] and [u] are frequently replaced by [e] and [o].[3] Varro[4] significantly regards Latin *speca* for *spica* ' ear of corn ' as ' rustic.' This sound change has left its impress on all Romance languages (except Portuguese) ; so much so that Meyer-Lübke[5] uses it as a criterion for what is to be styled a Latin or a Romance dialect. A number of further sound changes distinctive of various Romance languages is based on that original step. Cf. Latin *signum*, Ital. *segno*, Span. *seno* ; Latin *chrisma* (Greek *chrīsma*), Ital. *cresima*, French *crème*. Indo-European [u] became reduced, significantly enough almost exclusively in the peripheral districts, in Slavonic and in Old High German, where the influence of the ruling class was weak. In the Eastern borderland in Serbian and in Slovakian it changed into [o], cf. Latin

---

[1] Stein, L. (1942). *Speech and Voice*. Chapter ' Dyslalia.'
[2] Ament, l.c., p. 45.
[3] Meyer-Lübke, W. (1909). *Einführung in das Studium der Romanischen Sprachwissenschaft*. Winter, Heidelberg, p. 116.
[4] Varro, *De re rustica*, I. 48, 2. As quoted by Meyer-Lübke. *Ibid.*, p. 126.
[5] Meyer-Lübke. *Ibid.*, p. 120.

mus-cus, Old High German *mos* ' shoot ' ; Old Indian *sunus* ' son,' Lithuanian *sunus*, German *Sohn* ;[1] Latin *excutio*, Rumanian *scot* ' to take out.'[2]

The fact that English children at the age of about two years usually pronounce the word ' *no* ' in the standard manner, but change it into [*nau*] when a very strong negation is to be expressed casts some light on diphthongization. It calls to mind similar changes in several languages, dialects and idioms, for instance, old Slavonic *sәinu* from *sūnous*, Lithuanian *sūnous*, Gothic *sunaus* ' son,'[3] Indo-European *lòuquos*, Germanic *lauha* = Latin *lucus* ' grove,' Old English *séaw* from Germanic *sauwa* = Latin *sūcus* ' juice ' from a common base *souqo-s*.[4]

In baby talk unstressed syllables and endings are either shed, or their vowels are replaced by the indistinct vowel [ə] : German *Schokolade* > [glad, gəladə], *spiele* > [bil],[5] English *upstairs* > [tɛəz].

The London Cockney dialect of the sixteenth and seventeenth centuries exhibits numerous examples of words in which [i] was replaced by [e], for instance *kendred, wretten, tell, cheldern* for ' kindred, written, till, children.' This vocal change is paralleled by that from [o] to [ʌ] as in [mʌrou], [ʌspitɛl], [dʌki3] for ' morrow, hospital, Dorking.'[6]

Consonant changes are exemplified by the following instances : German *papa* > *babab*, Peter > *bedi*,[7] *selber*, ' self ' > *selfer, sieben* ' seven ' > *siwen*, *Schokolade* > *glad*, *Käse* ' cheese ' > *tes*, *koffer* > *toffer*, *Kaffee* ' coffee ' > *chaffi*, *Licht* ' light ' > *list*. English Sophie > [hovi] [vovi], *fault* > [vɔ : l], *song* > [to3].

Such examples can easily be supplemented by observations of children of other nationalities.

Dyslalia exhibits changes of the same nature. On close philological investigation we discover that the apparent sound chaos in this disorder is by no means devoid of form or rule. The dyslalic is not incapable of articulating the sounds of the mother-tongue, as, for instance, if an Austrian child of seven says [tifɛ] for *Kirche* [kiəxɛ] " church," alongside with [tje:ə] for *Scheere* [ʃe:rə] ' scissors ' ;

---

[1] Mikkola, J. J. (1913). *Urslavische Grammatik.* Winter, Heidelberg. I, p. 40.
[2] Tiktin, H. (1886). *Die Rumänische Sprache.* In Gröber's *Grundriss der Romanischen Philologie.* Trübner, Strassburg. I, p. 444.
[3] Vondrák, W. (1912), *Altkirchenslavische Grammatik*, Berlin, p. 114.
[4] Kluge, F. (1901). *Vorgeschichte der Altgermanischen Dialekte.* Paul's *Grundriss der Germanischen Philologie.* I/1, p. 404.
[5] Ament, l.c., pp. 46–47, 68.
[6] Matthews, l.c., pp. 19–20.
[7] Ament, l.c.

or if an English child says [ʃiːk] for 'cheek,' [ʃjiː] for 'she,' [ʃimpl] for 'simple,' as against [sjʌm] for 'some,' [tsaet] for 'cat,' [dɔːl] for 'girl,' [tjiː] for 'tree.' These sound changes are the result of the same process of 'palatalization' as accounts for the change which, for instance, Latin [k] was undergoing between the third and sixth centuries A.D.[1] The articulation of the Latin guttural stop [k] was influenced by a following palatal vowel [e] or [i], the articulation of which was anticipated. In the course of this process [k] was gradually changing into [kj], [tj], [ts], [s], [tʃ], [ʃ] ; cf. Latin *caelum* ' sky,' Rumanian *ceriu*, Italian *Cielo*, French *ciel*, Spanish *ciel*, Portuguese *ceo* ; Latin *canem*, French *chien* ; Latin *carum*, French *cher*, English *cheer* ; Cockney [dʒuːk], [tʃuːn] for ' Duke, tune.'[2]

The shedding of the final consonants as in [faun] for ' found,' [dʒʌs] for 'just,' [skwein] for 'strange,' is reminiscent of the modern English pronunciation of 'comb' [koum], and of fifteenth-century English *nex, husbon, uprigh, My Lor* for ' next, husband; upright, My Lord.'[3]

Changes such as *sum* [ʌm], *say* [ei], *school* [kuːl], *upstairs* [teəz], *some* [hʌm], *sweets* [hwiːts] call to mind that, for instance, all over the Indo-European area various words may be initiated sometimes with [s] and sometimes without it, for example, Old High German *spëhôn*, Latin *specio*, against Sanskrit *pac*, ' to see ' ; Gothic *stautan*, Latin *tundo*, Sanskrit *tud* ; Old High German *hinchan*, Greek *skázō*.[4]

The tendency to palatalize the [s] gives rise to a confusion of [s] and [ʃ]. This fluctuating articulation, illustrated by such changes as *brush* > [bjʌs], *chips* > [sips] is mirrored in Cockney pronunciations and spellings such as *shepter, sherche, fysse, marssys* for ' sceptre, church, fish, marshes.'[5]

Dyslalic change of vocal attack as in [houd] for ' old ' and the displacement of the explosives by the glottal stop as in [waebi'], [skwei'], [ski'], [wai'] for ' *rabbit, strait, skip, white* ' have their counterpart in such Cockney pronunciations as *hought, hese* for ' ought, ease,' current in the fifteenth century,[5] and [blou'], [ebaː'], [o'] for ' *bloke, about, hop*.'[6]

---

[1] Meyer-Lübke, W. (1909). *Einführung in die Romanische Sprachwissenschaft.* Winter, Heidelberg, pp. 139 ff.
[2] Matthews, l.c., p. 175.
[3] Wyld, H. C. (1936). *A History of Modern Colloquial English.* Blackwell, Oxford, p. 69.
[4] Kluge, l.c., I/l, p. 371, 39/b.
[5] Matthews, l.c., pp. 22, 184.
[6] The glottal stop is here represented by '.

The well-known substitution of [f] and [v] for [Θ] and [ð] in Cockney words such as [mauf,] [frʌst], [fevə] for *thrust, mouth, feather*,[1] is found both in baby-talk and in Dyslalia, e.g., *other* > [ʌvə], *with* > [wif], *three* > [fwi:]. It may be emphasized that such deviations can be discovered in children who cannot be assumed to have been influenced by the Cockney dialect. A correspondent of the *Sunday Express* (Dec. 8, 1946), points out that the natives of Southampton are glad to hear the name of the town pronounced *Suvampton*. They find it more homely.

Assimilation (a process by which unlike sounds are made more similar) of all kinds is frequent, e.g., *pot* > [pɔp], *prickly* > [krikli], *track* > [krack], *children* > [kwilgwən], *trick* > [pwik], *tried* > [pwaid], *cries* > [pwaiz], *queen* > [pwi:n], *dragged* > [bwɛgd], *broke* > [grouk]. The same process is betrayed in examples taken from the history of languages, e.g., Latin *lilium* < Greek *leirion* ' lily,' Latin *quinque* < Indo-German *pinque* ' five,' Latin *præcoquus* > Calabrian *krikopa* ' premature fruit,[2] Rumanian *apă* < Latin *aqua* ' water,' Rumanian *limbă* < Latin *lingua* ' tongue,' Provençal *celcle* > Latin *circulum* ' circle.'

In some cases we observe sound changes in opposition to such linguistic processes as, for instance, palatalization (see p. 138). They impress one as manifestations of a tendency to cling to past stages of development. In considering such examples as *church* > [txə:tx], *cheeks* > [kxi:ks], *jackal* > [gjaekɔ:l], *large* > [la:gj], *she* > [xi:] [3] one cannot help being reminded of regression to the past, since they seem to represent the reverse of the process observed in such changes as from Latin *caru* to French *cher* [ʃe:r], English *cheer*, or from Latin *galbinu* ' yellow ' to Old French *jalne*, Modern French *jaune* [ʒo:n], Italian *giallo* [dʒalo] ; Latin *gelu* ' frost ' to Rumanian *ger* [dʒer], Italian *gelo* [dʒelo].

A perusal of the foregoing examples shows that there is no genuine inability to articulate a given sound, but that often the *whole articulation basis* is shifted either forward or backward. The sound changes are merely the manifestations of an underlying general tendency affecting the whole articulation basis, i.e., the peculiar manner in which the speech organs are used to bring about certain conventional acoustic units.

---

[1] Cf. Matthews, l.c., pp. 22, 53.
[2] Meyer-Lübke, *Romanisches Etymologisches Wörterbuch*, No. 6712.
[3] My grateful thanks are due to my colleague, Miss Ruth Bennett, who has not only collected these examples, but has also ascertained the correlation between the dyslalic sound changes and the psychological attitude of the speakers.

It is worthy of note that Dyslalia is by no means confined to children. The same vehemently progressive sound changes can be found in such mental disorders as Paranoia or General Paralysis of the Insane if the patient's general attitude is child-like.[1] In other words, the dyslalic person has not reached or has fallen back from that level of bio-psychological maturation which exercises a checking influence on the lower levels of speech. This is corroborated by the fact that aphasic disorders are often combined with dyslalic ones, for instance, French [kikã], [titã], [papo], [tē], [poe] for *quittant, chapeau, train, bleu*.[2] The dominance of the lower level of speech which engenders dyslalic sound changes can be provoked if a normal speaker is, through hypnosis, taken back to early childhood.[3]

Dyslalia is often combined with a type of Aphasia (loss of the power of speech owing to an injury to the brain), known as Paragrammatism. The term indicates that patients so affected may utter words correctly but do not comprehend the idea and the use of grammatical forms and of syntactical constructions.

It is important to note the general attitude of dyslalic speakers. They usually display marked asociality in such aggressive behaviour as quarrelling with other members of their group, defiance against authority, preferring to be alone, refusal to eat, etc.[4] In other cases the attitude is a typically infantile one. The patients are easily frightened, attached to one person, usually the mother, and pampered; they do not want to grow up, pretend not to know their age, and so forth. In brief, their speech mirrors emotional rather than cognitive mentality.[5]

The comparison of sound changes found in baby-talk and Dyslalia with those detected in the history of languages shows that the infantile tendency to sound change plays an important part in the transmission and thus in the evolution of normal language. Many changes considered abnormal in regard to their too rapid development, i.e., their excessive deviation from the group speech, appear ' normal ' from the historian's and the linguist's point of

[1] Stein, L. (1940). " Disorders of Articulate Speech." *Brit. Med. Journ.*, vol. i, pp. 902 ff.—See also Liebmann, A. and Edel, M. (1903). *Die Sprache der Geisteskranken*. Marhold, Halle.
[2] Alajonanine, Th., Ombredane, A. and Durand, M. (1939). *Le Syndrome de Désintégration Phonetique dans l'Aphasie*. Masson & Cie., Paris.
[3] Winkler, F. (1929). *Zur Psychologie und Psychotherapie des Stammelns*. III. Congr. Intern. Gesellsch. f. Logopädie u. Phoniatrie. Deuticke, Vienna, p. 79.
[4] Miss Bennett's observation.
[5] Stein, L. *Speech and Voice*, pp. 146 ff.—Goldberger, E. (1933). *Mon. f. Ohrenheilk.* 67, pp. 73 ff.

NEW-FLEDGED LANGUAGE

view. Whether or not speech is permitted to strive forward more or less unbridled, depends on socio-psychological conditions. Left to develop by themselves within an isolated tribe, these deviations may become a ' new ' language spoken by the next generation. Among African tribes " speech is in a perpetual flux, and new dialects spring up with every swarm from the parent hive."[2] ' An offset from an Indian tribe in a few generations has a language unintelligible to the parent stock.'[3] Gabriel Sagard in his Grand Voyage du Pays des Hurons,[4] mentions that in North America the inhabitants of one village hardly speak the same language as those of another. Nay, two families of the same village do not speak exactly the same language. He adds that the language of the aborigines changes from day to day.[5] In South America the Guarani language is the only one that is widely understood. As to the rest, languages change from tribe to tribe, nay, from hut to hut, so that often only the members of the same family understand each other.[6]

Rousselot found that the French ' l mouillé ' (palatalized l, [lj]) as spoken in his native dialect, for instance in [filj] for *fille* ' girl,' had changed into [fij] from one generation to the next. And this must have been considered abnormal by the older generation. Lucian,[7] in a pleasant dialogue, referred to the sound change [s] > [t] (see above, p. 138), and facetiously described the Sigma (s) as the plaintiff against the Tau (t) which had expelled it step by step from the words of its inheritance " as when he took *tettarakonta* for *tessarakonta*, *temeron* for *semeron*, with little pilferings of that sort " (*tettarakonta* ' forty,' *temeron* ' to-day ').

Indefinite variability and instability of the speech sounds in primordial times has been assumed by several scholars.[8] ' No two consonants would seem to be more distinct than k and t. Nevertheless, in the language of the Sandwich Islands, these two sounds run into one, and it seems impossible for a foreigner to say whether what he hears is a guttural or a dental. The same word is written

---

[1] Müller, M., l.c., I. p. 59.
[2] Cliffe, Leslie, as quoted by Spencer, H. *First Principles*, p. 478.
[3] Rae, in Paget, l.c., p. 328.
[4] Paris, 1631.
[5] As quot. by M. Müller, l.c., I. p. 58.
[6] Azara, Voyages, vol. II. As quot. by M. Müller, l.c., II, pp. 35 ff.
[7] *Dike phoneenton*. Transl. by Fowler, H. G. and Fowler, F. G. (1905). Clarendon Press, i, pp. 26-30.
[8] Cf. Marr, Bernhard (1904). *Der Baum der Erkenntnis*.—Meyer-Rinteln, Wilhelm (1905). *Die Schöpfung der Sprache*.—Bréal, Michel, *Melanges de Mythologie et de Linguistique*, p. 375.—Kussmaul, A. (1877). *Die Störungen der Sprache*. Vogel, Leipzig.

by Protestant missionaries with k, by French missionaries with t. It takes months of patient labour to teach a Hawaian youth the difference between k and t, g and d, l and r.'[1] An analogous phenomenon can often be observed in Dyslalia (see p. 138).

Chamisso reported [2] that in observing a certain primitive language he had always wavered between d, dh and s, and between ch, k and g, although his ear was well trained.

A similar fluctuating articulation can be observed in the production of [l] and [r] so that travellers and natives alike often do not know how to transcribe the sound which, for instance, in Japanese deputizes for both of them. A booklet issued to American soldiers, which attempts to solve for them the problem of distinguishing between a Chinaman and a Japanese, stresses among other peculiarities that the latter ' cannot pronounce our liquid L and hisses on any S, so try him on lalapalooza.'[3]

AURIGNACIAN MAN

The Middle Pleistocene Age brought a new type of man into prominence who may have been in existence since the Penultimate Interglacial, about 250,000 B.C. (Swanscombe Man, Thames Valley).[4] In Upper Pleistocene times these people were already differentiated into several varieties, associated with cultural periods termed, in France, Aurignacian, Solutrean and Magdalenian.[5] They mark the intrusion of an entirely different racial and cultural type.[6] Europe and part of Palestine appear to have been populated by more or less pure Neanderthal people. That the two types were contemporaneous is suggested by the mixture of their characters in the skeleton found in the Skhul cave in Palestine [7] and by archaeological evidence.[8]

Aurignacian civilization ranged over an area from Southern France, Northern Spain, England (North and South-east), Italy, Central and Eastern Europe, to Palestine, Africa, Asia, Siberia and China.[9]

---

[1] Müller, M., l.c., II, 184.
[2] Werke II, p. 76.
[3] *Evening Standard*, March 3, 1943, p. 2.
[4] Zeuner, l.c., p. 298.
[5] Aurignac in the Pyrenées district (Haute Garonne), Solutré in the department of Saône-et-Loire, near Mâcon, La Madeleine on the river Vezère (tributary of the Dordogne).
[6] Burkitt, l.c., p. 139.
[7] Zeuner, l.c., p. 241.
[8] Zeuner, l.c., p. 299.
[9] Burkitt, l.c., pp. 145-6.

The new species, the so-called Neanthropic race (*Homo sapiens*) is represented by the remains excavated at Combe Capelle (near Montferrand, Dordogne), at Chancelade (Dordogne), and those found at Crô-Magnon, in the Grotte des Enfants (Grimaldi rocks, near Menton), Galley Hill, Paviland (Wales), Willendorf (Austria), Předmost, Brno (Brünn), Podbaba (Moravia), Cracow (Poland), Gagarino (Don, Russia), Podkumok (Caucasus) and in Siberia.[1]

Combe Capelle man differed widely from Neanderthal man in that he was of rather small stature (5 ft. 3 ins.) with straight and slender limbs. The brow ridges and the jaw were less and the chin more pronounced. The skull was long and narrow, the face broad.[2] The brain must have been fairly large.[3]

Of these varieties 'the Brünn man ... is the oldest, most primitive form in which the transition to *Homo sapiens* is completed. For the first time the calvaria [brain-pan] grows to a lofty vault, although the frontal bone is as yet only a weak approximation to the well moulded, strongly curved, refined forehead. The parietal region rises more steeply; the tenon-shaped prominent occiput is also more steeply arched. The neck is still conspicuously short.' ... 'the mouth is only slightly prominent.'[4] These features of Brünn men call to mind negroid and australoid races.[5]

As the ice was passing away the land remained marshy, humid and swampy. The winters were still so severe and snowy as to impede the growth of trees. The wintery storms brought masses of fine-grained soil, the so-called loess, while better drainage made the soil dry.

The loess played ' an important part in the rise of civilization. It is more suitable for the growth of grass than of trees, and, as the grass dies down and decays each winter, this soil has become very fertile. The fact that it has been free from dense forest, even when the climate was favourable to such growth, has always kept it open country. For these reasons, and especially the last, it has been a zone which men have chosen for movement and for settlement at many periods.'[6] And so ' Brünn man is the dweller in the broad, free steppe. In the loess-clad regions, cut through by broad river-valleys, where herds of large and wild beasts graze—mammoths,

---

[1] De Pradenne, l.c., p. 191.   Schmidt, l.c., p. 63.   Sollas, l.c., pp. 352 ff.
[2] Burkitt, l.c., p. 144.
[3] Keith, l.c., p. 100.
[4] Schmidt, R. R., l.c., pp. 63-65.
[5] Sollas, l.c., p. 456.
[6] Peake, H., and Fleure, H. J. (1927), l.c., pp. 31-2.

bisons, wild horses . . . loess-man created the earliest late Palæolithic culture, the Aurignacian, which lasted until . . . the mammoth had disappeared. . . . When the Magdalenian culture, the latest offshoot of the late Palæolithic, became extended over Europe, the Brünn men either were extinguished, or had become absorbed into the powerful Crô-Magnon race.'[1]

The Crô-Magnon people, living some 80,000 years ago,[2] were tall (from about 5 ft. 10 ins. to 6 ft. 4 ins.), with shins long in proportion to the thigh and the arms, long palms and short fingers.

The brain case was long and capacious (1590–1750 c.cm.),[3] the face disproportionately low and broad, the forehead higher, the chin better developed, the brow ridges less conspicuous, the nose is depressed at the root, rising rapidly, and is long and narrow. Crô-Magnon and Grimaldi people had a palatal arch (*torus palatinus*) like that of primitive negroid races.[4] (See Fig. 3, D_1, D_2.)

On the whole these people were distinguished from previous types by their more human and less brutish appearance, somehow reminiscent of the build of the Red Indians or the Sikhs of the Punjab,[5] and the Gauchos in the Canary Islands, perhaps their last survivors,[6] who were wiped out by the Spaniards in the 15th century.[7]

Chancelade man was of short stature (five feet)[8] and his posture was almost upright ; he had a long and lofty skull, probably with a better developed brain, a high and wide face, a well developed mastoid, strong and prominent cheeks, but lacked the snout-like jaw.[9] 'The elevation of the cranial vault . . . from Pithecanthropus to the Neanderthal, Brünn and Crô-Magnon races, has now reached its maximum. Among the Crô-Magnon people, the Chancelade skull, with a cranial capacity of 1,700 c.cm. excels all the men of the diluvium.'[10]

Sollas has emphasized the resemblance between the Chancelade skull and that of the Eskimo, alongside with similarities of culture.[11]

---

[1] Schmidt, l.c., p. 68.
[2] Tilney, l.c., p. 82.
[3] Burkitt, l.c., p. 144.   De Pradenne, l.c., p. 135.   Sollas, l.c., p. 449.
[4] Keith, l.c., p. 99.
[5] Henderson, l.c., pp. 68–9.
[6] De Pradenne, l.c., p. 135.
[7] Henderson, l.c., p. 77.
[8] De Pradenne, p. 136.
[9] Peake and Fleure. *Hunters and Artists*, p. 59.
[10] Schmidt, l.c., p. 70.
[11] De Pradenne, l.c., p. 185.

De Pradenne, however, points to certain differences of civilization which do not seem to admit of the conclusion that the modern Eskimos are surviving Chancelade people.

Grimaldi man was of short build ($62\frac{1}{2}$–64 inches). His legs were very long compared with his arms, his head bulky and long, the face wide and low, the nose wide ; the floor of the nose ends in two grooves as in negroids, the upper jaw shows marked alveolar prognathism (protrusion of the gums) and the lower jaw seems to recede owing to the hardly prominent chin.[1]

His teeth were of ' remarkable size ' ; ' in area of palate he measured half as much again as we do.' Keith[2] points out, however, that it is not so much the absolute, though modern, size of the brain, but the proportion between this large palate and Grimaldi man's brain which places him beneath modern man. Sollas[3] regards this race as allied to the Bushmen. De Pradenne quotes, with due reservation, Boule who finds " affinities " between Crô-Magnon, Chancelade and Grimaldi men on the one hand, and the existing white, yellow and black races on the other.[4]

The cave-dwellers excavated by Dubois in Wadjak (Java) had large brains in thick skulls, prominent brow-ridges, broad noses and powerful jaws, the latter reminiscent of those of the Rhodesians. Similar types were found in Boskop and T'zitzikama.[5]

Grimaldi people were contemporary with the woolly rhinoceros, mammoth (*Elephas antiquus*), Rhinoceros Merki, which suggests that ' the Grimaldi caves became inhabited at the close, or soon after the close, of a mild or warm period, during which Neanderthal man occupied Europe.' In the lowest stratum stone implements of the Mousterian culture were found . . . ' which record the last Arctic phase of the Pleistocene period—from a time when the French Riviera was warmer than it is in the present day until it fell almost to the temperature of Lapland.' [6]

The fauna of Aurignacian date consisted of animals adjusted to not too cold a climate such as the cave-bear, the cave-lion, the cave-hyena, the mammoth, the woolly rhinoceros, the wild pig, the Irish deer and the bison, while the reindeer was scarce.[7]

---

[1] De Pradenne, l.c., p. 136.
[2] Keith, l.c., pp. 101–102.
[3] Sollas, l.c., p. 452.
[4] De Pradenne, l.c., p. 136.
[5] Henderson, l.c., pp. 78, 8c.
[6] Keith, l.c., pp. 95–6.
[7] Keith, l.c., p. 72. Sollas, l.c., p. 348.

It is interesting to note that the bones of those animals were cut or artificially broken, and charred.

There is thus some indication that people of the Aurignacian period lived on a flesh diet, but by no means exclusively. Sir Arthur Keith calls attention to the molar teeth of Galley Hill men, which ' are worn—not deeply—in the manner seen in the dentitions of races living on a crude vegetarian diet.'[1]

Apart from charcoal, the remains of hearths, flint tools, barbed implements in bone, antlers of reindeer, ivory, necklaces of shells and of perforated teeth, and ornaments have been excavated at Aurignac.[2]

AURIGNACIAN CULTURE

In contrast to Mousterian flake or core tools, upper Palæolithic tools are chiefly made on blades.[3] Early Aurignacian tools are perhaps not so beautiful as the, albeit monotonous, Mousterian implements, but in Middle Aurignacian times the coups-de-poing, discs, side-scrapers, end-scrapers, gravers, and knife blades excel in elegance of the ' stepped ' short, scaly retouch. A further characteristic of this culture is the so-called fluting technique which suggests a high standard of craftsmanship and art.[4]

What may be regarded as distinctive of the Aurignacian age is the manufacture of *secondary* flint implements which enabled craftsmen to make dartheads, awls and pins of ivory or bone.[5]

The Aurignacian industry, although in all probability imported, seems to have been influenced by indigenous Mousterian models. This allows the inference that the people who manufactured them came into contact with one another.[6] The Aurignacians perhaps not only superseded but also mixed with their precursors. This interbreeding and the exchange of their traditional cultural accomplishments may well have raised the level of their civilization as a whole.

To the Aurignacians we can attribute ' the honour of being the world's first artists.'[7] In early Aurignacian times the drawings displayed simple designs such as rows of dots, spiral tracings and

---

[1] Keith, l.c., p. 284.
[2] Keith, l.c., p. 73.
[3] Burkitt, l.c., pp. 139 ff.
[4] Burkitt, l.c., pp. 141–2. Sollas, l.c., pp. 359, 513, footnote [2].
[5] Childe, G. V. (1944). *Progress and Archæology*, p. 14.
[6] Peake and Fleure. *Hunters and Artists*, p. 46.
[7] Davison, l.c., pp. 86–7.

silhouettes of hands.[1] Later on artists traced animal pictures with the finger on wet clay adhering to the walls. Then they began engraving and painting in red or black pigment. With increasing skill the drawing became more elaborate and realistic.[2] The two pictures on Plate No. 4 represent a hunting story. The picture below shows a rufous bison, his flanks transpierced by a javelin whose head lies broken off near him. His belly has been ripped open and his guts sag down bloodily. His head is drawn in and his horns are lowered as though to gore the prone figure of a man before him. On his head the man wears a bird-mask. In the foreground a bird on a pole. On the upper picture (originally on the left) we see a wicked-looking woolly rhinoceros. The two pictures mean to tell us that the hunter has wounded the bison. The bison has killed the man. The rhinoceros has torn open the bison. The man is dead. The bison is dying. The rhinoceros is ambling off. The bird looks on the tragedy from its pole.

Aurignacian artists also skilfully engraved and carved bone, bison's horn and ivory. They manufactured ivory rings, bone awls, pins, and ivory charms in the form of a phallus and its counterpart.[3] ' The animals they modelled in clay have had implanted on them the poise and spirit of life.' [4] (See Plate 5.)

Notable specimens of Aurignacian art are supplied by sculptures such as the two bisons modelled in clay (from the cavern of the Tuc d'Audoubert), and by small statuettes of fat women carved out of mammoth tusks such as the " Venus " figurines found at Brassempouy, Předmost and Willendorf.[5] (See Plate 7.)

Such artistic accomplishments were, at least originally, energized by magic ideas. Sollas[6] quotes Reinach as one who has pointed out that ' all the animals represented are such as are desirable for food : " undesirable " animals, such as lions, bears, and tigers, are never depicted. But it is a widely spread belief, once apparently universal, that the image of an object gives the possessor some sort of hold upon it, and thus, by drawing the likeness of these animals, primitive man might have thought to influence them in the chase. When we speak, M. Reinach remarks, of the magic of the artist's pencil, we use a metaphor which had once a literal meaning.' Similar

---

[1] Peake and Fleure. *Hunter and Artists*, pp. 82–3.
[2] Peake and Fleure, l.c., p. 83.
[3] Sollas, l.c., pp. 367 ff.
[4] Keith, l.c., p. 79.
[5] De Pradenne, l.c., p. 188   Keith, l.c., 106.
[6] Sollas, l.c., p. 423.

K

148   THE INFANCY OF SPEECH

FIG. 21
Sorcerer from Les Trois Frères.   (From Davison)

FIG. 22
(After Count Bégouen.   From Sollas)
Magical Symbolism of the Aurignacian Age.   Sorcerer from Lourdes.   Bearded man with a horse's tail, and lines above the head supposed to be meant for horns

considerations may apply to the drawings discovered in the cavern of Les Trois Frères, and at Lourdes. The former ' presents a remarkable combination of the horns of a stag, a face like an owl's, a long beard, the ears of a wolf, the tail of a horse, the paws of a bear and the feet of a man. The body and thighs are striped, probably to represent the pelt of some animal. It seems to symbolize in one person fleetness, wisdom, penetrating vision, and strength.' [1] (See Figs. 21 and 22.)

The Aurignacian culture resembles the Capsian culture (Capsa is the ancient name of Gofsa in Tunisia). The bearers of this culture and other groups may have migrated into Europe via Sicily and Italy, and settled down in Europe. (Cf. Fig. 23.)

FIG. 23
Capsian Art. Battle of archers. Figures in silhouette. (After Davison)

In some rock shelters in Eastern Spain a culture has been discovered which is cœval with Aurignacian Solutrean and Magdalenian art, but totally different from it, and believed to be of Capsian origin. It consists of usually small pictures of hunting *scenes* in which animals and *human* beings are represented in a most realistic, if inaccurate manner, reminiscent of the paintings of the Bushmen,[2] and of the naturalism of a modern Japanese picture.[3] (Fig. 24).

This art finally decayed into conventionalism [4] (see below, p. 170), a fact deplored by some, yet prophetic of some advance in the development of the rational approach to life as opposed to the purely libidinous one.

---

[1] Sollas, l.c., pp. 399 ff.
[2] Peake and Fleure, l.c., pp. 86-90.
[3] Burkitt, M. C. (1931). ' Most Primitive Art.' In *Early Man*. Benn, London, p. 90.
[4] Peake and Fleure. *Ibid.*, p. 90.

150   THE INFANCY OF SPEECH

Representational art, it is true, is essentially motivated by a need for the gratification of some desire. But the realistic drawings far exceed the results of such activities.

Pictorial art presupposes the ability to single out properties thought to be significant and therefore required to stand out in bright relief. Thus, through abstraction and classification, the

Fig. 24. Bushman Cave Art. A cattle-raid; pursuit by the Kaffirs and rear-guard action. (After Sollas)

hitherto impressionistic world picture assumed an increasingly descriptive, minutely detailed and circumstantial character.

Gilmour [1] has outlined the process of scientific classification as follows. " The classifier experiences a vast number of sense-data which he clips together into classes, each of which is definable in terms of certain specific data. Thus a class of blue things may be made for sense data exhibiting a certain range of colour, and so on. Any given series of data can, of course, be clipped together in a number of different ways, depending on the *purpose* of the classifier i.e., depending on which particular data he is interested in at the moment. . . . Classification, then, has always a pragmatic element, as well as an empirical and a rational one. . . . The purpose of all classification is to enable the classifier to make inductive generalizations concerning the sense-data he is classifying. . . . These generalizations are then used as guides to human action."

It would, however, be rash to assume that the people who had just begun to represent objects of their environment, realized minute *sense-data in isolation*, as the scientist knows them. Rather must we assume that they had to cope with large integral, little differentiated, but not simple wholes. Their activities were energized by primitive impulses either towards or away from an object within its setting. Hence the emotional element which still dominates rationality. But we must not anticipate events. Aurignacian people may be believed to have handled situations not by means of induction based on minute sense-data, but rather under the guidance of a ' *logique des sentiments* ' (Ribot[2]) the sole aim of which is to obtain gratification. In the course of development certain features associated with gratification came, rightly or wrongly, to be considered important and were given prominence in imagery and representation. This accomplishment marks the genesis of abstraction, individualization, recognition of details and complexity of thought, and alongside with it, of animism and magic.[3] It may be added that ' the more firmly man, with his increasing culture, makes an impression upon his environment, the mightier do the " things " which surround him become. . . . This new orientation in the spiritual life was certainly not completed earlier than the transition from Neanderthal man to *Homo sapiens fossilis*.' [4]

---

[1] Gilmour, J. S. (1939). ' Taxonomy and Philosophy.' *The New Systematics*. London, p. 465.
[2] Ribot, Th. (1908). *La logique des sentiments*. Alcan, Paris.
[3] See De Pradenne, l.c., p. 31.—Schmidt, l.c., p. 228.
[4] Schmidt, l.c., p. 93.

The features of Aurignacian and Solutrean cultures indicate the beginning of pictorial magic and of a crude logic as represented by figures of human hands, of hunted animals, of erotic scenes, etc. Ornaments and clothing perhaps imply the principle of possession. The specialization of technical skill probably went hand in hand with the growing complexity of the social structure.[1]

Valuable information as to the actual ways of thinking of Aurignacian man can be attained by interpolating what psychoanalysis has revealed through the investigations of modern primitive races comparable to Palæolithic man.[2]

We do not know whether the similarities of build and of culture were due to a common ancestry of both European, Asiatic and African Aurignacians, or to independent evolution, or to immigration. Be this as it may, we venture to draw some further inferences by interpolation. On a lower rung of the ladder we have Rhodesian man reminiscent of the ape and the negro, somewhere higher up the Aurignacians who foreshadow the now living Bushmen and Hottentots.[3]

Some genetic peculiarities found in both the Bushman and the negro are of value in our investigation. The Bushman is of short stature—a dwarf of not more than five feet. The negro, too, tends to give rise to dwarf varieties such as the pygmies in Uganda, the Akkas in the Sudan, the Malayas and the Philippines.[4] Other peculiarities of growth, for instance, the tendency to retain a forehead bulging forwards, a small mastoid process, the slight development of the brow ridges, a yellowish brown skin, are all embryonic features which the Bushman exhibits.[5] Now, Sir Arthur Keith reminds us that ' dwarf races are not primitive ; rather the opposite. They are races which have been shaped under the influence of a " Peter Pan " tendency—a tendency to retain throughout life the features of body and traits of mind which characterise the youths of a race.' [6]

It is not improbable that ' the American Indian, in all his varieties, is a descendant from a primitive Mongolian type of man,' as ' at various phases of both Pliocene and Pleistocene periods Siberia and Alaska enjoyed a 'temperate climate and were united by a wide land-bridge across which American and Asiatic animals could come

---

[1] See Schmidt, l.c., p. 228.
[2] See Róheim, G., l.c.
[3] Keith, l.c., pp. 360-367.
[4] Keith, l.c., p. 360.
[5] Keith, l.c., p. 360.
[6] Keith, l.c., pp. 358-9.

and go.'[1] The Patagonians, too, may be the survivors of a Palæolithic race, ' representatives of the pioneers who made their way into America from Mongolia in Palæolithic times.'[2]

' The Palæolithic races of Moravia are of great interest to us because of their resemblance to the native Australians. Their skulls have several features in common, and there are striking similarities in their ornaments, decorative patterns, and statuettes.

The only plausible explanation of this puzzling similarity seems to be that both the Australians and the early Moravians left a common home after a cultural tradition had been firmly established there. There is no reason to suppose that the aborigines reached Australia at a very early date, for they had the domesticated dog with them. We can trace Australoid skulls back through the Malay Archipelago to India, and a Central European type of art was practised in South Russia during the late Palæolithic times. So it is possible that the homeland lay between these two countries—perhaps somewhere south of the Caspian Sea. This region has been suggested as the original home of *Homo sapiens*.

Neanderthal men seem to have come from the east, and so again we may ask whether the Australoid branch of *Homo sapiens* became slightly mixed with them, while the Crô-Magnon branch remained pure.'[3]

In South Africa cave life and Palæolithic Aurignacian culture which at Grimaldi came to an end at the close of the Pleistocene period, have persisted into our time.[4]

The modern Australian native seems to be the descendant of the Talgai people which represent the ' earliest form of true *Homo sapiens*.'[5] The aboriginal Australian, in his turn, may have been the common ancestor of both African and European races.[6]

The conclusions drawn from a comparison of existing primitive peoples, dwarf races in particular, from fossils of Aurignacian man, from primitive languages, and from child language, should now facilitate an effort to conjecture the type of language spoken by the people of the Aurignacian type.

---

[1] Keith, l.c., p. 459.
[2] Keith, l.c., pp. 484–9.
[3] Davison, l.c., p. 98.
[4] Keith, l.c., p. 376.
[5] Keith, l.c., pp. 453–55.
[6] Keith, l.c., pp. 712–3.

AURIGNACIAN LANGUAGE

More or less vague surmises have been made as to the development of speech during the period following the experimental stage represented by the hominid types (Neanderthal and the like). The anatomist does not doubt that Aurignacian man, such as Galley Hill man, was able to speak since his brain was certainly of a conformation suggestive of the gift of speech. ' So far as concerns the convolutionary pattern, the Galley Hill man was not inferior to the average modern European. The areas or lobes which are specially associated with the senses of sight, hearing, and touch, were all there ; so, too, were the convolutions which are concerned in speech and in movements of the limbs and body.' [1]

In accordance with the naturalistic tendencies of the Aurignacians as displayed in their art we may expect a language which must have been highly individualistic, varying with the speaker's condition, mood and external circumstances. It was performed all along with postures and gestures, dramatizing these attitudes.

Phonetically we may presume a ' very delicately graduated series of vowels, all of which are capable of being nasalised,' a property still found in the Nama (Namaqua) dialect of the Hottentot language.[2] (See pp. 59, 80.)

The sound table very probably contained a considerable number of clicks and consonants, more often than not shifting to others of a similar sound or articulation. (See above, p. 101.) These noises occurred in beads either alternating with vowels or in ' jaw-breaking ' (= infantile !) agglomerations of consonants, or of clicks and consonants (see p. 71), as can still be found in the Nama dialect.[3]

The meanings of such sound sequences as wholes was greatly dependent on the intonation of the voiced elements, as is still the case in some languages (Chinese, Slavonic languages). This in its turn may have given rise to an immense variegation of sounds in the total patterns.

To say anything about the particular sounds occurring in man's primordial utterances would be mere guesswork. We shall therefore resort again to interpolating only the general pattern under the guidance of such linguistic forms as are still extant in primitive

---

[1] Keith, l.c., pp. 261–2.
[2] Hovelacque, A. (1877). *The Science of Language*. Chapman & Hall, London, p. 48.
[3] Hovelacque, l.c., p. 49.

languages. Let us conjure up the vision of a hungry tribesman who, having lost sight of his companions, is running about in search of them. As he casts his eye over the steppe and listens, the group, laden with the gatherings of the day, is approaching. His attention is riveted on the sight of food, a perception embedded in the emotional background of the event. This in its turn rouses up the gratification previously derived from feeding and awakens the babbling patterns which have for ages gone hand in hand with it. Let, for argument's sake, the following hypothetical example βογαδο βογαδο represent such a babble; in this and the following sound sequences the Greek consonants stand for *any* consonantal element, and the vowels for *any* vocalic element.[1]

On a subsequent similar occasion the same person may utter a *similar* sound sequence, let us say, βόγεζεγεζε, βογιαγια, βογοζογοζο, βοπεπε, βοκακι and so on.

In due course the element βο which happened to occur in some of the previous utterances became a new unit with actions leading to gratification, as this reaction had already been sensitized on previous occasions. The new speech units which man came to single out probably expressed the vision of all sorts of happenings connected with him, the food, the group and so on. Yet the Aurignacian mind had hardly conceived such generic ideas as food, walking, speed and so forth. The meanings which the recurrent components of a sound sequence adopted could therefore not be covered by the categories of modern logic.

The following examples may illustrate the point. In them βαγεδι denotes arbitrary sound sequences in which the phrases rendered in italics are embedded :—

βαγεδι—　*zobáfobafo*
　　　　　zobéhebehe
　　　　　zobiabia　—βαγεδι
　　　　　zobohoboho
　　　　　zodzedze
　　　　　zodadidadi

The first phrase describes (rendered in the European abstract way) that a small man's limbs move vigorously while he is walking. The second denotes the gait of a weak knock-kneed, bandy-legged

---

[1] It will presently become obvious that the example has been cunningly chosen, in order to facilitate the interpolation.

person. The third describes how a long-legged man pushes his legs forward in walking. The fourth describes the gait of a clumsy, slow, heavy and stout man. The fifth denotes brisk and nimble unhindered gait. The sixth version characterizes limping, wearisome and laborious gait. To these more than thirty similar expressions could be added.

They all engrave—to state it in a crude geographical simile—diverse channels in the nervous pathways concerned. A short piece of the route will be traversed by all of them. We mean the part

Fig. 25
The ruts leading from the road-fork towards the observer are deeper than those on the two side-tracks

representing in our Fig. 25 the syllable *zo* which happens to be common to all phrases.

It follows that the ' engram ' (i.e., " the abiding effect of transient stimuli on irritable living tissues ") [1] related to the utterance *zo* representing that which is alike in diverse processes, leads to the isolation of the common mental picture, i.e., abstraction, which is in our case the ' idea ' of *walking*, rendered by the syllable *zo*. The examples have not been made up, but are taken from the Ewe language.[2]

---

[1] Campion, G., and Elliot Smith, l.c., p. 67.
[2] See Westermann, D. *Grammatik der Ewesprache*. As quoted by Lévy-Brühl, l.c., p. 140.

In Aurignacian times utterance was probably still a mere part of a greatly fluctuating behavioural whole. Any part of that pattern could gain preponderance.

Speech was not the algebraic sum of two originally independent units, viz., utterance, on the one hand, and mental phenomena, such as emotions, perceptions, etc., on the other. Child speech and, to some extent, primitive languages suggest that the units which grammar has analysed out originally formed in the minds of the earliest ' homo sapiens ' *one* primary *indivisible whole*. His mental activities and gestures were firmly interwoven by what may here for convenience be described as *random* sequences of sounds. For this reason we are not permitted to assume that primitive man in his first fluctuating lalling consciously attempted to name or label classes of external objects, actions, or other events.

The following example suggests that utterance is fundamentally part and parcel of manipulative behaviour. Esquimaux hunters having killed a whale shriek in a hoarse voice and beat the water with their hands. . . . Here the hunter . . . probably performs homæopathic magic by copying the sounds and gestures of the dying whale.[1]

We can thus far agree with Heyse[2] who almost 100 years ago averred that speaking and thinking are to man according to his nature *one and the same*, one integral act, of which the former is the outer, the latter the inner side. This conception conforms with the theory of identity which we ourselves have made the basis of our considerations. (See p. 11.)

It is, however, not permissible to apply Heyse's assertion to more highly developed forms of speech, as this would lead us to accept the idea of ' speaking ' as mere ' loud thinking,' an idea which is not tenable in the light of further evidence.

How did his fellows react to Aurignacian man's utterances and gestures ? Probably in a manner similar to that of the speaker. Yet not in a mere attempt at mimicking other people's utterances. Our story reveals that such conventional accompaniments of certain behaviours must not be taken as engendered *thesei*, but *physei* ; that is to say, patterns of communication were not intentionally *set up* by man, but *sprang up* perforce as ' collective '[3] responses.

---

[1] Frazer, G. (1933). *The Golden Bough.* Abridged edition, p. 221.
[2] Heyse (1856). *System der Sprachwissenschaft,* p. 40 : ' Sprechen und Denken ist für den Menschen seiner Natur nach *eines*, ein einfacher Akt, von welchem jenes nur die aussere, dieses die innere Seite ist.' As quoted by Marty, l.c., p. 130.
[3] See Lévy-Bruhl (1922). *Les fonctions mentales dans les sociétés inferieures.* Paris.

The dominant feature of babbling expressed the social linkage and the give and take involved in it. Utterances were not 'invented' but found ; they were performed without a preconceived plan.[1]

THE SECOND RUNG OF MEANING

So far we have been looking upon the newly integrated type of speech as the manifestation of psycho-biological *tendencies*. Clicks and consonants are now emotionally linked to a given situation, their 'meaning' being the gratification arising from the intake of something satisfying. Vowels initiated by the soft or by the aspirated attacks (fundamentally grunts or sighs) also lend themselves to expressions of satisfaction. They arise when a danger from within (see p. 57) is being or has been averted (relief, contentment).

Utterances which were originally elicited mainly by vegetative stimuli were later on evoked by occurrences which accompanied and conditioned them. In the further course of development, human beings who primarily *tended* to utter certain sounds began to *intend* them, as soon as they ' expected ' the same sequence of events with the final gratification.

A certain disposition to this change of attitude can be observed in animals. A cat mews, a dog whines, waiting for the door to be opened. The ' meaning ' of these ejaculations is, at first, purely emotional as is confirmed by signs of unrest and seemingly senseless random behaviours, indicative of perplexity. If the door is opened on subsequent occasions, the animal begins to utilize its utterance as a means to an end; the utterance has a ' purpose.' It and the accompanying gesture become ' pointers.' Sound and gesture are originally parts of a whole, enjoying equal rights.[2]

It has been pointed out above (p. 157) that primordial utterance with its accompanying gesture was the socio-affective link between the members of a group, and was therefore ' collective.' The miming action made others ' understand ' the utterance in so far as it made them *do* something. Once this had been realized by the community utterance became an intentional signal.

The ' meaning ' of utterance thus rose to the second rung of the evolutionary ladder : *intention*. Sounds became a means to an

---

[1] ' Man cannot invent, but only find and imitate.' Herder. ' Nicht " wahllos " sondern " planlos " ist also die Devise.' Marty, l.c., p. 158.
[2] Cf. Marty, l.c., p. 45 : ' In Wahrheit sind Laut und hinweisende Bewegung . . . gleichberechtigte Teile eines Ganzen von Verständigungsmitteln. Der Schrei sucht die Aufmerksamkeit anderer auf meine Bewegung zu richten. *Und die Bewegung ist hinweisend, der Laut nicht.*'

NEW-FLEDGED LANGUAGE

end, one could ' will ' something with them. Just as the relation between speech behaviour and consciousness was progressing, i.e., growing by adding level to level, so the ' meaning ' of the word ' meaning ' changed in accordance with the level of consciousness in which it was embedded.

It is worthy of remark that the use of the term ' meaning ' (which is, of course, of much later origin) mirrors that development of its own meaning. In the chapter on onomatopœia (see p. 162 and p. 163) we venture the conjecture that ' meaning ' took its origin from a base kindred to Old German *minne*, ' love.' At the present juncture we recall phrases such as English, ' to mean business,' ' to mean what one says,' ' to mean to do something,' ' to mean no harm ' ; German, ' *ich habe es nicht böse gemeint*,' and the like in which the meaning of ' intention ' is still preserved.

The growing infant furnishes a parallel to the evolutionary ascendancy from pure feeling to aiming. Mme. Spielrein ' has tried to prove that the baby syllables, *mama*, uttered in so many tongues to call the mother, are formed by labial sounds which indicate nothing more than a prolongation of the act of sucking. " Mama " would therefore be a cry of desire and then a command given to the only being capable of satisfying this desire. . . . In so far as it is the continuation of the act of sucking, it produces a kind of hallucinatory satisfaction. Command and immediate satisfaction are in this case, therefore, almost indistinguishable, and so intermingled are these two factors that one cannot tell when the word is being used as a real command and when it is playing its almost magical role.' [1]

Other babbled utterances, such as [*dada, vavava, nana, mamamam*] appearing towards the end of the baby's first year of life, certainly ' mean ' wish fulfilment ; they do not aim at ' labelling ' the objects of the child's desires.[2] Gardiner has elaborately shown that adult speech in our days has ' at first definitely utilitarian aims.' [3]

MAGIC SPEECH

The recognition that an utterance was followed by a gratifying event must have had a miraculous and startling effect on primitive people.

---

[1] *Intern. Zeitschr. f. Psychoanal.*, Vol. VI, p. 401. As quoted by Piaget, l.c., pp. 3-4.
[2] See Bühler, l.c., p. 178.
[3] Gardiner, l.c., pp. 62 ff.

They may have had the same experience as they had when they were discovering the power of the tools, harpoons, arrows, etc., which they had fashioned, or when they conceived the causal relation between the hunting scenes they had drawn in the darkest recesses of caves, with successful hunting.

Just as they had become tool-makers, they became ' language-makers ' a conception still preserved in the word ' poet ' derived from the Greek word *poietés* ' he who makes,' to wit language. Clark has recently pointed out that in medieval English ' maker ' meant ' poet.' [1]

We shall probably not be far off if we locate the event at a period when other factors had already paved the way for the ' creative ' attitude, that is to say, from late Mousterian times, about 100,000 B.C. onwards.

How did the richness of meaningful utterance increase in conformity with the fuller recognition of the vicissitudes and diversities of life ? I am inclined to assign an important, although not all-pervading, rôle in this advance to onomatopœia. It was one of the several imitative gestures which in the world of primitive man were of fundamental importance. To the minds of primitive people any part of another being such as hair, nails and so forth, anything that resembles it in any respect, colour, form, size, behaviour, etc., anything that represents it, is in a mystic, but none the less ' real ' way linked with it, even if separated from it. To be in possession of such parts or representations means power over the original object. And this mastery of the surround is Magic. Just as the drawings, engravings and clay sculptures of the Palæolithic age were the effluence of man's magic attitude so were his utterances. They were audible gestures which in conjunction with and embedded in visible mimetic magic (animal dances and disguises), ' dramatized ' his wants ' that the Powers may be constrained to act imitatively.' [2]

Man found himself multipotent in releasing unseen devices which could themselves exercise power over the animals around him and his mates. He began to master the surround by his utterances which, like all other things, he conceived as mystic spirits flying through the air, the *epea pteroënta*, " the winged words " of Homeric times.

In all these activities Palæolithic ' man being in union with all nature, feels himself closely akin to the beasts also. In his animal

---

[1] Clark, J. M. (1943). *Our Language.* Craig & Wilson, Glasgow. p. 17.
[2] Cf. Schmidt, R. R., l.c., p. 4.

dances and disguises he is himself the animal which he mimics, and through whose voice he " plays the spook." '[1]

Thus we can assume that besides human sounds crude as they were, animal sounds were the most significant and important noises which hunters copied and utilized in the making of language. This stage of meaning—intention—is reflected in the child's speech development. Child psychologists (Meumann, Stern, Piaget and others) have good reasons to believe that such ' words ' as the child copies, by no means signify the objects for which they are employed in adult language. Rather do they express the child's emotional attitude and desires which centre round a given object or event. The child does not mean to name, represent or record them by the sounds he emits, just as the Aurignacians did not paint and draw animals for the sake of making pictures of contemporary beasts for the benefit of posterity. To primitive man as well as to the child, speech is in the first place a magic link between the one who utters and the objects or events he ' means,' i.e., loves or desires. This link between the speaker and the surround has, at the stage under consideration, become a magic tool with which man can handle, through which he can control and direct the movements of animals and of his mates. So much is the union felt that the savage does not find it contradictory to assert that he ' is ' the bird whose name he bears or which is his totem (an object or natural phenomenon mystically linked with primitive man).

The following example demonstrates the growth of ' manipulative speech ' (M. M. Lewis). The expression [mam : am :] was first used by a girl on her 206th day, seemingly as a sign of tenderness. From the 354th up to the 602nd day any person, any kind of food (e.g., bread, bretzel), any other object (e.g., a key to a drawer where chocolate was kept) and any occurrence connected with them (e.g., the dropping of a toy), which served the gratification of the child's desires, evoked the same response. It is thus evident that at this stage the ' word ' defies every attempt at including it in any current grammatical (logical) category.

ONOMATOPŒIA

Just as imitation in general is traceable back to remote ages, so is one of its applications, viz., onomatopœia. The term denotes the faculty to form words by imitation of natural sounds associated with the object named, as well as the words so formed.[2]

---
[1] Schmidt, R. R., l.c., pp. 4-5.
[2] Wyld. Universal Dictionary of the English Language.

Examples of onomatopœia can easily be detected in all languages, e.g., cock-a-doodle-doo, buzz, hum, dangle.[1] Such infantile utterances as [gn-gn] for drinking [2] or such 'standard' expressions as *pitter-patter*, *huff-snuff*, *helter-skelter*, *flogging and flagging*, *murmur*, show how onomatopœia and reiteration collaborate in the formation of words. A parallel is furnished by Polynesian *huhu* 'anger,' literally ' swelled out.' [3] (See also the examples on pp. 124 ff.)

The influence of onomatopœia has been minimized or even denied by many writers. I cannot share this scepticism; it is to be admitted that evidence which Comparative Philology has hitherto supplied is comparatively scanty; yet this may only indicate that the effluences from this tendency are rooted in such deep layers as are beyond the reach of philology. A few examples may illustrate this contention. The French word 'mignon' and the Italian word 'mignolo' (little finger) are assumed to be derivations from the German *minna* 'Liebchen' (sweetheart), which in its turn can be traced back to Old High German *minna* 'love,' 'remembrance,' kindred to English *mind*, *mean*. Yet it remains to be proven that *mignon* was really borrowed from German. The word belongs to a family of words extending over a vast area of the Romance languages.

It appears that—to mention only a few of them—French *minon*, Genoese *miño*, *miñin*, *miñana* denote a little kitten, a pussy.[4] These words are to all appearances onomatopœic petnames, i.e., they depict the mewing of kittens [mimi]. Thence has emanated the meaning of ' dainty girl ' in many dialects of Italy, Northern and Southern France (Provence) and Switzerland (Jura). The petname *mimi* is only used when implicit reference is being made to the daintiness of the beloved. Just as the modern English word *sweetheart* denotes the beloved person by stressing the 'sweetness,' so the children's word *min-nie* itself indicates ' sugar.' [5] The primeval [mamamam] may have converged with [mimimi] and so may have given rise to a sound pattern which served the formation of numerous derivatives. Is it, then, not possible that the Indo-European base of Old German *minna*, ' love,' Greek *ménos*, Latin *mens*, ' desire,' ' longing,' ' wish,' ' craving,' ' will,' ' impulse,' ' pluck,' ' passion,' ' wrath,' and the cognate Greek words *mainás*, ' enthusiastic, inspired, in raptures, in ecstasy, raging,' *mainó*, ' I rage, I rave, I am

---
[1] Graff, l.c., p. 81.
[2] Graff, l.c., p. 298.
[3] Rae, J., in Paget, R., l.c., p. 329.
[4] Meyer-Lübke, W. (1911). *Romanisches Etymologisches Wörterbuch*. No. 5581.
[5] Per Lady Malise Graham. As quoted by Paget, l.c., p. 138.

passionately agitated,' *maiomai*, ' I strive, I aspire,' *maomai*, ' I strive, I intend,' as well as Sanskrit *mánas*, *manyús*, ' wrath, pluck,' *mányate*, ' he thinks,' Latin *memini*, ' I remember,' and Gothic *munan*, ' to mean ' sprang from the same source ? That Latin *mens* and Modern English *mind* mainly denote ' reason ' or ' thinking power ' is no contradiction; there is evidence that these terms originally had an emotional rather than a rational meaning. Erotic linkage was probably the prevailing mode of reference up to the time of the birth of the modern idea of ' meaning.' The term ' meaning ' itself may have been derived from such onomatopœic sounds as expressed feelings of love and tenderness. It is, therefore, not improbable that in late Palæolithic times man was still conscious of the lowest ' meaning of its meaning.' Considering that the magic attitude has not even vanished in our own days, we can readily conceive of those two lower rungs of meaning: affection and intention. The well known, and often misunderstood Old German phrase " Freiheit die ich meine " (freedom that I love) exemplifies this trend of development most clearly. The context in which this phrase occurs leaves no doubt that the poet did not refer to freedom that he *meant*, that is to say a certain kind of freedom to which he was referring among others, but freedom which he *loved* or longed for. If it startle the reader to find that contradictory emotions are assumed to spring from the same base, be he reminded of Catullus' poem

' I hate and love. Why I do so you may perhaps inquire.
I do not know: but I feel it happening, and I am tortured '.
This is one of the pithiest expressions of the modern concept of ' ambivalence.'

In other cases historical comparison speedily uncovers the onomatopœic origin. The sound of the English word ' pigeon ' [pidʒən], from French *pigeon* [piʒõ] does not call to mind any onomatopœic utterance. Yet in conjunction with Italian, New Provençal [pizun], Piedmont, *piviun*, Lombard, *pivion*, Italian *piccione*, *pippione*, Spanish *pichon*, it proves to be derived from Latin *pīpio* [1] in which we can easily detect the onomatopœic sequence [pi : pi] which is a baby-word and a call for chickens in many languages (Italian, German, etc.). This base is also found in Latin *pipilare*, ' to pipe,' Sicilian, *pikkiari*,[2] and can be traced in many other words, e.g., Italian, Catalan, Spanish *pipa*, ' pipe,'

---

[1] Meyer-Lübke, W. (1911). *Romanisches Etymologisches Wörterbuch*. No. 6522a.
[2] *Ibid.*, No. 6522.

L

piva, ' bagpipe,' South-east French *piva*, ' fir-cone,' and its derivations, Italian (Piedmont) *piola*,' tap of a cask,' (Bergell) *pigot*, ' little whistle,' French *pipeau*, ' shawm,' Italian *pipare*, Provencal *pipá*, Spanish *pipar*, ' to smoke,' (Friul) *piva*, ' to whistle,' French *piper*, ' to blow the bird-whistle.' [1]

The above derivations from the primary sucking noise, from the mewing and from the piping sound, as well as many other words, such as the offsprings from Latin *cuculus*,[2] ' cuckoo,' Italian *vecchio cucco*, ' silly old man ' [vet∫ kyk], ' impotent old man ' (Milan dialect) [oef kuk], Provencal *iou kugieu*, ' addled egg,' demonstrate that the power of onomatopœia operates at all times and in all races, which justifies the assumption that it constitutes a hoary linguistic tendency the effluences of which cannot at the present stage be fully assessed.

Although this cannot reasonably be doubted, onomatopœia cannot be assumed to have given birth to the faculty of *producing* sounds. It was only after that faculty had come into existence that man could have availed himself of his ability and proceeded to the intentional and purposive copying of sounds. The manner in which sounds were copied or rendered was seemingly fluctuating and ' arbitrary.' That is why the above examples do not seem to obey the ' sound-laws ' which, according to the Young Grammarians, ' admit of no exceptions.' It is, however, evident that sound-laws can only come into operation after a coherent auditory and articulatory basis of speech has been established. On the rather low level of speech which engenders onomatopœia, articulatory and auditory patterns, the conventional appraisal of the bounds within which their identity is felt to be preserved [3] are only just sprouting.

As regards the correlation between a given mental picture and its sound-pattern, certain predilections can be noted which still await elucidation. In the Ewe language the reiterated [l] sounds in the verbs : *zohloyihloyi*, ' to go about with many dangling objects or clothes,' *zolumolumo*, denoting the hurried running of small animals like rats or mice, *zoŵlaŵla*, ' to walk away, fast and unhindered,' [4] seem to depict the same fluctuation, as was seen in the [lululu] of the girl cited by Steinthal. (See p. 124.) The Ewe verbs *zatakataka*, ' to walk blindly and carelessly,' *zatyatya*, ' to

---
[1] Meyer-Lübke, W. (1911). *Romanisches Etymologisches Wörterbuch*. No. 6520.
[2] Meyer-Lübke. *Ibid.*, No. 2360.
[3] See Graff, l.c., pp. 224-5.
[4] Westermann, D. *Grammatik der Ewesprache*. As quoted by Levy-Bruhl, l.c., pp. 140 ff.

NEW-FLEDGED LANGUAGE 165

walk fast,' bring to mind the obviously onomatopœic English expression *pitter-patter* and others. Words of the Dieyerie language [1] such as *boonoonoo*, ' itching,' *bunyabunyina*, ' trotting pace,' *doomoodoomoora*, ' round,' *koodakoodarie*, ' very crooked,' *kunthakunthuna*, ' shaking,' *nokooloonokooloo*, ' continually repeating,' call to mind the repetitive gestures which may have accompanied them originally. Here the sound elements as such are of no import as it is only the large aggregate that is ' descriptive ' in the manner of *tweedledum and tweedledee*.

SYMBOLIC LANGUAGE

It has repeatedly been pointed out that the individual, his utterances, his gestures, and behaviour originally formed one integral unit with the surround. The integration of voicing and clicking brought greater multiformity alongside with differentiated mental experiences. The primitive grouping of experiences into classes of like and unlike events is motivated by the need to discriminate between what is aimed at and what is to be avoided.

The noises that have so far been traced back to their source were first embedded in behaviours involving mental states which the rational mind ' classifies ' as feelings of love and later of power.

At a still later stage of man's cultural development emotional and intentional language became pictorial.[2] This ornamental epithet needs some comment. If a given utterance is—at the level under consideration—said to be a ' picture ' of an object or event, this can be taken literally only in the case of onomatopœic noises. A baby-word like [tata], [mama] in conjunction with other gestures, however, can be styled a picture from the angle of the magic mind which feels the ' likeness,' the unit of the utterance and its reference, viz., sucking, i.e., the union with the mother ; in other words, to the magic mind such words picture or ' mean ' the occurrence which engendered them, and in which they were embedded.

The nominalist who holds that words of modern language are realities merely within their own right but have no close and invariable association with other realities (objects, events, ideas), is aware that magic picture-thinking and picture-speaking is what is generally meant by symbolism, i.e., the employment of symbols for representation. A symbol is a sensual unit, an ultimate, indivisible, and above all un-willed (involuntary) pattern of a distinctive

---
[1] Curr, E. M. (1896). *The Australian Race*. See above, pp. 125ff.
[2] Cf. Howe, l.c., p. 37.

significance. It is a section of reality inasmuch as it has sprung from the primary mode of reference, and is now embedded in a more differentiated field of reference. The ' objects ' within the referential field are classified and related to the symbol in a magic manner. That is why symbols ' mean ' something that cannot be communicated rationally. The culture of a given social group is ' felt ' by its members through their common symbolism.[1] This is clearly borne out by the present-day fashions of name-giving. From time immemorial persons have been given names which are meant to endow them with certain outstanding qualities, e.g., English *Constance*, *Prudence*, *Strong*, *Dare*; Greek *Kleisthenes* (strong in calling). For the same reason children in our days are given names of their forebears, which are to perpetuate their ' spirit ' and the qualities implied. The *Sunday Express* has recently [2] reported this Yugo-slav custom : ' When a Yugo-slav soldier dies for his country and his body cannot be found, his *name*, spoken into an open grave by a relative, is buried instead.' Here we can still observe the primeval thing-word unit which is still tyrannizing the populace of the world, with the exception of some philosophically-minded savants and poets who have severed the bond between words and things.[3]

We shall now follow up the development of symbolism during the Magdalenian Age.

THE MAGDALENIAN AGE

Aurignacian culture was gradually superseded by the so-called Magdalenian type, except in those dry loess areas which, during the second maximum of the last (Würm II) glaciation (about 70,000 B.C.) were invaded by the Solutreans. These foreign hordes probably came from the East, and imported their peculiar industry.[4]

Magdalenian culture was for some time cœval with Aurignacian culture, the latter making its way in the South of France, Central Europe and South-West Russia, the former thriving in France (La Madeleine) and Southern England (Creswell Crags in Derbyshire, Kent's Cavern in Devonshire).

---

[1] See Spengler (1917). *Der Untergang des Abendlandes*, pp. 223 ff. As quoted by Eisler, *Handwörterbuch der Philosophie*.
[2] 1944, July 2, p. 6.
[3] See Christian Morgenstern's poems and their interpretation, by Spitzer, L. (1918). *Die groteske Gestaltungs-und Sprachkunst Christian Morgensterns*. In *Motiv und Wort*. Reisland, Leipzig.
[4] Burkitt, l.c., p. 152. Keith, l.c., p. 224.

The Solutreans dwelled in hut-shelters at a time when Europe was covered first by tundra and later by steppe and forest. They hunted wild horse, cattle and reindeer which were their principal animal food. The first intruders were not skilled in the forging of weapons. They had brought with them, however, a new technique (pressure flaking) which they later on combined with the Aurignacian technique. They probably held the position of great folk in the midst of the Aurignacian crowd with whom they intermingled little by little.[1]

The advance in craftsmanship brought about implements with good points and sharp edges and of beautiful design known as laurel-leaf and willow-leaf patterns. (See Fig. 26.)

Only a comparatively short period of independent existence was allotted to the Solutreans when they were superseded by the Magdalenians. These enjoyed a longer life span, enduring the closing phase of the Ice Age up to about 20,000 B.C.[2]

The chief representative of the Magdalenian Age is Chancelade man (Chancelade, Dordogne). These people were perhaps the descendants of the Aurignacians who had withdrawn into the mountains before their Solutrean oppressors and who had finally driven them out towards the East.[3] ' They returned to their old hunting grounds, but in the meantime the forests had grown up, so that they developed as isolated communities, having few, if any, relations with one another in different parts of the Eurasiatic continent.'[4]

' The face of the Chancelade man appears to be flat because of the peculiar configuration of his cheek bones and Zygomatic arches. . . . These bony struts give attachment to a pair of principal chewing muscles ; the stronger these muscles are, the stouter, and more prominent are the bony arches.' This feature is particularly developed in the skulls of the Eskimos. Yet his projecting jowls and chin, and the palate within the modern range of measurements [5] bring Chancelade man nearer to highly evolved man.

Among the animals (mammoth, bison, horse, fish) the reindeer was abundant. The fact that it penetrated as far south as Mentone indicates the arctic climate of the period,[6] with forest (pine followed

---

[1] Peake and Fleure, l.c., pp. 35-52.
[2] Zeuner, l.c., p. 294.
[3] Henderson, l.c., p. 89.
[4] Peake and Fleure, l.c., p. 58.
[5] Keith, l.c., pp. 85-7.
[6] Burkitt, l.c., p. 155.

168   THE INFANCY OF SPEECH

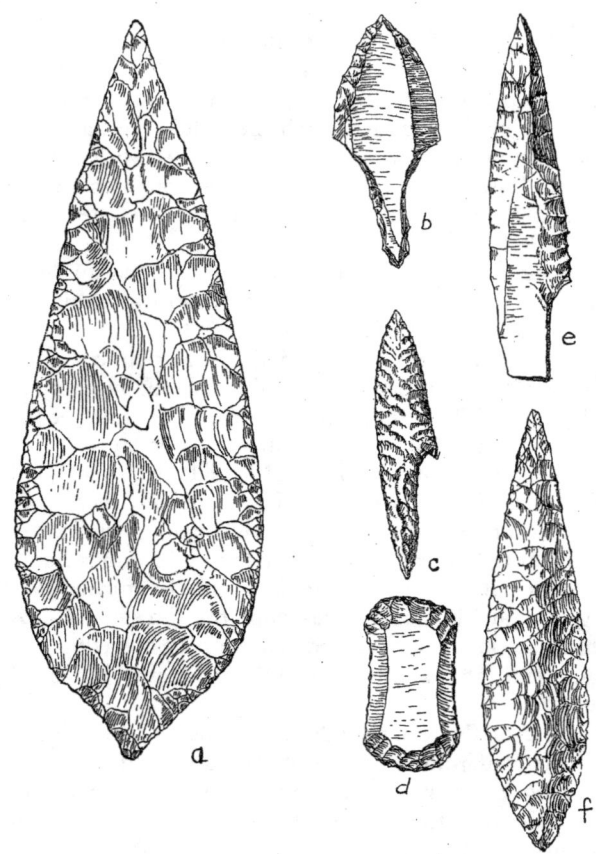

FIG. 26
Solutrean Flints.   (After Davison)
a, Large votive ' laurel leaf ' flint.   d, Double scraper.
b, c and e, Shoulder points.   f, Small ' laurel leaf.'

by oak)[1] and tundra ensuing the steppe conditions of Solutrean times.[2] It may be assumed that the Magdalenians were not only Eskimo-like in appearance but may have lived a life similar to that of the present-day Eskimos, Algonkians and Athapascans.[3]

Early Magdalenian implements which evolved out of the

---
[1] Peake and Fleure. *Hunters and Artists*, p. 95.
[2] Burkitt. *Ibid*.
[3] Sollas, l.c., pp. 591, 596.

NEW-FLEDGED LANGUAGE 169

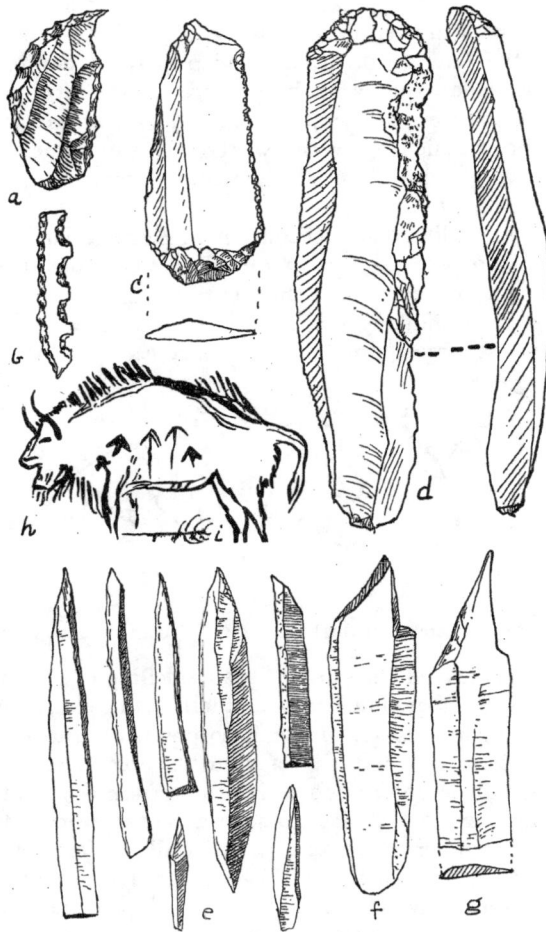

FIG. 27
Magdalenian Flint Implements. (After Davison)

a, 'Parrot-beak' graver.
b, Notched flint for smoothing spear or arrow shafts.
c, Combination scraper and graver.
d, Scraper, front and side views.
e, Small gravers.
f and g, Graver.
h, Bison, with arrows painted on its side.
i, Drawing of a feathered arrow (?)

Aurignacian tools[1] were mostly bone lance points, which later on were supplemented by more and more elaborate types of harpoon,

---

[1] Peake and Fleure. *Hunters and Artists*, p. 53.

besides beautiful scrapers, gravers, awls, made of blades, bone, horn, antler and ivory, and shell-necklaces.[1]

Towards the end of the Magdalenian period round scrapers, curved knife blades, the parrot-beaked graver, the large pyramidal core-scraper and core-graver, and small shoulder-points characterized by a ' nibbling ' retouch, appear in Northern Spain, France, Belgium, England (Devon, Derbyshire), Switzerland, Germany, Poland and Moravia.[2] (Fig. 27.)

Magdalenian art like that preceding it in Aurignacian time is extremely concrete. (See Fig. 28.) ' This need not mean that Magdalenians were incapable of abstract thinking. It does probably indicate that their thinking was habitually as concrete as possible,[3] Such traits are still recognizable in African races.

Fig. 28
Magdalenian Art. Sketches of the human face. (After Breuil. From Sollas)

Towards the close of the period ' the modelling of the inner part of the figure was abandoned. Nevertheless, the clearly indicated outlines give an impression of living corporeality, and of unusual command of form. . . . . It is a return to the archaic, but with that commanding skill in delineation which came from the zenith of the coloured mural art.'[4] ' At last to such an artist, who included all tones in his instrument, and who wrought all his forms to reality, the naturalistic presentation of life was no longer the ultimate aim.'[5] A highly conventionalized style developed, the naturalistic representations of the objects were replaced by symbolic pointers. ' Thus a horse's head viewed full-face degenerated by stages into a trident, that is, into a symbol indicating mane, two ears, and length ; or simple geometric patterns and " suggestion " pictures, such, for example, as a herd of reindeer of which the foremost and hindmost

---

[1] Burkitt, l.c., p. 154.
[2] Burkitt, l.c., p. 157. Sollas, l.c., p. 513, footnote 2, p. 593.
[3] Childe, V. G. *Man Makes Himself*, pp. 63-4.
[4] Schmidt, l.c., pp. 141-2.
[5] Schmidt, l.c., p. 139.

animals alone were figured, the rest of the picture being merely a maze of lines indicating a forest of antlers.'[1] (See Plates 5, 6.) Such patterns alongside linear meanders of the late Magdalenian period (Isturitz) constitute ' a sort of shorthand in animal representation.[2] A similar artistic approach is still maintained by the Bushmen.[3]

The high incidence of very useful and variegated, but by no means beautiful stone tools may be regrettable from the artist's point of view.[4] Yet, to the impartial onlooker Magdalenian culture marks the time when active pictorial magic underlying cave-painting was changing its motive and was thus indicating the birth of rational thought. In the Magdalenian world an entirely different mode of classification was taking root : Man's thousandfold experiences came to be sorted, listed, and strung together according to new principles of relevance, among which those of form, number, possession, and happening played a prominent part, whilst the temporal aspect and the idea of mere existence were—significantly—absent.

MAGDALENIAN LANGUAGE

We can, under the guidance of the foregoing considerations, conjecture the unfurling of utterance during the Magdalenian period.

Every fresh attempt at artistic representation is naturalistic. The artist depicts his surround as it appears to him and as he wishes it to appear to others. In a more advanced stage he, as well as the thinker, tends to single out what *he* deems essential. In giving the distinctive features due prominence he produces a more or less stylized picture.

In the same manner utterance loses its onomatopœic realism ; its symbolism, originally highly descriptive, becomes merely suggestive of the picture it used to conjure up and so opens up the way to " shorthand speaking."

Magdalenian art does not, however, warrant the assumption that such highly abstract verbalization had reached its zenith. Some linguistic patterns which are still preserved in some African and Asiatic languages seem to constitute a fair analogue to Magdalenian art and technique. To begin with a simple though by no means

---

[1] Burkitt, M. C. (1931). *Most Primitive Art. In Early Man,* p. 88.
[2] Schmidt, l.c., p. 144.
[3] Sollas, l.c., p. 410.
[4] De Pradenne, p. 112.

172   THE INFANCY OF SPEECH

primeval pattern, let us have a glance at a phrase taken from a tale in the Ssubija language (a Bantou dialect).[1]

ba	kazana	abo		ba
Persons	girls	here they persons		they persons
		'these girls'		
	mu-ntu		*mu-lotu*	
	person man		person beautiful	
		'a beautiful person'		
bumwe		*bu*	*siku*	*ba-*
she quality one		quality	night	persons
	kazana	*abo*		
	girls	the they persons here		
ba		*ti*	*ba*	*ya*
they (persons)		say	they (persons)	go
	'one night the girls decided to go out'			
n	–	*tsi* – *tsi*	–	*samo*
it is		thing thing		tree
		'it is a tree'		
n	–	*zi* – *zi*	–	*samo*
it is		things things		tree
		'they are trees'		

In Zulu the English sentences : (1) 'our handsome man whom we love, appears' and (2) 'our handsome men whom we love, appear,' would run :

(1) *umuntu*	*wetu*	*omuchle*	*uyabonakala*	*simtanda*
man	ours	handsome	appears	we love
(2) *abantu*	*betu*	*abachle*	*bayabonakala*	*sibatanda*
men	ours	handsome	appear	we love

Jespersen,[2] in quoting the above examples from W. A. I. Bleek's Comparative Grammar, emphasizes the luxuriant growth of concord and the redundant repetitions of reminders (as he significantly terms the prefixes), but does not hint at the origin of the grammatical customs. If, furthermore, Sir Harry Johnston[3] tells us that, for instance, the prefixes *ba* and *bu* were formerly *baba* and *bubu*, i.e., babbling patterns, we have here the ' missing link.'[4]

These 'reminders' tell of the all-pervading power of the two previous epochs of erotic and conative meaning. The then

---
[1] Finck, F. N. (1910). *Die Haupttypen der Sprachbaus.* Teubner, Leipzig, pp. 48–68.
[2] Jespersen, O. (1922). *Language.* Allen & Unwin, London, p. 353.
[3] *The Uganda Protectorate* (1902), 2.891. Quoted by Jespersen, l.c., p. 315.
[4] Cf. p. 129.

prevalent phonetic patterns are still in force, but are employed for less emotional and more cognitive purposes.

Traces of the same tendency can—I submit—be found even in highly developed and more 'logical' languages. In Turkish one says *ben-im ev-im*, 'my house,' actually : of me, house me ; in Hebrew the article recurs in phrases such as *hajōm hazē*, 'this day,' literally 'the day the here (and now)' ; *hā-ir hagǝdōla*, 'the big city,' literally 'the city the big.'

Although these idioms have attained to a comparatively high degree of grammatical specialization in which endings and the like play a prominent part, the primary rhythmical recurrence of sound sequences, i.e., the babbling character, is still shining through. Reiterative speech, once the offspring of primordial erotic feelings, now proves to be capable of serving entirely novel purposes. It has greatly contributed to the differentiation of language into parts in their own right, although still embedded in the whole of the utterance. Soon they will take their stand and lay claim to more freedom of movement.

In our, though by no means primeval, examples we have seen how one distinctive sound aggregate endowed with conceptual meaning has emerged. It is still embedded in a rather long sequence, as the crystal in the making is still immersed in the liquid. As soon as it has emerged it gains prominence whilst the original solution is more or less losing significance.

The original unity is still noticeable in many primitive languages. For instance the language of Greenland cannot claim to be capable of constructing sentences, i.e., utterances, in which only free forms and no bound forms occur. (A speech form which can be uttered alone with meaning is a free form ; one that cannot be uttered alone with meaning is a bound form, e.g., *-ish* in 'boyish,' *-s* in 'hats.' A free form such as 'boy,' which does not consist entirely of lesser free forms, is a word.)[1] In the language of Greenland the parts of speech can never present themselves as independent forms; they help to build up huge agglomerates of bound forms which are all pregnant with lucid pictorial meaning, for instance: [okxakx] 'tongue,' [okxa-luzpokx] 'he spins long yarns, swaggers, blusters, talks big,' where [luzpokx] denotes possession founded on abuse and thus gives the term an ironical connotation, in contrast to [okxaRpokx] 'he says something,' [okxa-lu-tuakx] 'a certain

---

[1] See Bloomfield, L. (1939). *Linguistic Aspects of Science.* The University of Chicago Press, pp. 23–30.

narrative,' the suffix [tuakx] denoting individuality, thus literally 'an individual abuse of the tongue.' The suffix [šhakx] ' fitted for,' and one denoting negation bring about [okxa-lu-tua-sha-kxa-jilakx] ' something not endowed with something fitted for a certain narrative,' that is to say, he has or had nothing to narrate.[1] Similar conditions are found in certain North American languages.[2]

It can be seen that even in the comparatively advanced primitive languages the phonetic body is still rather exuberant and carries a highly specialized pictorial meaning. Viewed from the angle of modern language ' the bigger and longer the words, the thinner the thoughts.'[3]

The Ssubija language furnishes an example of what aspects of relevance may be singled out and become the principles of grammatical classification. There are no less than seventeen categories expressing person, persons, living being, living beings, piece, quantity, thing, things, organism, organisms, individual, small, small ones, quality, direction, besides several forms of the personal pronoun.[4] (Cf. pp. 180 ff.)

So far we have been viewing language as an activity the evolution of which ' finds expression not merely in the structure of the individual but also in those associations of individuals which we call communities.'[5] We have not overlooked the awakening of the ' self,' but note that the self has so far remained embedded in the community like the individual cell in the tissue.

Anthropological investigations make it at least not improbable that in the primeval community there was no differentiation of rank.[6] In the Aurignacian and Magdalenian ages, however, evolution produced certain human beings in whom the mental faculties so far described were developed to a degree far surpassing that attained by their fellows. Those Proto-individuals emerged as spontaneous variations, assumed leadership and became sorcerers and ultimately priest-kings.[7]

The crowd, no doubt, were in possession of many facts concerning their walks of life, they knew their crafts and trades such as fishing, hunting, tool-making and they had a personal and social culture.

[1] See Finck, N., l.c., pp. 31-46.
[2] See Spencer, l.c., pp. 269 ff.
[3] See Jespersen. *Language*, p. 432.
[4] Finck, l.c., pp. 52 ff.
[5] Kerr, l.c., p. 197.
[6] Cf. Davison, l.c., p. 77.
[7] See Heard, Gerald (1929). *The Ascent of Humanity*. Jonathan Cape, London, p. 67.

The sorcerer, however, was 'in the know,' he was aware of the 'essence' of things. In his mind events were organized in a coherent framework, there was a 'system' in his knowledge of the surround. He was able to single out essential characters from the bulk of trivial things, and he probably brought order and stability into behaviour, custom, trade and sex relationships. In order to do this he had to establish a kind of unwritten code which was henceforth handed down to posterity by tradition.

Such requirements of social, economic, and religious life necessitated a language of a fairly stable form and meaning. The sorcerer became not only the first book-keeper, but also the first poet, the 'maker' and preserver of such linguistic forms as custom had engendered.

The above interpolation is somehow mirrored in the growth of speech in early childhood. There are many 'sorcerers' around the small child; his parents, nurses, elder brothers and sisters and so forth perform things strange, miraculous and overwhelming. They form a social group which is quite different from the undifferentiated social union in which he has hitherto been living. That group is characterized by a more or less conspicuous hierarchy of ranks, and by an, albeit unwritten, code of behaviour to which all members of the community adhere. They utter words which work wonders inasmuch as these utterances bring about fulfilments with so much certainty as to make them appear infallible magic formulas. No doubt the child in an endeavour to overcome his inferiority and in his striving after aggrandisement, tries to emulate his elders as best he can. He grows into the social group by adjusting his behaviour to theirs. It is here that the child's individualism comes to grips with sociality, and it is the first time that his mode of uttering is yielding up to it.

The results are usually said to be due to imitation. In view of the diverse meanings of the term 'imitation'[1] it will be well to elucidate *how* this somewhat lengthy and, to all appearances, laborious process takes place. That the child simply throws his babble overboard and adopts adult speech is, we believe, a priori unlikely because it is contrary to all we know about learning. All 'new' functions are based on old and well established ones, as walking, writing and pointing are based on crawling, grasping, reaching for things and so forth. The child in an endeavour to use words imposed upon him begins to bridle his impetuous and

---

[1] See Valentine, l.c., pp. 185 ff.

everchanging language and singles out the nearest babble. In this manner ' stomach,' ' garden,' ' chocolate pudding ' are rendered as *tum-tum*,[1] [*gaga*], [*kokopumpum*].

Somehow the sorcerer and priest handled the vulgar tongue comparable to a meadow which flourishes and blossoms almost without man's aid, and turned it into artificial language analogous to a garden fenced in by the hand of man and demanding unremitting attention if it is to produce good fruit.[2] Parallels suggestive of this further development will be given presently (see pp. 180ff.).

The next chapter will, after briefly summing up the natural evolution during the Old Stone Age, contrast the collective, spontaneous, although no longer brutish yet still irrational, undesigned trend of linguistic evolution with the more rational, intellectual, cognitive and purposive line of development of the next period, when man is found to be more alive to the needs of his cultural achievements.

---

[1] Jespersen, O. *Language*, p. 179.
[2] See Weise, l.c., p. 181.

CHAPTER VI

FULL-FLEDGED LANGUAGE

THE AZILIANS

THE LAST link in the chain between what Elliott Smith[1] termed Experimental Types of Mankind, and *Homo Sapiens*, is perhaps represented by the " Lady of Lloyds," excavated when the foundation of Lloyd's building in Leadenhall Street, London, was laid. This woman lived in Mousterian times or earlier, but did not belong to the Neanderthal race.

The hind part of her skull and the part covering the " association areas " of the brain are well developed and the bone is thinner than in previous races.[2] These had been evolved during the upheavals of the glaciations, played their part for a longer or shorter period, bred more or less adapted variants and vanished. The human types of the ensuing period show that man was becoming ' modern ' [3] in respect of physique and culture.

Towards the close of the Pleistocene period a change of climate adverse to hunting [4] took place which turned steppes partly into desert, partly into forests. This made the reindeer of Magdalenian time migrate, and caused some Magdalenians to follow them up north. Their place was again taken by invaders from the East, the Azilians, the remains of whom were found in a stratum which follows the Magdalenian strata in orderly sequence.[5] These hordes perhaps intermingled with the remaining Magdalenians who had turned more or less into food-gatherers and were leading a life of extreme poverty and destitution perhaps like that of the natives of Tierra del Fuego. The only achievement seems to have been the domestication of the dog and the introduction of rough pottery.[6]

The Azilians, dominant from about 15,000 to 8,000 B.C.,[7] took over the Magdalenian technique of making flint and bone tools ; the wonderfully made Palæolithic implements gave way, however, to somewhat " degenerated " small and poorly fabricated ones. This

[1] Smith, Elliott, *Human History*, p. 98.
[2] Davison, l.c., p. 75.
[3] Fallaize, l.c., p. 30.
[4] Burkitt, l.c., p. 240. Sollas, l.c., p. 594.
[5] Keith, l.c., pp. 78-9.
[6] Peake and Fleure, l.c., pp. 96-98, 120.
[7] Cf. Zeuner, l.c., p. 200.

decay in artistic culture marked a break which was followed by the so-called mesolithic or Epipalæolithic civilization. Azilian achievements, although negligible from the artist's point of view, have, however, a strong bearing on the development of man's outlook which is in marked contrast to that of previous periods of the Old Stone Age.[1]

Among the implements, curious rounded pebbles marked with

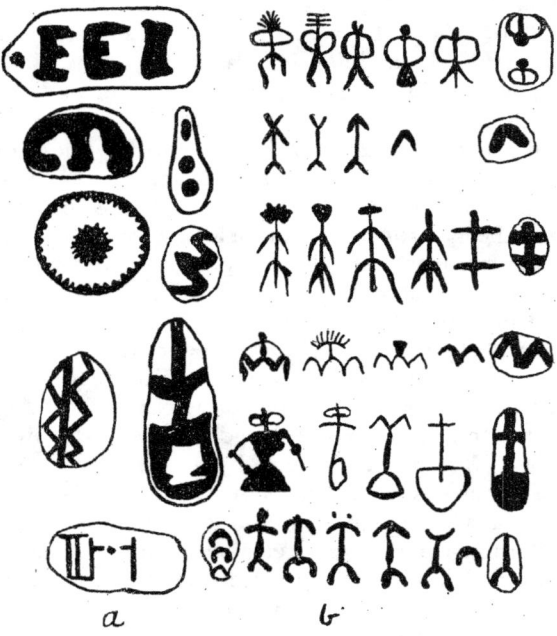

FIG. 29
Azilian Art. (After Davison)
a, Painted pebbles.
b, Diagrammatic drawings of the human figure from Spanish rock-paintings similar to the designs on Azilian pebbles.

painted signs resembling hieroglyphics were found.[2] (See Fig. 29.) It has hitherto not been possible to decipher them or to give any interpretation of their meaning; they seem to bring to light, however, that the Azilians had abandoned realistic representation. The soul of Primitive Imagery became Symbolic Thought.[3]

[1] See Schmidt, l.c., pp. 128, 202.
[2] Burkitt, l.c., p. 241. Keith, l.c., pp. 78–9. Peake and Fleure. *Hunters and Artists*, pp. 98–101.
[3] Schmidt, l.c., p. 147.

A similar trend is manifest in the rock-pictures of the Sierra Morena, in Southern Andalusia, and in Western Spain. Here also ' the human and animal conventionalized figures of the latest Palæolithic, stiffen into purely geometrical abstractions. . . . For the first time . . . figures with rays, suns, and stars, diagrams of points and circles appear among these symbols.' [1]

The evolutionist cannot permit himself to regard the magnificent drawings of Magdalenian times as superior to the schematic ones of Azilian time, if he intends to classify them from the purely temporal angle and in respect of intellectual evolution. Realistic and naturalistic representation indicates that the artist is enthralled by his surround. It is noteworthy that the present-day Bushman or Eskimo child, like his forebears, does not exhibit any inclination to transgress the boundary within which nature confines him.

Modern negro children and the children of white races draw in a more abstract and less realistic fashion like the Azilians. They do not copy naïvely, but transform reality in conformity with an idea or scheme, as when, for instance, people's legs are attached to their heads, or a person's stomach or legs can be seen through the outer covering.

Psycho-analytical experience has revealed that the child places in the foreground those details which are of positive emotional interest to him. He neglects, lets slip into the background or represses such objects as would conjure up unpleasant experiences, frustration and tabooed ideas. This is particularly true in respect of the human body as the focus of the child's primitive libidinous impulses. If the child is not supposed to know anything about his parent's sexual organs (which to the child's mind include also the whole digestive and urinary tracts), then they do not appear in his drawings. If digestion stands in the foreground of the child's interest, the stomach will be drawn rather than the neck. If a child fears his father's penetrating and searching look, he will not draw his eyes, but may, for example, put several long lines down the face to indicate that the father is buck-teethed.

This ' ideoplastic ' approach in advanced races, as opposed to the ' physioplastic ' fashion of Magdalenian fame, goes hand in hand with the growth of the faculty of abstracting and of forming general concepts out of percepts.[2]

---

[1] Schmidt, l.c., p. 202.
[2] See Giese, F. (1922). *Kinderpsychologie. Handbuch d. Vergleichenden Psychologie*. Reinhardt, München. I, p. 414 ff. Verworn, R. (1917). *Zur Psychologie der Primitiven Kunst*. Jena. Schmidt, l.c., p. 204.

It seems that in pre-Azilian times behaviour was only little inhibited, an assumption which is corroborated by Róheim's observations on Central Australian natives who give free rein to their primal demands, so that " there is an immediate transition of the direct genital libido from the parents to their playmates, to all the children of the same age. . . . Repression has not reached so far into the depths of the human psyche as in civilization." [1]

Seen from the primal libidinous angle the drawings of children of the savage and of pre-Azilian man are as ' true ' to nature as the ' flowery,' lucid, pictorial languages of primitive races are and probably were up to some thousands of years ago.

AZILIAN LANGUAGE

In Azilian time, however, repression or inhibition set in and with ,it the purely emotional and the more conative meanings of pictorial and symbolic representation and of human utterance were being overridden by cognitive meaning. The referential modes of erotic linkage and of desire and intention gave birth to that of mere ' indicating ' in the same way as a child's grasping and reaching for an object turns at the age of about fourteen months [2] into pointing. Language ascended the third rung of meaning where it is pre-eminently, or at least ostensibly, used as a *sign*, *label* or *pointer*.

Any part of the whole bulk of linguistic forms as had outlasted the emotional and conative stage could be used for this purpose. A child may indicate water by a sucking noise, or reiterative gurgles like *gu-gu*,[3] a horse by *click-clack* and later by *gee-gee*, a chicken by *kwak-kwak* (Fenton).[4] Many examples of that predilection for onomatopœia and alliteration can be found in the literary records of all ages. The Homerian *polyphloisboio thalasses*, ' the uproarious sea,' is distinguished by the recurrence of [l] calling to mind *lululu* of Steinthal's girl (see p. 124), and of hissing and aspirated sounds indicative of noisy sipping. The poet seems to have compared the rushing of the sea with sipping and lapping noises.

Such labels were at first embedded in gesture. A child aged one year and two months who accompanies the utterance *wound and wound* (round) by rotational movements with the hand, a cry by shaking the head, and so forth,[5] goes over the same ground.

---

[1] Róheim, l.c., p. 98.
[2] Valentine, l.c., pp. 401–2.
[3] See above, p. 115.
[4] Valentine, l.c., pp. 413–4.
[5] See Valentine, l.c., p. 416.

FULL-FLEDGED LANGUAGE

Inhibition tends to hide the overt symbolic aspect of human activities and contents itself with mere hints. Thus representation and utterances grew more and more colourless; the latter were divested of their mimicking accompaniment. The process of reduction did not stop here. So much did inhibition take off the edge of utterance itself as to render its original palpable reference to sucking and crying with all its implications, more and more obtuse and obfuscated.

In the Azilians this result was probably aided by another concurrent process. So far we have seen man as driven by his impulses and enthralled by the surround. ' With the revolutionary change, from man-enslaved-by-nature to man-dominating-nature, the mental transformation is completed, and the original unity becomes divided into two regions : World and Ego, outer and inner.' [1]

This achievement is the outcome of the struggle between man's inherited tendencies (Id) and his surround. Man had become a subject as opposed to objects. This is " the primary division in the process which leads to the acquisition of knowledge." It " consists not only of those sense-impressions which go to form what we call the external world, but also of all the past and future states of the thinker (including feelings). Thus the primary duality is not one of mind as opposed to matter, but of the ever-present subject 'I,' as opposed to the objects of thought of that subject, these objects including both ' mind ' and ' matter '." [2]

Yet the Azilians merely set the ball in motion, and it has by no means reached its goal.

THE UPPERMOST RUNG OF MEANING

It was thus through inhibition, abstraction and analysis of qualities that integral responses involving emotion, intention, and perception in a hierarchy, underwent dissociation.

In reshuffling and recombining the elements, more often than not disregarding the original meaning-compound (see above, pp. 79ff.), man created two henceforth distinctive and more or less separated classes of sense data, viz., objects and events on the one hand, and symbols denoting them on the other. Some such symbols are termed ' names,' i.e., linguistic expressions for an object, an

---

[1] Schmidt, R. R., l. c., pp. 13-14.
[2] Gilmour, John, l.c., p. 463.

individual, or a class of objects. Properties of 'interest' usually guide us in giving a name.[1]
Other 'parts of speech' act as 'instruments of noting'[2] properties, modes of acting, relations and so on.
Here again the growing child demonstrates how it is done. He hears long sound sequences uttered by the ' sorcerers ' around him at a speed so terrific as to make it impossible for him to make out more than a blurred symphony of sounds. In it some noises stand out which the child later on recalls to have heard before under similar circumstances. And whenever they were uttered changes in the situation took place. It will be the peaks within a whole sequence of sounds, marked by rhythm, intensity, and/or pitch which the child first picks up. In this way the child learns to correlate the complex sound aggregates with more or less complex situations. The ' word ' as a more or less long sequence of noises (sounds) crystallizes out. The single word, therefore, is a relatively late phenomenon in both the phylogeny and ontogeny of language. It sprang from such sequences as have to be styled ' sentences ' inasmuch as they express the *whole* of an emotion, or thought. That the sentence was earlier than the word is maintained by most philologists, and evidenced by observations of speakers belonging to communities up to a comparatively high standard of culture. To the Ashanti a word *per se*, cut from its sound group, seems almost to cease being an intelligible sound.[3] ' The Golahs of Liberia, according to O. F. Cook, do not know that their language is made up of words. Their unit of consciousness is the sentence.'[4] The ancient Celts thought and spoke in whole sentences rather than in words ; so much so that ' words ' as analysed out by the modern grammarian may have different initial consonants according to the final sounds of the preceding ' word,' for instance, kymr. *penn*, ' head ' ; *dy benn*, ' your head ' ; *fy mhenn*, ' my head ' ; *ei phenn*, ' their head.'[5] ' In Sanscrit, the language of the most acute grammarians the world has ever seen, we sometimes find a series of words run into one whole which ends only with the end of the sentence or with some other natural break.'[6] Even in our days illiterate people often write in

[1] See Eisler, *Handwörterbuch der Philosophie*, s.v. *Name*.
[2] See Buchanan, S., l.c., p. 8.
[3] Rattray, R. S. As quoted by Chadwick, M. (1928). *Difficulties in Child Development*. Allen & Unwin, London, p. 139.
[4] Quoted by Piaget, l.c., p. 133.
[5] Zimmer, H. (1909). ' Die keltischen Literaturen.' *Die Kultur der Gegenwart*. Teubner, Leipzig, I/XI/1, p. 38.
[6] Giles, P. (1895). *A Short Manual of Comparative Philology*. Macmillan & Co., London, p. 176.

this manner. As regards primitive languages it is difficult for the grammarian to decide whether a given sound sequence is to be classed as a sentence or a word. Terms like *sentence-word, one word-sentence* and the like indicate the dilemma.[1]

These multifarious notations which his prolific mind has engendered man has ' imposed ' on the capricious and perfidious events around him in an effort to exercise his influence over them and bring them in his train. " The manner how speech serveth to the remembrance of the consequence of causes and effects, consisteth in the imposing of ' names ' and the ' connection ' of them." [2]

Near the lower end of the evolutionary scale we met such long sound sequences as *zobafobafo* (see p. 155), which bear the mark of primitivity. Towards its upper end we find an elaborate system of syllables appended to a base which indicate a variety of grammatical categories. Formative elements such as the ones quoted on pp. 172–173 or Greek *tato* used for the formation of the superlative as in *hystatos* ' last,' and the reduplicated forms of the verb in many Indo-European languages (cf. p. 188), still betray their origin in reiterative speech. Others are the weakened forms of words which have been deprived of their independent standing. They have been welded into new wholes with neighbouring words after the fashion of French *chanterons* where the ending *-ons* no longer betrays its origin from Latin *habemus*, French *avons*, ' we have.' Thus the meaning of *chanterons* corresponds to that of English *we have to sing* ' we shall > we are obliged > we are going to sing.' In the Middle Ages the objective pronoun could still stand between the main verb and the auxiliary verb in Southern French.[3] It, therefore, stands to reason that the people still conceived the construction as consisting of two meaningful units. In Modern French the original meaning of the truncated auxiliary verb has paled and the speaker is no longer conscious of the etymological source of what is now a mere ' ending.' In other languages, such as Chinese, the unification has not yet taken place. In the Chinese sentence lai^2 la san^1 ko $z\wedge n^2$ $la,$ ' three people have come,' literally ' come finish three piece men finish,' the word *la* (shortened form of $li\bar{a}o$ ' to finish '), occurs both after the verb denoting ' coming ' and after

---

[1] Cf. the discussion of the relationship between word and sentence in Gardiner, l.c.
[2] Hobbes, Th. *Leviathan, IV*.
[3] Meyer-Lübke, W. (1913). *Historische Grammatik der Französischen Sprache*. Winter, Heidelberg, pp. 251-2.

the noun denoting ' man.' It must, therefore, not be assumed to correspond, for instance, to the English suffix -*ed*, indicating the past tense. Rather does it stand for such phrases as ' that finishes it,' ' that's that ' and the like.[1] The urge to reiterate in the analogous examples cited on p. 124 may also be noted here.

Since the original speech-thought unit was split up, utterance and thought have been assuming forms peculiar to each of them. So dissimilar are they in some respects that fantasy must come to the aid of the inquirer who desires to unveil their common origin. Utterance has been more or less divested of its pictorial properties, liveliness and perspicuity, and thought tends to indulge in generalities. So it has come to pass that present-day man, ' the living repository of a profound knowledge of language,'[2] finds himself in possession of an all-round tool, that is to say, words that fit many occasions, according to the different modes and fields of reference which they indicate.[3] The speaker no longer feels a constant need for words like the ones quoted on p. 155, but is content with the ' general ' word for the act of walking. True that in this way speech has become a formidable instrument of thought, yet it remains a fact that a language can never overtly express with precision all the ideas and sentiments of the speaker. This state of affairs entails the danger of ambiguity which man avoids as best he can by peculiar arrangements of the verbal labels. So much so that Graff finds it necessary to state explicitly that " it is not the function of the single word to be communicated or to communicate." [4] Timothy Shy, commenting on the phrase " this is capital expenditure " used by a Big Business Man in *The Times*, brings this home to us in his facetious manner when he says that " As generally used in the City (our spies report) the adjective ' capital ' attached to the noun ' expenditure ' means not ' involving loss of life ' but ' averting dirty looks from blondes.' Just one more example of the richness and subtlety of the English language, as the cockatoo said to the booksy girl ! " [5]

It is, however, true that words can never entirely cast off their emotional significance which is then handed down to posterity by tradition. The ways of feeling and thinking as well as the language of those upholding the tradition undergo divers changes, so that

---

[1] See Finck, l.c., p. 22.
[2] Gardiner, l.c., p. 5.
[3] Cf. Graff, l.c., pp. 101-2.
[4] Graff, l.c., p. 117.
[5] *News Chronicle*, 26.6.43, p. 2.

in the end ' words ' and ' things ' are imbued with ' nuances ' that have not developed on parallel lines. The history of the terms for ' love ' in the Romance languages illustrates this principle most forcibly. The Romans had the verb *amare* and the noun *amor* which as babbled words (see below, p. 193) lent themselves as terms of endearment for the psycho-somatic process styled by Chamfort as " the exchange of two fantasies and the contact of two cuticles." Yet the idea of love had already been dissociated from its verbal counterpart in Indo-European times. In Sanskrit erotic desire is denoted by a base which has been preserved in the Germanic and Slavonic languages : Sanskrit *lubhyati*, ' he desires strongly ' ; Old Slavonic *ljubiti*, ' to love ' ; *ljubə*, Gothic *liufs*, ' dear ' ; Old English *lēof*, ' dear,' ' beloved ' ; *lufu*, ' love ' ; Middle English *luve*, ' love ' ; from the same base has sprung English *lief*, ' gladly, willingly, dear,' now archaic and obsolescent ; German *lieb*, 'dear ' ; *Liebe*, ' love.' Allied with *lief* is English *to leave*, originally ' to favour,' hence ' to permit.' In our days the English compound verb *to believe* and the noun *belief* has a different shade of meaning, but the idea of ' something one holds dear,' from which it was derived, is still discernible. In Latin the base of these words is represented by *libet*, originally *lubet*, ' it pleases ' ; and *libido*, originally *lubido*, ' lust, desire, urge.' Its full meaning embracing all the forces emanating from the primary sexual urge has been restored by Freud who showed that most psychological processes can be derived from, and are energized by it.

In the further course of development Latin *amare* retained its libidinous value in the South, among more sensual and voluptuous people, as is vividly testified, for example, in Catullus' love poems.

The word retained its *central* mode of reference all over the area of the Romance languages, even when the idea of libidinous union became sublimated and etherealized. In Spain, however, the element of erotic desire gained the upper hand again, and so the old Latin verb *quærere*, ' to will, to desire ' in its Spanish form *querer* replaced the Catullian *amare*. In Catalan *voler*, cognate with English *to will*, has undergone the same change of meaning, whilst spiritual love is denoted by *estimar*, ' to esteem,' sublime love by *amar*, and stilted love by the archaic form *aymar*.[1]

---

[1] Spitzer, L. (1918). *Über einige Wörter der Liebessprache*. Reisland, Leipzig, pp. 5–30.

NON-REITERATIVE SPEECH

Let us, after this digression, take up the thread. The overemphasis on abstraction which we have seen in Azilian art may well have left its impress on other features of language too. Abstraction consists in the mind's attending to those properties for which there is a need (positive abstraction) and in its compulsory discarding of such properties as are not demanded for action, or are harmful (tabooed). It is thus a struggle between two main classes of impulses : the ancient striving after pleasure, undifferentiated emotional linkage and gratification on the one hand, and the flight from frustration, displeasure and isolation on the other.[1] Thoughts rise phœnix-like out of the mingling of emotions, a process which is far from being completed. Every thought bears the marks of the peculiar emotions from which it has accrued.

The utterances correlated to cognitive thinking are, naturally, still endowed with such features as hard or soft attack, a peculiar pattern of intonation and articulation, and so forth. But it is not to be wondered at that concurrent with the development of conceptual thought, certain structural changes began to take place which have reached their climax only in few languages.

The history and the pathology of language as well as the growth of infant speech show that the trend of development has been from reiterative, i.e., babbled, i.e., emotional speech, to non-reiterative, i.e., cognitive speech. It now remains to elucidate how this change has taken place and is still taking place under our very eyes.

Let us first consider baby talk. During the babbling stage we first find a variety of reiterative beads. They ' mean ' something merely in so far as they are a segment of the whole of the occurrence as an *emotional* event. Such utterances are merely expressive of the ' pleasure principle.' The baby is, however, constantly confronted with the non-reiterated speech of those around him.

At a later stage the reiterated utterances are seemingly discarded in favour of non-reiterated ones. Thus [klokloklo], [gagaga] finally become ' clock,' ' garden.' Here (as in respect of the adjustment made by singling out the nearest babble, see p. 99) it would be rash to content ourselves with the statement that the child has acquired more ' skill ' or ' mastery.' Moreover, there is considerable evidence that non-reiterative speech is entirely alien to the small

---

[1] See Schiller, F. C., l.c. Ferenczi, l.c., ch. viii.

child. One boy of two when asked to say [ba] remained completely mute, but readily and correctly responded to the request to say [bababa]. Another boy aged two and a half said [fa] in response to the first request, but answered correctly in the second instance. This example also rules out the assumption that he was not as yet capable of articulating [b]. It shows, however, that the sounds [b] and [f] could be distinguished only in their natural context, i.e., in rhythmical speech.

The modern child usually hears non-reiterated ' words,' and yet, if an attempt at imitation is made at all, such words are at first converted into babbles. Valentine's girl turned the ' request word ' [ta] into more or less prolonged babbles, as late as the age of one year and two months. I quote part of his report : " Held her hand towards a cigarette case I had. I withheld it : a sharp cry : then a kissing sound ; then cry again ; I said ' Ta ' and at once she said ' Ta.' I gave it her and she repeated ' Ta ta ta.' " [1]

This example appears to be of great significance. It shows two entirely diverse modes of utterance and of reference in succession. The babble refers to the longing for an object, the ' sharp ' cry (glottal stop) to frustration. Then the girl regressed to the primeval sucking noise in the form of kissing expressive of union and incorporation, followed by a cry as the response to frustration. Under the guidance of the pattern [ta] offered to her, she managed to harmonize the two impulsive patterns. As soon as the stress of the situation had vanished, the newly emerged pattern significantly disappeared to give way to the more primitive [ta ta ta] expressive of gratification.

The situation in which this girl found herself at the age of fourteen months was *partly* new and different from anything ever experienced before : ' a *problematic* situation that raises questions, arouses doubts, induces hesitations, and suggests alternatives.' [2] It is *capable* of evoking thought, and the stress of this particular case has led to the first and most difficult step towards thinking as ' *stopping to think* ' that is to say, ' the inhibition or arrest of the natural impulse to react at once.' [3] This stoppage involves the integration of conflicting antagonistic behavioural acts including both mental and linguistic patterns.

We are coming nearer the solution of the problem when we say

---
[1] Valentine, l.c., p. 409.
[2] See Schiller, F. C., l.c., p. 198.
[3] Schiller, F. C. *Ibid.*

that in the child rhythmical utterance is gradually shortened and finally reduced to one single ' syllable ' through the interaction of the pleasurable babblings with sound patterns signifying displeasure. The conflict between pleasure and reality is manifest in the gradual emergence of non-babbled, non-reiterative speech.

This struggle has been raging for thousands of years. It set in comparatively recently, perhaps in the Azilian period, at a time when with the vaulting of the frontal part of the skull the forebrain became better convoluted, and affective-pictorial expression was superseded by reflective and abstract verbalization. This assumption is made probable not only by the foregoing psychological and artistic considerations (see p. 170), but also by some extant linguistic records. The enormous prevalence of reiterative speech in prehistoric times is mirrored in the present-day languages of races that have remained on a lower rung of the evolutionary ladder. We owe much anthropological evidence to Sir John Lubbock's (Lord Avebury's) painstaking investigations. According to his perhaps not quite accurate scoring, the Maori vocabulary contains 169 words consisting of reiterated syllables per thousand words, Tonga contains 166, Hottentot 75, Brazilian Tupi 66, whilst relatively 'modern' languages like Greek, French, and English exhibit only two or three such words.[1] Up to several thousands of years ago the phylogenetically young Indo-European languages clung to the customs of reiteration for purposes of inflexion. The old Oscan and Umbrian dialects of Italy for example, displayed a stately series of verb and noun forms, such as *mamers, deded, fefure, fefaced*, whose Latin equivalents show no trace of reduplication. Such few forms as did persist in classical Latin soon disappeared in composite verbs where the intrusion of the reduplication between the preposition and the stem of the perfect was felt to be irregular, e.g., *con-tigit* as against *tetigit.* In Vulgar Latin *curri* took the place of Classical Latin *cucurri*.[2] The same process of shortening may have taken place when independent words were fused into a compound.

For these and other reasons meaning became attached to a new unit, the ' syllable,' that is, in the modern sense of the word, a continuous stream of vocal sound the sonority of which is interrupted only once, e.g., [ap] or [pa], each new interruption giving the impression of a new syllable. It was this newly emerging unit that

---

[1] Lubbock, J. (1889). *The Origin of Civilization.* Longmans, Green & Co., London, pp. 523–5.
[2] Weise, l.c., pp. 57, 58, 149.

FULL-FLEDGED LANGUAGE 189

was represented when writing had passed the stage of figurative and symbolic notation and became phonetic. The single speech sound as a reality had not been discovered yet.

In modern English the shortening of words has been carried very far. So much so that the majority of words are monosyllabic and 'long' words are felt as strange, un-English, cumbersome and unnecessary. Thus Nathaniel, Mephistopheles become Nat, Mephy.[1] Even the highly educated classes cannot escape that tendency as is evident from the following quotation.[2] ' " We are now witnessing," wrote Pearsall Smith in 1912, " the struggle of the Genius of language with the popular but somewhat indigestible word cinematograph." The language has done it by ejection. The word is not heard to-day. We go to the pictures or the flicks. But what can the Genius do with the octosyllabic names of modern science ? Teachers have long given up trying to prevent children saying streps and staphs, and polys vie with polymorphs. But now we subdivide the streptococci, and perhaps the paper shortage will come to the assistance of the genius of language by compelling us to write hæmostreps (57) for the 57th of Griffith's types of Lancefield group A of the hæmolytic streptococci. Certainly we should speak of hæmostreps. It is the same with the new drugs. The ageing brain cannot remember all their names ; the young one should not attempt to do so for many will soon disappear. Generically we should speak about the Sulphs. Often we need to discuss whether we should use them at all before deciding which one to employ, and for " The question is whether we should exhibit chemotherapy " we may well ask " Shall we put him on a Sulph ? " ' The inclination to shorten words, condemned by Swift and others, seems to have been popular in the Cockney dialect of Edward Ward's days (1667-1731). In his writings we find *mob* alongside with mobility, *cits, non-con, mump, skip, blab, bub, strum, rep, qual* for ' citizens, non-conformist, mumper, skipper, blabber, bubble, strumpet, reputation, quality.' [3]

GRAMMATICAL CATEGORIES

Throughout the course of this inquiry utterances have been said to refer to objects or events. The modern mind, such as it has been moulded since the times of the Indian and Greek grammarians, has

---
[1] *Sunday Express*, 16.1.44.
[2] *Lancet* (1943). May 22, p. 660.
[3] Matthews, l.c., p. 126.

arrived at a certain vision of the world which culminates in the all-embracing conception of space-time relationships. Classifying events according to the space-time principle the logical mind has established categories such as that of agent, action, time (past, present, future), number, things, qualities, sex and so forth. Such ideas have been claimed to correspond to universal categories of words, word-forms (nouns, cases, pronouns, adjectives, gender, case, tense, person, mood, number, etc.) and syntax (subject, predicate, object, etc.). In fact, however, such grammatical categories vary with the mode of reference. An Eskimo, for instance, cannot make the statement ' he rides the kajak ' where the pronoun ' he ' denotes the agent, ' rides ' the action, and ' kajak ' the object. In his language he says *kajaktorpok* literally, ' kajak-riding-his.' After this fashion he conceives of the whole of an occurrence which is so divided into parts as to make it appear ' as if the active subject were passively suffering the action.'[1] The individual is assailed, ' affected,' and his statement expresses this emotional tuning. After the same fashion the Eskimo says in Thalbitur's translation ' *my being stabbed by him is* ' instead of ' he stabs me.'[2] The translation does not, however, do justice to the original text, as shall be illustrated by a few Greenlandish phrases. The expression *tusad-pu-ya* would, for convenience, be translated ' I hear ' but the English translation would by no means render the real meaning. The phrase does not belong to the category of verbs, but actually refers to the mere occurrence of ' sounding,' and the suffix *-ya* does not denote a personal pronoun ' I ' but the ' being-possessed-by.' The distinction between personal and possessive pronouns ('I' against ' my ') is non-existent, as is demonstrated by *tusaslu-tik* ' sounding theyness ' = ' they hear,' as against *ilu-tik* ' houses theyness ' = ' their houses.'[3] It thus appears that in Greenlandish the idea of the Ego as the perceptive, evaluating self is only poorly developed and expressed. Furthermore, the analysis into such abstract logico-grammatical categories as are expressed by verbs, nouns and so forth is only in its teens.

The language of the Wintu tribe of California contains a considerable number of suffixes which implicitly inform the listener of details essential to the Wintu mind, but by no means worthy of note to the modern European mind. The Wintu cannot, for instance,

---

[1] Werkmeister, l.c., p. 359.
[2] Quot. by Werkmeister, l.c., p. 363.
[3] Finck, F. N., l.c., pp. 36 ff.

simply declare that he is drunk ; the Wintu statement *tsoyilake ni*, formed by means of the suffix *-ke*, implies that the information is based on hearsay. Lee translates it : ' I am drunk (I hear) ; they tell me I'm drunk.'[1] In a similar manner visual and other sensory evidence (smell, touch, etc.), logical inference, approximation, purpose, desire or effort, idle wish, necessity, obligation, etc., are categories which the Wintu *must* express by special suffixes. The European mind does not always find it necessary to be so explicit.

Likewise the highly abstract notion of ' object ' or ' person ' does not seem to have sprung up in Amerinidian thinking and uttering. Algonquian suffixes, for instance, denote categories in respect of states of matter, such as, wood-like, stone-like, string-like, solid, liquid, or with regard to tools, parts of the body, animals, women, child (but not, apparently, adult males).[2]

The abstract idea of mere ' tense ' (past, present, future) is absent in the above languages. This does not imply that the Greenlander or Red Indian cannot think of an event taking place, say, in the future. Yet the suffix *-le* indicating the future shows itself to be derived from a verb denoting ' dwelling ' and to imply the idea of necessity and duration. In a love-song a man and a woman, lovers, are about to part finally. They sing : *pelen tosmalitors belebom* : the sleeping place which you and I hollowed out *shall* remain. The Wintu explains that this really means : ' You and I can put an end to our relations ; but we cannot obliterate the place on the hill where we have slept. It is that *-lebom, it shall despite ourselves*, which gives poignancy to the song.'[3]

In most archaic languages it is the notion of aspect, the category of duration, rather than of tense that prevails. The Hebrew verb, for instance, has no forms for the tenses. An event is conceived and expressed as either occurring or having occurred, as incomplete or complete. ' There are languages, such as Russian, in which the concept of aspect preponderates so far as to become the main principle of the whole verbal system ; but in French, as in Latin, it is but an isolated survival, or responds only to an accidental need.'[4] . . . ' Nevertheless, the notion of aspect is not unknown in those of our modern languages which best express the notion of tense. For example, in order to express the durative, which they lack, the

---

[1] See Lee, D. D. (1938). ' Conceptual implications of an Indian Language.' *Philosophy of Science*, Vol. 5, pp. 89 ff.
[2] Bloomfield. *Language*, p. 241.
[3] Lee. *Ibid.*, p. 97.
[4] Vendryes, l.c., p. 111.

Germanic languages have utilized the present participle with the substantive verb as an auxiliary. In Middle High German there already existed expressions like : *all die mich sehende sint,* " all those who see me " (Der Arme Heinrich, v. 673) or *der riter . . . mit dem der lewe varend ist,* " the knight . . . with whom the lion travels " (Iwein, v. 2986). From the same need arose the English expressions *I am going, I was reading,* which are so extensively employed. We know that in the French of the sixteenth century an attempt was made to create a durative of the same type as the verb *être* (to be) or *aller* (to go), but, as it was not countenanced by Malherbe and Menage it came to nothing. Nevertheless, Voiture still used : *Cette prison qui va vous renferment,* and La Fontaine : *Je me vais désaltérant.*' [1]

The infinitive (a form of the verb denoting action or existence without limitation of person, number or tense [2]), too, is a fairly recent accomplishment. Many extant primitive languages as well as the Indo-European mother-tongue do not know it. One of the offsets of the latter, Celtic, was still on that level which does not provide for the expression of an action as independent from the actor. The ancient Indians, the Greeks and other Indo-European races attained the goal of severing the Ego from happening, and so hammered out the infinitive.

Archaic languages lacked the copula (see above, pp. 6f.) ' is ' or ' are,' probably because the highly abstract idea of mere ' existence ' had not arisen as yet. The copula was, for instance, not expressed in Hebrew, nor in Old and Middle Egyptian.[3] In Greek and Latin the use of the copula is by no means obligatory. *Hortus pulcher,* for instance, means both ' lovely garden ' and ' the garden is lovely.' The relationship between two concepts thus remains veiled. It is noteworthy that the omission of the copula is encountered mainly in proverbial, archaic, and poetic expressions.

WORD COINAGE

In considering words the question is often put to us as to why a given language uses special metaphorical modes of expression which differ from those found in others. It is safe to say that the employment of certain sound patterns for the formation of verbal labels denoting certain notions depends on the speaker's or the community's

---
[1] Vendryes, l.c., pp. 109-110.
[2] Wyld. *Universal English Dictionary.*
[3] Gardiner, l.c., p. 219.

mentality. Owing to the lack of written records it is, of course, impossible to reconstruct the original patterns. In some cases, however, it is possible to hazard a fair guess. A number of words are obviously of onomatopœic origin. French *coquet* " coquettish," *cocarde*, " cockade," *cocotte*; *coco*, term of endearment for children, English *cocky* are derived from a reiterative baby word *coco*, which may be the onomatopœic base of the standard word *coq*. French *bibelot*, " knicknacks," is derived from the babbled pet-name *bibi* for *biche*, " hind." [1]

It is still easy to trace Old Italian *smanziere*, " lover " ; *smanzieria*, " caresses," back to the Latin verb *amare*, " to love." Other offshoots from the same stem such as Italian *amore*, French *aimer*, Provençal Catalan, Spanish, Portuguese *amar* are less disguised. Latin *amator*, " lover " derived from *amare*, and Latin *amor*, " love " which is cognate, have yielded Italian *amatore*, Old French *ameour*, Provençal Catalan, Spanish, Portuguese *amador*, French *amadouer*, " to cuddle " ; Italian *amore*, French *amour*, Spanish, Portuguese, Provençal Catalan *amor*, " love." Yet only philological skill can unveil the same base in the Old Lombardian phrase *per mo de zo*, " anyhow," [2] from *per amorem de deo*, " for the love of God."

The Latin base *amare* itself clearly reveals itself to be a babbled word like its cognates *mamma*, " mother " ; *amma*, " wet-nurse " ; *mamilla*, " nipple " ; *nanna, ninna, monna, amita*, " aunt " ; and *pappa*, " father " ; *pappare*, " to eat."

Among the offsets of these babbled words we find quite a number which, as to sound and/or meaning, more or less patently betray their origin from the above sources, for instance, French *tante*, southwest Provençal *tata*, where the babbling feature was imposed on old French *ante*, English *aunt* ; Spanish *mamella*, " hill " ; Rumanian *nani*, Italian *niuna, ninna, nanna*, " lullaby " ; Italian *niunolo*, " toy " ; Old Italian *niuna*, " girl " ; Italian *niumma*, " little doll " ; Spanish *nino*, " child " ; *nina*, " eye-ball " ; Portuguese, *nunha*, " cradle " ; Venetian *papota*, " chubby cheek " ; Spanish, Portuguese *papo*, " goitre " ; *papado*, Italian *pappagorgia*, " double chin." [3]

The elimination of waste products too is denoted by words derived

---

[1] See Spitzer, L. (1918). *Über einige Wörter der Liebessprache*. Reisland, Leipzig.
[2] See Meyer-Lübke, W. *Romanisches Etymologisches Wörterbuch*. Nos. 399, 407, 427.
[3] The list is not complete, the obvious derivations having been left out. See Meyer-Lübke, l.c., Nos. 424, 425, 5276, 5277, 5817, 6213, 6214.

from a babbled word, Latin *cacare* (Greek *kakkáō*, Rumanian *cacà*, Italian *cacare*, French *chier*, Spanish, Portuguese *cagar*). Their derivatives hardly betray their origin from a tabooed vulgar word referring to a vegetative function : Venetian *kagon*, " coward, weakling " ; Rumanian *cacă-frică*, " timid man " ; Middle French *cagot*, " wretch " ; French *cagot*, " hypocrite " ; hence name of a caste living in Béarn ; Bret. *kakó, kagó*, " leprous " ; Italian *cacapuzza*, " a species of milkweed " (*Euphorbia*) ; (Abruzzi) *kataputtseo*, " turpentine-tree." [1]

The transfer of meaning from Latin *mamilla*, ' breast ', to Venetian *mamella*, ' hill ' (cf. also English *paps*, ' rounded conical hills side by side ') [2] casts some light on the general principles ruling the change of meaning. To the analytic mind it seems obvious that the similarity of form between the female breast and a hill may have invited the metaphor. Yet the psychologist and the philologist, admitting that the change of meaning is logically understandable, cannot be content with this answer. The point at issue is not only whether a change of meaning is possible ; it must also be demonstrated why a given metaphor has been chosen whilst others have been rejected. From reasons not far to seek it can be surmised that here the ancient conception of ' Mother Earth ' manifested itself in a virile, and highly erotic people. This leads to the conclusion that the whole cultural outlook of a given social group is to be taken into consideration if we are to comprehend a given choice of route. Cf. also the meanings of mama (p. 131).

As words are continuously coined afresh we can gather the principles governing word coinage from what is happening under our very eyes and what has happened in recent historical times. In focussing on the process of word coinage as main feature of mental events recorded in historic times we can profitably peruse the writings of authors whose individual make-up is known. The study of Gustav Meyrink's works (born in Prague in 1868, died 1932), yields illuminating results. In a thorough examination of Meyrink's novels Sperber [3] has ascertained the statistical frequency of certain words and phrases. It appears that in the first place the motif of suffocation runs through most of his literary works. The writer displays remarkable skill in employing words and phrases which depict the agony of not being able to breathe. Sperber seems to

---
[1] Meyer-Lübke. *Ibid.*, No. 1443.
[2] Wyld. *Universal English Dictionary*.
[3] Sperber, H., and Spitzer, L. (1918). *Motiv und Wort*. Reisland, Leipzig, pp. 1–52.

have found that the idea of not being able to breathe constitutes in Meyrink's case only a section of the wider topic of impeded bodily functions. Expressions referring to depriving someone of, or reducing someone's sight, of blinding, dazzling and so forth, play a predominant part. Another group of mental pictures centres round the idea of the vampire in the sense of an evil spirit which sucks blood, life, out of men, animals and plants.

Two questions force themselves on the enquirer's mind. First, how did it happen that Meyrink was driven to invent tales in which the ideas of hanging, shutting in a vessel void of air, blinding, blood-sucking and so forth constantly recur. Secondly, what led this author to employ expressions referring to suffocation even where the reader cannot detect a cogent reason for their use?

The present writer is fortunate in having obtained such information on Meyrink's life as bears on his predilections for the above-mentioned means of literary representation. Dr. E. Popper, under whose care Meyrink had been for many years, tells me that constitutionally he was a strange mystic type, full of anxieties and inner problems. By his fear of life, probably based on birth trauma, he was constantly driven to contemplate suicide. From his thirties onwards he was suffering from a severe nervous disease which affected mainly the vegetative nervous system and so brought about visceral dysfunction of all kind.

What is true of an individual writer or poet applies also to families, tribes, social groups, and nations which have a certain cultural outlook in common. We may thus conjecture that the language of the late Stone Age probably contained words which were derived partly from onomatopœic utterances, partly from sounds and noises accompanying gestures indicative of the primary interests and motives, and of the magic aspect of the surround. A glance at the modern Figs. 30 and 31 may give an intimation of how the transfer of meaning is brought about, and how pictorial language becomes abstract and metaphorical.

The sound and the vocabulary of those bygone ages were perhaps more fluctuating than they are in civilized languages, owing to the more unbridled natural tendencies of sound change (see p. 141). The speed at which words changed their form and meaning was perhaps decreasing with the growing significance of tribal laws and customs. Thus natural tendencies came to grips with social institutions, the latter imposing more and more inhibitions on the former.

196   THE INFANCY OF SPEECH

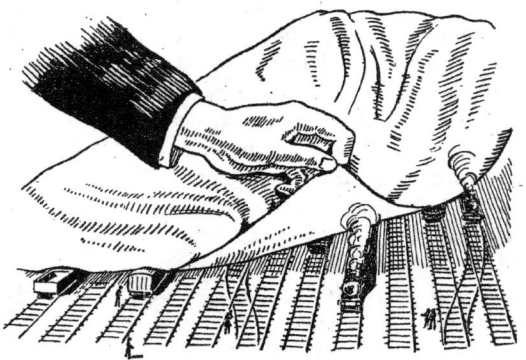

By courtesy of British Railways
FIG. 30
"Under Cover"

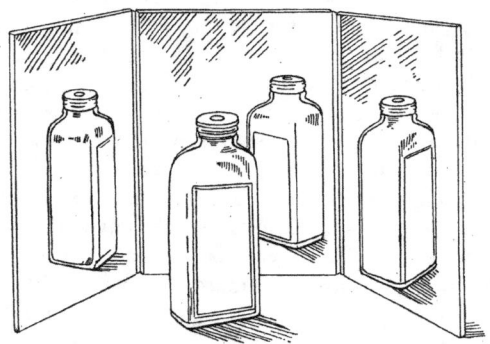

By courtesy of W. Warner & Co. Ltd.
FIG. 31
" From whatever angle you look at it "

HERE ENDETH THE NARRATIVE

For some time we have been considering types of language which can be said to be truly " cultural " achievements as opposed to mere " natural " functions. The latter still underlie the speech of present-day man, who, under the guidance of traditional models, utilizes them as raw material for more or less artificial and/or artistic speech. The story of the infancy of human language ought, therefore, to have ended with the period when the babbling tendency had become capable of being transmitted through inheritance. That was the epoch illustrated by such early archæological records as open our eyes to the daybreak of culture. Those were the days when natural, crude speech patterns came to be purified and refined.

It is, of course, difficult to establish a clean-cut borderline between natural and cultural tendencies which have been overlapping and interacting throughout the ages. However that may be, the motive power which has prompted the extension of the story is the same as is found in fairy tales. The narrator while delving into the remote past, and feeling himself into the behaviour of the then living speakers, cannot help peeping into the ensuing age, part of which, as it happens, is his own lifetime. Thus he can satisfy his fantasy and tell how the speakers ' lived happily ever after.' And what about the future of language ? The narrative means to answer the question by showing how in Kipling's words

' We prepare it to-day,
And inherit it to-morrow.'

INDEX

Abaelard, 6.
Abbevillian culture, 89.
Abercrombie, L., 75, 126.
abstract thinking, 170.
abstract verbalisation, 188.
abstraction, 14, 150, 151, 179, 181, 186.
abstractions, geometrical, 179.
Abu Zachariya Hayudj, 14.
accentuation, 64.
accessorius nerve, 69.
Acheulean culture, 95, 105, 111.
acoustic fibres, 69.
African languages, 70.
agglutination, 15.
aggression, 140.
air, 67, 114, 115.
air-bladder, 27, 53.
Alajonanine, T., 140.
alimentary tract, 49, 66.
Allaire, 80.
alliteration, 126, 180.
ambiguity, danger of, 184.
ambivalence, 163.
Ament, W., 22, 135, 136, 137.
amœba, 44.
amphibians, 27.
Andersen, H., 132.
animal language, 30.
animal pictures, 147.
animals, 28, 30, 31, 34, 35, 36, 44, 45, 47, 48, 49, 50, 52, 57, 58, 68, 93, 147, 152, 158, 160, 161, 167.
animism, 151.
annal, 19, 22.
anthropoid apes, 36, 40, 42, 89, 113.
anthropology, 24.
anthropomorphic approach, 3.
anxiety, 57.
aortic arches, 21.
ape, baby, 120.
ape-man, 42.
apes, 28, 29, 32, 35, 68, 69, 87, 93.
apes, anthropoid, 36, 40, 42, 89, 113.
aphasia, 54, 102.
archaic expression, 170, 192.
archaic languages, 191.
Aristotle, 10.
art, 146, 147, 170.
art, Magdalenian, 171.
art, mural, 170.
art, pictorial, 150.
art, representational, 150.
articulate speech, 35, 84, 91, 92, 113, 118.
articulated language, 99.
articulateness, 99, 113.
articulation, 5, 65, 84, 101.
articulation basis, 139, 164.

articulatory changes, 114.
articulatory movements, 49.
asociality, 136, 140.
aspect, concept of, 191.
aspect, magic, 195.
aspect, symbolic, 181.
assonance, 126.
Aston, W. G., 115.
Atkinson, B. P. C., 64.
attack, aspirated, 56, 65, 158.
attack, hard, 56, 57, 58, 62, 63, 65.
attack, soft, 56, 62, 79, 186.
attack, vocal, 56, 61, 79.
attitude, emotional, 53, 64.
auditory patterns, 164.
Augustinus, 2.
Aurignac, 146.
Aurignacian culture, 149, 166.
Aurignacian man, 154, 161.
Aurignacian period, 105, 108, 111, 142, 144, 145, 146, 147, 152, 155, 157, 161, 167, 169, 174.
Australian aborigines, 101, 105, 109, 153.
Australoid races, 143.
Australopithecus, 38.
autogenesis, 118.
autonomic nervous system, 46.
auxiliary verb, 183.
Avesbury, Lord, 188.
Azara, 141.
Azilian art, 186.
Azilian man, 177, 181.
Azilian period, 170, 180, 188.
Azoic, 26.

babbling, 99, 100, 103, 104, 113, 114, 115, 117, 118, 119, 121, 126, 130, 133, 134, 158, 159, 173, 185, 186, 187, 188, 193, 194, 196.
babies, 68, 80, 93, 96, 119, 121, 131.
baby talk, 130, 135, 137, 140, 186.
baby words, 131, 165, 193.
Baily, E. B., 27, 29, 38, 39, 42, 45, 85, 89.
Basu, G. C., 60.
Beach, D. M., 81, 115.
behaviourism, 46, 79.
belching, 67.
beliefs, magical, 101.
Bennett, R., 139, 140.
Biogenetic law, 21, 53, 100, 115.
birds, 27, 29, 36, 37, 52.
birth, 102.
Blanshard, B., 14, 30, 31, 79.
Bleek, W. A. I., 172.
Bloomfield, L., 15, 62, 63, 64, 129, 130, 173, 191.

body and mind, interrelation of, 11.
Bolton, H. C., 36.
Boskop man, 105.
Boule, 87, 107, 145.
Boyer, P., 8.
brain, 4, 28, 33, 40, 41, 48, 82, 87, 88, 105, 108, 112, 144, 145, 154, 177.
brain case, 143, 144.
Bréal, M., 141.
breathing, 49, 52, 73, 102.
Brickner, R. M., 73.
Briffault, R., 121.
Britain, 42, 86.
Broca's area, 73.
bronchi, 50.
brow ridges, 107, 144, 145.
Brown, G. B., 90.
Brünn, 144.
Brünn man, 143.
Buchan, J., viii.
Buchanan, S., 9, 182.
Bühler, C., 65, 75, 81, 159.
bulb, spinal, 69.
burial, 45, 91, 109.
Burkitt, M. C., 90, 91, 112, 142, 143, 144, 146, 149, 166, 167, 168, 170, 171, 177, 178.

Cainozoic, 27.
calls, musical, 65.
calvaria, 143.
canalisation, 120.
Canello, 131.
Capell, A., 126, 127, 128.
Capsian culture, 149.
Carnap, R., 11.
categories, grammatical, 189, 190.
Catullus, 62.
causation, 4, 126.
cave-dwellers, 108, 145.
cavity, oral, 92.
centres, motor, 34.
centres, subcortical, 69.
Chadwick, M., 182.
chamber, labial, 67.
chamber, palatal, 67.
chamber, velar or laryngeal, 67.
Chamberlain, 55.
Chamisso, 142.
Champion, G. G., 70, 156.
Chancelade man, 144, 145.
Chatterji, S. K., 71.
Chauveau, 58.
Chellean culture, 89, 90, 91, 96, 100, 105.
Chellean implements, 95.
Chellean industry, 111.
Chellean language, 91.
Chellean people, 93, 94.
chewing, 69.
child, 104, 179, 182.
child's language, 104, 157, 161.

Childe, G. V., 17, 41, 84, 85, 86, 89, 101, 109, 134, 146, 170.
chimpanzee, 28, 29, 31, 36, 42, 58.
chin, 88, 92, 113.
chronicle, 19.
civilisation, 143.
civilisation, Epipalæolithic, 178.
Clark, J. M., 160.
classification, 150, 151.
classification, grammatical, 174.
clicks, 68, 70, 71, 74, 80, 81, 82, 96, 98, 100, 102, 113, 115, 118, 119, 134, 154, 158.
Cliffe, L., 141.
climate, 68.
clothing, 152.
cockney, 62.
code of behaviour, 175.
cognition, 78.
cognitive element, 94.
cognitive meaning, 79.
cognitive mentality, 140.
cognitive speech, 186.
cognitive thinking, 186.
collective responses, 157, 158.
colliculi, inferior, 69.
combination, sound, 101.
communication, 157, 166.
communities, 174.
completion of action, 126.
concepts, 104, 179, 192.
conceptual thought, 186.
conditioned stimuli, 158.
configurations, 29.
consciousness, 112.
consonants, 34, 80, 97, 100, 101, 115, 117, 118, 154, 158.
consonants, shedding of, 138.
conventionalism, 149, 170, 179.
conversation, 86.
convolution, anterior central, 69.
convolution, inferior frontal, 41.
convolution, third frontal, 88.
convolutions, 105, 113, 154.
co-operation, 103.
copula, 6, 7, 192.
cortex, 32, 48.
coup de poing, 90, 91, 112, 146.
crafts, 174.
cranial vault, 144.
cries, 53, 74, 181.
Crô-Magnon race, 105, 144, 145, 153.
culture, 89, 166, 176, 194, 195.
culture, Aurignacian, 149, 166.
culture, Capsian, 149.
culture, Magdalenian, 144.
culture, stone, 89.
Curr, E. M., 125, 165.
Curry, R., 59.

dances, animal, 161.

danger, from within and without, 57, 102, 103, 158.
Davison, D., 42, 47, 86, 92, 104, 109, 112, 113, 146, 153f., 174, 177.
deaf and blind, 121.
dementia, senile, 117.
Democritos, 1.
Dent, J. Y., 74.
dental sounds, 141.
desire, erotic, 180, 185.
dialects, 132.
diction, poetic, 103.
digestive tract, 65.
dilatators of larynx, 52.
diluvium, 144.
Dittrich, O., 8.
Douglas, L. C., 49.
Dubois, 42.
Durand, M., 140.
dwarf races, 153.
dyslalia, 136, 138, 140.

early man, 44, 93, 102.
Earth, Mother, 194.
earth, origin of, 25.
eating, 49.
Economo, 33.
Edel, M., 140.
efflux of air, 115.
Egger, E., 22, 56, 135.
ego, 114, 181, 190, 192.
egocentric, 104.
Eisler, R., 2, 6, 11, 19, 24, 166, 182.
ejaculations, vocal, 158.
ejection of noises, 122.
Elliot-Smith, G., 41.
embryology, 124.
embryonic features, 152.
emergent evolution, 17, 35, 97, 98.
emotion, 48, 53, 54, 64, 79, 140, 151.
emotional copula, 122.
emotional language, 165.
emotional linkage, 186.
emotional oneness, 117.
emotional power, 128.
emotional response, 80.
emotional speech, 186.
empiricists, 2.
encephalitis, 80.
ending, 183.
engram, 156.
Ennius, 19.
Eoanthropus, 86, 94.
Eocene, 27, 42.
epiglottis, 58.
Epipalæolothic civilization, 178.
equilibrium, 57, 79.
eros, 102.
erotic feelings, 104, 173, 180, 185.
erotic meaning, 121.
erotic scenes, 152.
Estienne, H., 14.

Ettmayer, K., 130.
etymology, 14.
Eunomius, 121.
evolution, 15, 17, 19, 25, 38, 43, 57, 79, 133, 188.
evolution, emergent, 17, 35, 97, 98.
evolution of language, 37, 72.
exclamations, 53.
experimental types of man, 92, 177.
expression, affective-pictorial, 188.
expressions, poetic, 192.
expulsion of air, 114, 115.

facial nerve, 69.
Fallaize, E. N., 42, 89, 92, 106, 107, 108, 109.
Faust, 125, 126.
Fayum, 28.
features, embryonic, 152.
Ferenczi, S., 122, 186.
fibres, acoustic, 69.
field of reference, 76, 78, 81, 82, 83, 96, 104, 166.
Finck, F. N., 127, 130, 172, 174, 184, 190.
fire, 86, 109.
Firth, J. R., 48, 70.
flaking, 167.
Fleure, H. F., 143, 144, 146, 147, 149, 167, 168, 169, 177.
flexional languages, 15.
flint implements, 89, 90, 95, 109, 111, 146.
fluting technique, 146.
food gatherers, 177.
forebrain, 188.
form, sense of, 112.
formants, 55.
formative elements, 183.
forms, grammatical, 126, 128.
formulæ, magic, 125.
fossils, 6, 38.
Fowler, N. G. and F. G., 141.
Fox, M., 34, 36, 44.
Fraser, J. G., 71.
Frazer, G., 157.
Freud, S., 79, 185.
fricatives, 117.
frontal lobe, 88.
Fröschels, E., 31.
frustration, 186, 187.
fundamental tone, 55.

Galley Hill, 154.
ganglia, 47.
Garbini, A., 80.
Gardiner, A. H., 8, 78, 159, 183, 184, 192.
gargling, 71.
Garstang, W., 21.
Gassner, H., 135.
General Paralysis of the Insane, 140.

generalisation, 14, 151.
genetically fixed structures, 22, 100, 121.
genu inferius, 32.
geometrical abstractions, 179.
Gerber, 2.
Gesell, A., 35, 100.
gestures, 34, 71, 122, 158, 160, 180, 195.
gestures, mouth, 30, 31, 71, 84.
gestures, repetitive, 165.
gesture-utterance, 83.
gibbon, 28, 36.
Gibraltar skull, 107, 108.
Giese, F., 179.
Giles, P., 182.
Gilmour, J., 157, 181.
Ginneken, J., 67, 72, 115.
glaciations, 42, 84, 108, 109, 110, 111.
glossopharyngeus nerve, 69.
glottal stop, 58, 62, 187.
glottis, 49, 58.
Goethe, J. W., 11, 23, 126.
Graff, W. L., 70, 98, 101, 127, 128, 162, 164, 184.
Graham, M., 162.
grammatical categories, 189.
grammatical classification, 174.
grammatical forms, 126, 128, 129, 190.
grasping, 50, 96, 103.
gratification, 122, 150, 151, 158, 161, 186, 187.
gravers, 146.
greed, 68, 69.
Gregory of Nyssa, 121.
grimaces, 48, 71.
Grimaldi people, 144, 145.
groans, 98.
group, social, 102, 104, 166, 175, 194, 195.
Grunwald, 49.
Günz glaciation, 84.
gurgles, reiterative, 180.
gurgling, 115.
gustatory sensations, 70.
Guthrie, D., 119.
guttural sounds, 141.
gyri, central, 105.
gyrus hippocampi, 69.
gyrus, third frontal, 108.

Haeckel, E., 21.
Hagemann, 2.
Haldane, J. B. S., 17.
Halle, 2.
hand, 89, 95, 109, 152.
hand-axe, 90.
handling, 96.
hard attack, 57, 62, 63, 65, 108, 186.
Harris, P. G., 125.
Hawkes, J., 112.
Hayoudj, Abu Zachariya, 14.
Head, Sir Henry, 48.

heard, 69, 174.
hearing, 154.
hearths, 146.
Heidelberg man, 88, 89, 91, 92, 104, 107.
hemispheres, 42.
Henderson, K., 28, 29, 35, 92, 105, 108, 110, 115, 144, 145, 167.
herd instinct, 120.
Herder, 3; 158.
Hetzer, H., 82, 96.
Heyse, 157.
hieroglyphics, 178.
history, 15.
Hobbes, 78, 183.
Höber, R., 69.
holding, 50.
Homer, 15.
Homeric times, 160.
Hominid types, 92.
Homo, 35, 55.
Homo Sapiens, 24, 91, 106, 143, 151, 153, 177.
Hornell, J., 125.
Hottentotism, 94, 117.
Hottentots, 71, 106, 152.
Hovelacque, A., 154.
Howe, G., 103, 131, 165.
Howes, F., 73.
human fossils, 38.
human stem, 42.
human types, 41.
Humboldt, W., 3.
Humphreys, 135.
hunger, 103.
hunters, 161.
hunting life, 120.
Huxley, A., 46, 93.
Huxley, J., 11, 36, 37, 53, 66.
hypoglossus nerve, 69.

ice age, 85, 86, 108, 110.
ice sheet, 38, 39.
Id, 181.
ideas, 104, 113, 184.
identity, theory of, 157.
ideoplastic approach, 179.
imagery, primitive, 178.
imbecility, 117.
imitation, 136, 161, 175, 187.
implements, 112, 167, 168, 177, 178.
implements, Acheulian, 95.
implements, Chellean, 95.
implements, flint, 89, 95.
implements in bone, 146.
implements, secondary flint, 146.
imposing of names, 183.
impositions of words, 9.
impressionistic world picture, 151.
impulses, 99, 186.
incorporation, 115, 187.
independence, 57.

INDEX 203

individual, 104, 174.
individualisation, 151.
individualistic tendencies, 136.
infant, 94, 186.
infant speech, 186.
infantile attitude, 140.
infantile cry, 55.
infantile utterances, 162.
inferior colliculi, 69.
inferior frontal convolution, 41.
infinitive, 192.
infix, 129.
influx of air, 115.
inheritance, 196.
inhibition, 180, 181, 187, 195.
inspiration, 52.
institutions, social, 195.
instrumentality, 126.
instruments of noting, 182.
integers, 29.
integral wholes, 34, 45, 54.
integration, 112.
intelligence, 67, 83.
intensity, 64, 126, 182.
intention, 9, 34, 158, 159, 161, 180.
intentional and emotional language, 165.
intentional signal, 158.
interglacial period, 84, 86, 99, 107, 142.
interjection, 99.
interpolation, 18, 44, 59, 93, 152, 154.
intonation, 65, 80, 154.
isolation, 186.

Jagger, J. H., 83.
Jaques, 112.
Java man, 41, 105.
jaw, 6, 33, 34, 69, 87, 88, 91, 92, 107, 113, 145.
Jespersen, O., 14, 15, 101, 172, 174, 176.
juxtaposition, 98.

Kant, 53.
Katz, D., 68.
Kehrer, 54.
Keith, Sir Arthur, 38, 39, 42, 45, 84, 87, 88, 89, 91, 92, 105, 106, 107, 108, 109, 111, 113, 143, 144, 145, 146, 147, 152, 153, 166, 167, 177.
Kellogg, N. N., 120.
Kerr, J. G., 12, 21, 26, 38, 41, 124, 134, 174.
kicking, 72.
Kipling, R., 10, 108, 110, 197.
kiss, 70, 81.
Kluge, F., 127, 128, 137, 138.
knives, 105.
Koch, L., 11, 53, 66.
Kreibig, 3.
Kuppers, E., 47.
Kussmaul, A., 22, 141.

labelling, 159, 180, 192.
labial chamber, 67.
Lach, R., 74, 125, 126, 127, 131.
Lady of Lloyds, 177.
lalling, 134, 135.
lanceolate points, 111.
language, 1, 4, 8, 15, 24, 36, 48, 49, 59, 70, 82, 83, 101, 133, 175, 182, 184, 186, 196.
language, animal, 30.
language, articulated, 99.
language, Chellean, 91.
language, child's, 104.
language, emotional and intentional, 165.
language, evolution of, 37, 72.
language, Magdalenian, 171.
language, makers of, 160.
language, pictorial, 195.
language, symbolic, 165.
languages, archaic, 191.
languages, primitive, 100, 101, 103, 157, 183.
laryngeal sound, 30, 67, 101.
laryngeal or velar chamber, 67.
laryngeus superior nerve, 69.
larynx, 34, 50, 52, 57, 58, 59, 67, 69, 97.
laughing, 48.
laws of sound change, 136, 164.
laws, tribal, 195.
Layard, J., 20.
Lazarus, 3.
Leakey, 24.
Lee, D. D., 191.
Lenzen, V. F., 6.
Leroy, C. J., 96.
Lévy-Bruhl, 94.
Lewis, J. H., 106.
Lewis, M. M., 122, 133, 135, 161.
libido, 149, 180.
Liebmann, A., 145.
Liebmann, O., 18.
linguistic patterns, 84.
linkage, emotional, 186.
linkage, erotic, 180.
linkage, social, 158.
lips, 32, 50, 67, 69, 97, 103, 107, 118.
listening, 68, 82.
Lloyds, Lady of, 177.
lobe, frontal, 88.
lobe, temporal, 69, 105.
Locke, 2.
loess, 143.
logic, 152.
logical mind, 190.
logico-grammatical categories, 190.
logique des sentiments, 151.
logos prophorikos, 24.
Louis, 6.
love, 103, 185.
Lubbock, J., 29, 188.

Lucretius, 2, 45.
Lytton, viii.

MacColl, D. S., 19, 20.
MacCurdy, J. T., 73, 90, 91.
macrocosmos, 79.
Magdalenian age, 166, 174, 179.
Magdalenian art, 171.
Magdalenian culture, 142, 144.
Magdalenian language, 171.
Magdalenians, 167, 168, 170, 171, 177.
magic, 2, 11, 101, 147, 151, 159, 160, 161, 166.
magic aspect, 195.
magic formulæ, 125.
magic mind, 165.
magic, pictorial, 152.
magic speech, 159.
magic symbolism, 148.
magical beliefs, 101.
makers of language, 160.
mammals, 27, 28, 57, 108.
man, 6, 29, 35, 72, 86, 87, 89, 99.
man, Boskop, 105.
man, Brünn, 143.
man, Chancelade, 144.
man, early, 44, 93, 102.
man, experimental types of, 92, 177.
man, Heidelberg, 88, 91, 92.
man, Java, 41, 105.
man, Mousterian, 108.
man, Neanderthal, 105, 106, 108, 113, 151, 153.
man, Palæolithic, 71, 152.
man, Piltdown, 85, 86, 88, 89, 92, 104, 105.
man, primitive, 44, 53, 73, 102, 120, 122, 160, 161.
man, Rhodesian, 104, 105, 107, 110, 152.
man, Swanscombe, 142.
mandible, 92, 113.
manipulative language, 122.
Marr, B., 141.
Marty, A., 2, 3, 24, 100, 119, 157, 158.
mastication, 69.
Matthews, W., 129, 132, 137, 138, 139, 189.
maturation, 136.
maturation, retarded, 93, 117.
Mead, M., 124, 125.
meaning, 8, 76, 78, 79, 101, 102, 104, 122, 128, 154, 159, 161, 163, 166, 172, 180, 185, 194, 195.
meaning, cognitive, 79.
meaning, erotic, 121.
meaning, personal, 121.
meaning, pictorial, 174.
me-ness, 114, 115.
Menes, 134.
mental pictures, 195.
mentality, cognitive, 140.

Mephistopheles, 125.
mesolithic age, 178.
Mesozoic, 27.
metabolism, 52.
metaphorical expression, 192, 194.
Meumann, 161.
Meyer, K., 125.
Meyer-Lübke, W., 130, 131, 135, 136, 138, 139, 162.
Meyer-Rinteln, W., 100, 141.
Meyrink, G., 194, 195.
Mikkola, J. J., 63, 64, 137.
mimesis, 37.
mimicking, 181.
miming, 84, 158.
mind, 11.
mind, magic, 165.
miocene, 27.
mode of reference, 78, 79, 82, 104, 132, 166, 180.
mode of relatedness, 114.
mode of utterance, 187.
monism, 3.
Moore, J. H., 45.
Morgan, C. L., 12.
Morgenstern, C., 166.
Mother Earth, 194.
motor centres, 34.
Mousterian language, 112.
Mousterian, man, 108.
Mousterian period, 105, 106, 110, 111, 112, 113, 114, 145, 146, 160, 177.
mouth, 57, 65, 67, 97, 113, 143.
mouth activities, 105.
mouth gestures, 30, 31, 71, 84.
movements, 34.
movements, rhythmical, 47.
Much, 131.
Müller, J., 119.
Müller, M., 1, 10, 14, 15, 141, 142.
multitude, 126.
mural art, 170.
Murphy, J., 35.
musical calls, 65.
muzzle, 107.
mysticism, 160.

name-giving, 166.
names, 181.
names, imposing of, 183.
nasal vowels, 80, 154.
nasalisation, 59, 60.
nasopharynx, 59, 65.
nations, 195.
nativism, 2.
naturalistic representation, 170, 171.
naturalistic tendencies, 154, 195.
Naunyn, B., 4.
Neanderthal man, 105, 106, 107, 108, 109, 110, 111, 112, 113, 142, 144, 145, 151, 153, 154, 177.
Neanthropic race, 143.

necklaces, 146.
need, 68.
negation, 126.
Negroes, 106.
negroid types, 105, 143, 144.
Negus, V. E., 50, 58.
Nernst, W., 26.
nervus laryngeus superior, 69.
neuro-physiology, 46.
new-born, 53, 67, 68.
Niessl-Mayendorf, E., 4.
nipple, 82.
noises, 43, 52, 72, 80, 94, 96, 123, 182, 195.
noises, ejection of, 122.
nominalism, 165.
non-reiterative speech, 186, 188.
Noreen, A., 63.
notation, 183.
notation, symbolic, 189.
noting, instruments of, 182.
noto-chord, 21.
number, 192.
nystagmus, 73.

object, 104, 114, 166, 181, 189, 191.
œsophagus, 49, 50, 67.
Ogden, C. K., 76, 183.
old testament, 1.
olfactory nerve, 70.
Oligocene, 27, 28, 42.
Ombredane, A., 140.
oneness, emotional, 117.
onomatopœia, 113, 159, 160, 161, 162, 164, 180, 193, 195.
ontogeny, 21, 22.
oral cavity, 50, 92.
ornaments, 146, 152.
Osborn, H. F., 84.
outlook, cultural, 194, 195.
over-specialisation, 112.
overtones, 55.

packs, 46.
Paget, Sir Richard, 2, 3, 4, 30, 31, 40, 71, 162.
pain, 48.
Palæocene, 27.
Palæolithic age, 91, 108, 110, 144, 146, 160, 179.
Palæolithic man, 71, 152, 153.
Palæonthropus, 89.
Palæozoic, 27.
palatal chamber, 67.
palatalisation, 138, 139.
palate, 57, 58, 65, 92, 107, 108, 115, 145.
paragrammatism, 140.
Paranthropus robustus, 38.
parthenogenesis, 118.
participle, 192.
parts of speech, 182.

Passavant's cushion, 65, 66.
pathology of speech, 54, 92.
patterns, linguistic, 84.
patterns, phonetic, 173.
patterns, reiterative, 124.
patterns, sound, 67, 188, 192.
patterns, vocal, 52, 54, 55.
Paul, H., 100, 128.
Peake, H., 143, 144, 146, 147, 149, 167, 168, 169, 177.
Pearsall Smith, 189.
pebbles, 178.
perception, 78.
percepts, 179.
person, 191, 192.
personal meaning, 121.
Peter Pan, 152.
Petersen, E., 72.
petnames, 162.
pharynx, 50, 69, 118.
philology, 24, 124.
phonation, 59, 67.
phoneme, 62, 63.
phonetic body, 174.
phonetic functions, 102.
phonetic notation, 189.
phonetic patterns, 173.
phonetics, 65.
phylogeny, 21.
physioplastic fashion, 179.
Piaget, J., 104, 159, 161, 182.
pictorial art, 150.
pictorial expression, affective, 188.
pictorial language, 165, 195.
pictorial magic, 152.
pictorial meaning, 174.
pictorial properties, 184.
pictorial representation, 180.
picture speaking, 165.
picture thinking, 165.
pictures, animal, 147.
pictures, mental, 195.
Pienaar, P., 67.
Piers Plowman, 126.
Piltdown man, 85, 86, 88, 89, 92, 104, 105.
Pirson, L., 130.
pitch, 63, 64, 65, 182.
Pithecanthropus, 39, 41, 42, 43, 45, 54, 55, 56, 59, 68, 69, 79, 80, 81, 82, 83, 84, 85, 92.
Plato, 1, 2.
pleasure, 79, 186.
pleasure-pain principle, 79, 186.
Pleistocene, 38, 42, 86, 87, 88, 89, 106, 109, 142, 145, 152, 177.
Pliocene, 27, 84, 87, 113, 152.
poetic diction, 103.
poetic expressions, 192.
poets, 126.
pointers, 158, 180.
pointers, symbolic, 170.

Popper, E., 195.
posture, 48.
Poulton, 118.
Pradenne, A. V. de, 23, 38, 39, 45, 90, 92, 105, 111, 112, 143, 144, 145, 151, 171.
pragmatic element, 151.
predicates, 6.
pre-logical, 94.
pre-magical, 94.
pre-Palæolithic times, 68.
presentation, naturalistic, 170.
pressure flaking, 167.
priest, 176.
priest-kings, 174.
Primary period, 27.
Primates, 28.
primeval utterances, 101.
primitive imagery, 178.
primitive languages, 100, 101, 103, 157, 183.
primitive man, 44, 53, 70, 102, 122, 130, 153, 159, 160, 161.
primitive races, 59, 104.
primitive speech, 102, 123.
primordial man, 72, 74.
primordial sounds, 100.
primordial utterances, 76.
problematic situation, 187.
Propliopithecus, 28.
prosimian, 32.
proto-Australian, 106.
proto-individuals, 174.
protrusion of lips, 32, 33.
proverbial expressions, 192.
psychic energy, 103.
psycho-biological tendencies, 158.
psycho-somatic, 117.
purpose, 158.
Pygmies, 106.

quadrigeminal bodies, 69.
quadrupeds, 35.
qualities, analysis of, 30, 91.
Quaternary, 27.

race, Crô-Magnon, 144.
race, Eoanthropic, 94.
race, Neanderthal, 177.
race, Palæolithic, 153.
races, Australoid, 143.
races, dwarf, 153.
races, negroid, 144.
races, primitive, 59, 104, 145.
Rae, J., 3, 141, 162.
Raleigh, Lord, 26.
rarefaction of air, 67.
rational self, 48.
rationality, 54, 149, 151.
Rattay, R. S., 182.
reactions, total of, 78.
Read, C., 35, 36.

realistic drawings, 150.
realistic representation, 178, 179.
recent geological systems, 27, 38.
reduplication, 98, 131.
reference, field of, 76, 78, 81, 82, 83, 96, 104, 166.
reference, mode of, 78, 79, 82, 104, 132, 166, 180, 187.
Regnaud, P., 53.
regression, 117.
Reinach, 147.
reiterated syllables, 98, 134.
reiteration, 126, 128, 129, 130, 133, 184, 186.
reiterative beads, 186.
reiterative gurgles, 180.
reiterative patterns, 124.
reiterative speech, 173.
reiterative tendency, 131.
reiterative words, 125.
rejection, noises indicative of, 72.
relatedness, mode of, 114.
relief, voiceless utterance of, 59.
religious theories of language, 1.
Renan, 3.
repetition, rhythmical, 123.
repetitive gestures, 165.
representation, realistic, 178, 179.
representation, symbolic, 180.
representational art, 150.
repression, 180.
respiratory tract, 27, 49.
response, emotional, 80.
retarded maturation, 93, 117.
Réthi, L., 69.
Révész, G., 5, 81.
Rhodesian man, 104, 105, 107, 110, 152.
rhythm, 26, 34, 65, 72, 73, 182.
rhythmical chewing, 34.
rhythmical movements, 47.
rhythmical repetition, 123.
rhythmical speech, 187, 188.
rhythmical tendency, 124.
Ribot, T., 151.
Richards, I. A., 76, 183.
rock pictures, 179.
Róheim, G., 71, 82, 109, 125, 127, 129, 130.
Romanes, 22.
root of the tongue, 66.
roots, 7, 14.

safety valves, 50, 61.
Schiller, F. C., 7, 17, 186, 187.
Schlegel, 128.
Schleicher, A., 128.
Schmidt, R. R., 39, 45, 80, 83, 84, 85, 86, 95, 107, 108, 109, 110, 112, 113, 123, 143, 144, 151, 160, 161, 170, 171, 178, 179, 181.
scholastic grammarians, 9.

INDEX

cholastic philosophers, 14.
Schwidetzky, G., 32.
science, definition of, 1.
scrapers, 105, 146, 170.
secondary flint implements, 146.
secondary period, 27.
self, 114, 115, 190.
self, rational, 48.
self-assertion, 57, 114.
semi-vowels, 60.
senile dementia, 117.
sensations, gustatory, 70.
sense data, 78, 151.
sense of form, 112.
sense, olfactory, 58.
sensorimotor nervous system, 46.
sentences, 64, 182.
sentiments, 126, 184.
sentiments, logique des, 151.
Seth, G., 119.
sexuality, 74, 185.
Shakespeare, 129.
shedding of final consonants, 138.
Shepherd, W. Y., 29.
Sherrington, Sir Charles, 15, 19, 26, 27, 32, 79.
shortening of words, 188, 189.
shorthand speaking, 171.
Shotwell, 15, 16, 17, 19, 20, 24.
Shy, T., 184.
sibilants, 60.
Sievers, E., 63.
sighing, 56, 61, 98.
signal, intentional, 158.
signs, intentional, 34, 180.
simian type of man, 107.
Sinanthropus, 40, 45, 80, 83, 84, 85.
situation, problematic, 187.
skull, 87, 93, 105, 145, 177.
skull, Gibraltar, 107, 108.
skull, Talgai, 105.
Smith, E., 28, 70, 83, 85, 106, 109, 156, 177.
Smith, Pearsall, 189.
Smuts, 13, 14.
social group, 136, 166, 194, 195.
social institutions, 195.
social life, 104.
social linkage, 158.
social structure, 152.
social unity, 115.
soft attack, 56, 62, 79, 158, 186.
soft palate, 57, 58, 65, 115.
Sollas, 38, 42, 85, 89, 90, 105, 107, 111, 117, 120, 123, 143, 149, 168, 170, 171.
Solutrean culture, 142, 152, 166, 167.
Sommer, I., 33.
songs of primitive races, 59.
sorcerer, 148, 174, 175, 176.
sound change, 60, 136, 140, 141, 195.
sound combination, 101.
sound, laryngeal, 30, 67, 101.

sound laws, 164.
sound patterns, 67, 188, 192.
sound, primordial, 100.
sound production, 164.
sound sequence, 182, 183.
sound table, 72, 102, 115, 136.
sounds, 30, 52, 53, 115, 123, 158, 161, 165, 182, 195.
sounds, speech, 55, 73, 119, 141, 189.
sounds, vocal, 53, 61, 71, 80, 97.
space-time principle, 190.
speaking, picture, 165.
speaking, shorthand, 171.
specialisation, 112.
speech, 5, 35, 42, 50, 65, 66, 71, 73, 89, 92, 94, 103, 104, 112, 118, 135, 154, 158, 175, 196.
speech, articulate, 91, 113, 133.
speech centres, 112.
speech, child's, 157, 161, 186.
speech, cognitive, 186.
speech disorders, 94.
speech, emotional, 186.
speech, magic, 159.
speech, non-reiterative, 186, 188.
speech, parts of, 182.
speech pathology, 54, 92.
speech, primitive, 102.
speech, reiterative, 173, 187.
speech sound, 55, 73, 119, 141, 189.
Spencer, H., 15, 53, 174.
Spengler, 166.
Spéranski, N., 8.
Sperber, H., 194.
Spiegel, E. A., 33, 69.
spinal bulb, 69.
Spinoza, 11.
spirants, 60.
spiritus lenis, 63.
spitting, 71.
Spitzer, L., 166, 185, 193, 194.
St. Basil, 121.
stammering, 118, 133.
Stein, L., 57, 61, 65, 95, 97, 133, 136, 140.
Steinthal, H., 2, 3, 100, 117, 124, 126, 164, 180.
Stern, W., 5, 96.
stimuli, vegetative, 158.
stone age, 89, 90, 91, 176, 195.
stop, 116.
stop, glottal, 57, 58, 62, 187.
Strack, H. L., 134.
stress, 80.
striatal system, 37, 47, 48.
subcortical centres, 69, 82.
subject, 6, 114.
substantia nigra, 69.
substantive verb, 192.
substitutes, utilisation of, 90, 91, 94, 109.

sucking, 67, 68, 71, 74, 82, 99, 102, 119, 159, 181.
sucking movements, 115.
sucking noises, 68, 80, 81, 93, 96, 97, 118, 164, 180, 187.
sucking stage, reversion to, 118.
suffixes, 190.
suffocation, 57.
sulcus centralis, 32.
surround, 79, 121, 160, 161, 165, 175, 181, 195.
Süssmilch, 1.
swallowing, 57, 69.
Swanscombe man, 142.
Swift, 189.
Swinburne, 126.
Swinnerton, 21.
syllables, 64, 97, 98, 99, 102, 156, 183, 188.
syllables, reiterated, 98, 134.
symbolic aspect, 181.
symbolic expression, 57, 74.
symbolic language, 165.
symbolic notation, 189.
symbolic pointers, 170.
symbolic representation, 180.
symbolic thought, 178.
symbolism, 165, 166.
symbolism, magical, 148.
symbolization, 59, 68, 80, 101.
symbols, 181.
symphysis, 92.
syntax, 190.
synthesis, 103.
system, sensorimotor nervous, 46.
system, striatal, 37.
system, vegetative, 46.

tabooism, 101.
Talgai skull, 105.
Tambimuttu, M. J., 131.
Tarsioids, 29.
Tasmanians, 110.
tasting, 69, 80.
temporal lobe, 69, 105.
tendencies, individualistic, 195.
tendencies, natural, 195.
tendencies, naturalistic, 154.
tendencies, psycho-biological, 158.
tendency, babbling, 196.
tendency, reiterative, 131.
tendency, rhythmical, 124.
tension, 48, 126, 191, 192.
Tertiary, 27.
testament, old, 1.
thalamus, 47, 69.
Thalbitur, 190.
theories of language, 1.
theory of identity, 157.
"things," 6, 185.
thinking, abstract, 170.
thinking, cognitive, 186.

thinking, picture, 165.
Thorndike, L., 1, 29.
thought, 48, 184, 186, 187.
thought, conceptual, 186.
thought, symbolic, 178.
throat, 65.
Thucydides, 15.
Tiktin, H., 137.
Tilney, 89, 144.
tone, fundamental, 55.
tones, 55.
tongue, 5, 6, 32, 33, 35, 67, 69, 50, 92, 103, 113, 115, 118.
tongue, root of, 66.
tongue, vulgar, 176.
tonicity, 64, 80.
tool-maker, 160.
tools, 85, 86, 89, 90, 109, 110, 111, 113, 121, 160, 161, 169.
tools, flake, 111, 112.
tools, flint, 111, 146.
tools, utilization of, 94.
torus supraorbitalis, 39.
totemism, 123.
touch, 154.
tracheotomy, 67.
tract, alimentary, 49, 66.
tract, digestive, 65.
traditionalistic theories of language, 1.
tribal laws, 195.
tribes, 195.
trigeminus nerve, 69.
truncated words, 183.
Tudor-Hart, B., 3, 82, 96.
Tumbian culture, 89.
Twisleton, E., 6.
Tylor, E., 3, 15, 30, 45.
types, hominid, 92.
types, human, 41, 93.
types, negroid, 105.
types, simian, 107.

uncus, 69.
union, 187.
unity, social, 115.
universals, 2, 14, 114.
utilization of substitutes, 90, 91, 94, 109.
utilization of tools, 94.
utterance, gesture, 83.
utterance, rhythmical, 188.
utterances, 48, 71, 72, 74, 92, 101, 117, 158, 160, 165, 189.
utterances, infantile, 162.
utterances, mode of, 187.
utterances, primeval, 101.
utterances, primitive, 123.
utterances, primordial, 76.

vagus nerve, 69.
Valentine, C. W., 35, 81, 94, 99, 115, 120, 122, 175, 180, 187.
Van Reit Lowe, C., 89.

INDEX

variability of speech sounds, 141.
Varro, 136.
Veda, 1.
vedic language, 59.
vegetative stimuli, 158.
vegetative system, 46.
velar or laryngeal chamber, 67.
Vendryes, J., 7, 8, 24, 49, 70, 120, 121, 123, 128, 191, 192.
Venus statuettes, 147.
verb, 192.
verb, auxiliary, 183.
verbal labels, 192.
verbalization, 171, 188.
Vergil, 19.
Verworn, R., 179.
vocal attacks, 56, 58, 79.
vocal cords, 51.
vocal ejaculations, 53, 55.
vocal patterns, 53, 54, 55.
vocal sound, 53, 61, 71, 80, 97.
vocalic change, 65.
vocalization, 36.
voice, 36, 52, 53, 56, 71, 75, 80, 82, 97, 98, 99, 102, 113, 114, 118, 123, 134.
Vondrák, W., 137.
Vossler, 17.
vowels, 54, 64, 65, 80, 94, 97, 98, 113, 115, 154, 158.
vulgar tongue, 176.

Ward, E., 189.
Ward, I. C., 62, 63, 64, 116.
Warren, S. H., 111.
weapons, 167.
Weekley, E., 131.
weeping, 48.
Weir, J., 27, 29, 38, 39, 42, 45, 85, 89.

Weise, O., 9, 125, 176, 188.
Wells, H. G., 26, 28, 91.
we-ness, 114, 115.
Wentworth, H., 132.
Werkmeister, W. H., 109, 190.
Westerman, D., 62, 63, 64, 116, 156, 164.
Whitney, 2, 127.
wholes, 45, 54, 151.
Wieland, 9.
will, 67, 159.
Wilson, R. A., 4.
Wilson, T., 55.
windpipe, 50, 57.
Winkel, J., 63, 135.
Winkler, F., 140.
wish fulfilment, 159.
word, 181, 182.
word, baby, 131, 165, 193.
word coinage, 133, 192, 194.
word-deafness, 54.
word formation, 128.
word-forms, 190.
words, 161, 185, 187, 190, 193, 194, 195.
words, reiterative, 125.
words, shortening of, 189.
writing, 50.
Wundt, W., 2.
Wyk, N., 9.
Wyld, H. C., 72, 74, 99, 128, 132, 138, 161, 192, 194.

Yerkes, R. M., 30.

Zeuner, F. E., 25, 26, 27, 39, 88, 107, 111, 142, 167, 177.
Zilsel, E., 17.
Zimmer, H., 182.

PLATE 1

A   B

C

MOUTH GESTURES IN APES. (*From Fox and Schwidetsky*)

    A. [y   'What's that?'
    B. [m   'What a pity. I am disappointed.'
    C. [u   'You are a dear!'

PLATE 2

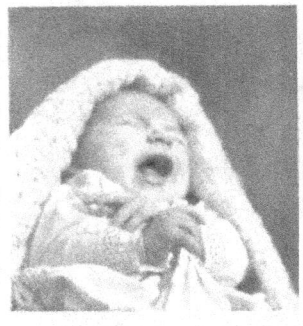 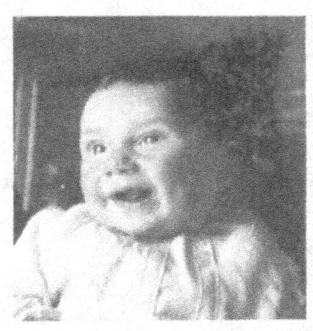

A B

 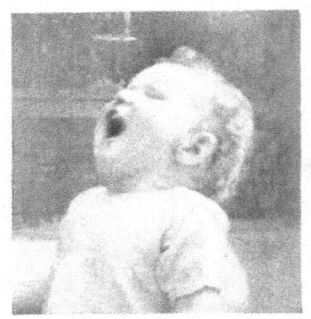

C D

MOUTH GESTURES IN CHILDREN

A. 'ae 'ae   ' I detest you.'
B.   ĕ   ' Not bad.'
C.   ' Do you really ? '
D.   ɔ   ' How amusing.'

PLATE 3

   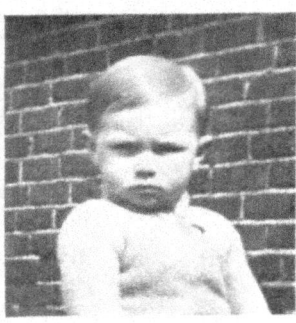

A   B

   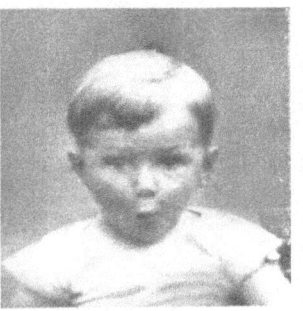

C   D

MOUTH GESTURES IN CHILDREN

A. [e]   'Nice to be alive.'
B. ['m] 'We are not amused.'
C. [i]   'Dear one."
D. [u]   'What about me?'

PLATE 4

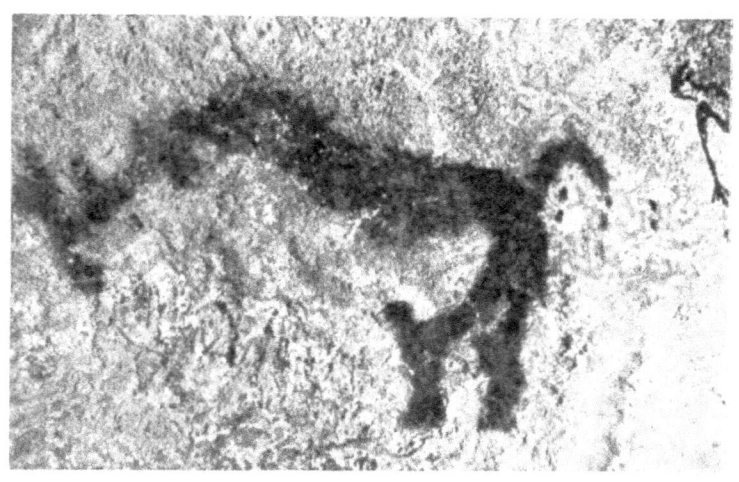

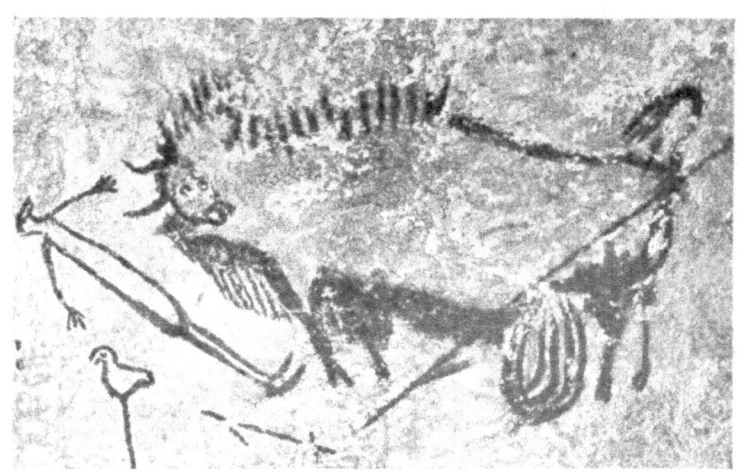

EARLY AURIGNACIAN OUTLINE-PICTURES
HUNTING STORY

(*After Breuil. From Alan Houghton Broderick*)

PLATE 5

A
AURIGNACIAN SCULPTURE
Two bisons modelled in clay.
(*After Count Bégouen. From Sollas.*)

B
SUPERPOSED PAINTINGS
a, deer, Lower Aurignacian (in red); b, b, horse and some kind of ox, Upper Aurignacian (in red); c, c, horses, Lower Magdalenian (in black); d, deer, Magdalenian (in red); e, horse, Upper Magdalenian (in red, with part of the outline of the head in black, an early stage of polychrome).
(*After Breuil. From Sollas.*)

PLATE 6

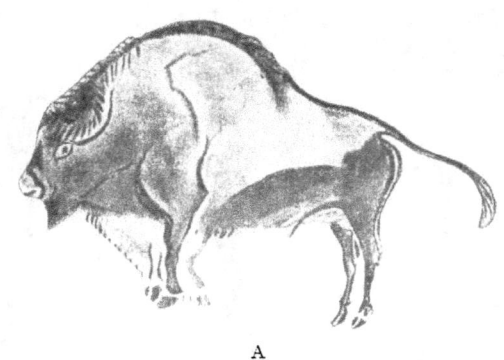

A

B

MAGDALENIAN ART
(After Sollas and Leakey)

'VENUS' STATUETTES
(*From Hawkes*)

PLATE 8

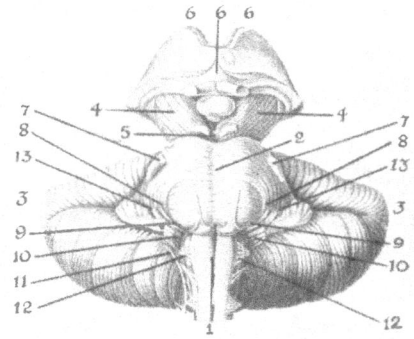 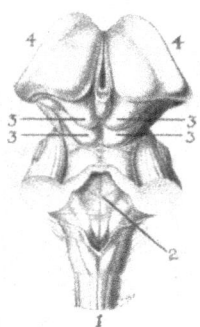

A BRAIN-STEM FROM BELOW
1. Spinal bulb.
2. Pons.
3. Cerebellum.
4. Cerebral peduncles.
5. Substantia nigra.
6. Thalamus.
7. Nervus Trigeminus.
8. Nervus Facialis.
9. Nervus glossopharyngeus.
10. Nervus vagus.
11. Nervus accessorius.
12. Nervus hypoglossus.
13. Auditory nerve.

B BRAIN-STEM FROM ABOVE
1. Spinal bulb.
2. Rhomboid fossa.
3. Colliculi.
4. Thalamus.

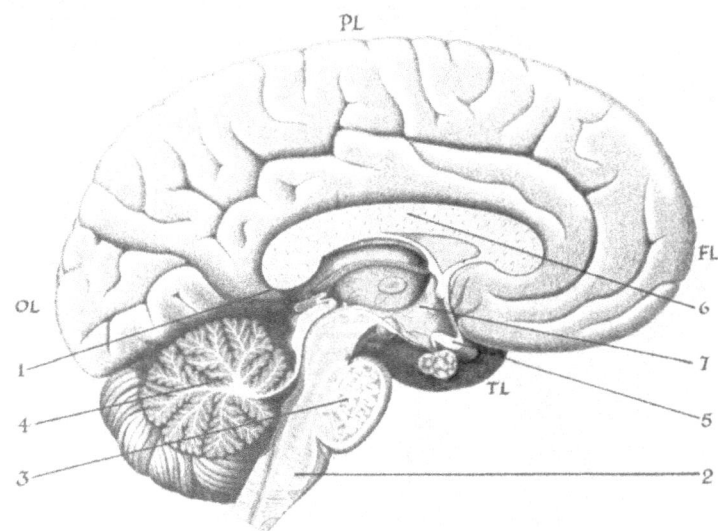

C INNER SURFACE OF THE BRAIN
FL Frontal Lobe.
PL Parietal Lobe.
OL Occipital Lobe.
TL Temporal Lobe.
1. Gyrus hippocampi.
2. Spinal bulb.
3. Pons.
4. Cerebellum.
5. Optic nerve.
6. Corpus callosum.
7. Thalamus.

(*All after Reichert*)

For Product Safety Concerns and Information please contact our EU representative GPSR@taylorandfrancis.com
Taylor & Francis Verlag GmbH, Kaufingerstraße 24, 80331 München, Germany

www.ingramcontent.com/pod-product-compliance
Lightning Source LLC
Chambersburg PA
CBHW071834300426
44116CB00009B/1534